Shakespeare's Chaucer

A STUDY IN LITERARY ORIGINS

Shakespeare's Chaucer

A STUDY IN LITERARY ORIGINS

ANN THOMPSON

*Lecturer in English Literature
in the University of Liverpool*

BARNES & NOBLE BOOKS · NEW YORK
(A division of Harper & Row Publishers, Inc.)

Published in the U.S.A. 1978 by
HARPER & ROW PUBLISHERS, INC.
BARNES & NOBLE IMPORT DIVISION

ISBN 0-06-496832-4

First published 1978

Set in Monotype Sabon 11D/12 pt by
The Lancashire Typesetting Company Limited, Bolton
and printed and bound in Great Britain by
R. & R. Clark Limited, Edinburgh

For my father

Preface

This book arose primarily out of an interest in two of Shakespeare's most 'problematic' plays, *Troilus and Cressida* and *The Two Noble Kinsmen* (written in collaboration with John Fletcher). The interest was a critical rather than a scholarly one, but further exploration convinced me that the peculiarly dark, cynical atmosphere prevalent in both these plays (though more obvious in *Troilus and Cressida*) could not be considered without taking account of Shakespeare's source-materials, in both cases extended poems by a man more famous today for his comic than for his tragic skill, Geoffrey Chaucer. I discovered to my great surprise that there existed no comprehensive study of the literary relationship between these two men; indeed there were scholars who maintained that Shakespeare had never read Chaucer at all. An attempt to remedy this omission became a more important challenge than my original desire to add to the more general critical debate, and as I went on I found ample rewards in the Chaucerian background to plays such as *Romeo and Juliet* and *A Midsummer Night's Dream* in addition to the interest of the plays with which I began.

Like most people whose interest in Shakespeare stems from an enthusiasm for the plays themselves rather than an interest in their social and cultural background, I have tended to be sceptical at times about the value of source-studies and to feel that they are a remote and pedantic backwater. I have found however that my work on Shakespeare's use of Chaucer has in many ways intensified my critical interest in the plays as well as satisfying my more 'academic' curiosity as to their origins. A source-study should always provide insights into Shakespeare's working methods, and especially into the way his astonishing memory and rich powers of association enabled him to construct such complex and evocative texts. In this particular instance one has the added fascination of being able to compare Shakespeare's methods and attitudes with those of his greatest predecessor. When I went on to study some other Elizabethan and Jacobean dramatists in order to place Shakespeare more securely in the context of his contemporaries, I found that by comparing their use of Chaucer with his I was able to perceive some specific reasons for his evident but ill-defined superiority. I hope that I have been able to convey in this book some of the unusual interest that the topic itself holds.

Contents

Appendix
Chronological table of Shakespeare's
references to Chaucer
page 220

Acknowledgements

Much of this book is based on my London University PhD thesis, and I am particularly grateful to Richard Proudfoot who supervised the work at that stage and has continued to give advice and encouragement. Subsequent assistance has been given by Geoffrey Bullough, Kenneth Muir, and Philip Edwards, all of whom have read and commented on various chapters most helpfully. The section of Chapter 3 on *Romeo and Juliet* appeared as an article in *The Yearbook of English Studies*, vi (1976) and I am glad to have the editor's permission to reprint it. I have used the resources of the British Museum, London University Senate House, King's College and Liverpool University Libraries, and I am grateful to the staff of those institutions for their help. Finally I should like to express my thanks to Liverpool University Press, to my husband and the many friends who have given support of various kinds, and to Catherine Rees who typed the final version.

A. T.

Liverpool 1978

I

Introduction

'Malvolio in the Twelfth Night of Shakespeare hath some expressions very similar to Alnaschar in the Arabian Tales: which perhaps may be sufficient for some Criticks to prove his acquaintance with Arabic.' Thus, in 1767, Richard Farmer warned his contemporaries against over-enthusiastic source-hunting in the works of Shakespeare, already described as 'a vast garden of criticism'. His own aim, however, was to explore the English corner of the garden, a hitherto neglected patch, and to make substantial claims for vernacular sources as against 'all such reading as was never read' in Latin and Greek which had been attributed to Shakespeare by such men as his eighteenth-century editors: Pope, Theobald, Hanmer, and Warburton. Farmer admitted that he might err in the opposite direction in his effort to redress the balance, but most of the English books and translations he suggested as Shakespeare's sources are still accepted by modern critics, and his essay contained several important discoveries, such as his evidence for believing that, far from reading Plutarch, 'our Author hath done little more than throw the very words of North into blank verse'.[1]

Farmer has remained something of an exception. In the twentieth century, as in the eighteenth, critics have shown more interest in trying to define the exact meaning of Jonson's famous ascription to Shakespeare of 'small Latine and lesse Greeke', and many books and articles on 'Shakespeare's learning' and 'Shakespeare's reading' have been produced which make little or no reference to literature in the vernacular; if they do, they nearly always concentrate on the works of Shakespeare's contemporaries rather than on those of

1. Richard Farmer, 'Essay on the learning of Shakespeare' in D. Nichol Smith (ed.), *Eighteenth Century Essays on Shakespeare* (Oxford, 1903), pp. 151–202.

earlier native writers. Shakespeare is no longer virtually denied an acquaintance with the literature of his own language, and the heat has gone out of the argument which made the classical and native traditions seem almost mutually exclusive, but we still have no satisfactory account of the latter. F. P. Wilson summarized the position in 1950,[2] and his conclusion that 'what Shakespeare read he read for the most part in English' would probably still find unanimous acceptance, but his article is nevertheless more concerned with limiting even more precisely Shakespeare's use of works in other languages than with attempting to detail this extensive English reading.

There are, of course, reasons for the more advanced state of research into the dramatist's use of the classics, the most important being the existence of objective, external evidence as to what he might have read. The emphasis on classical and foreign writers in a book like V. K. Whitaker's *Shakespeare's Use of Learning*[3] is a natural consequence of the long opening section on Shakespeare's education, and it has been possible for T. W. Baldwin to reconstruct Shakespeare's probable school curriculum.[4] A large amount of research has been done on Tudor education in general, but, unfortunately, vernacular literature was not read at school,[5] and there is no sure way of ascertaining when, how, and in what variety a middle-class schoolboy might have come across English books; for the most part we are thrown back upon the internal evidence of the plays themselves, and critics have been reluctant to tackle this in anything other than a very piecemeal way.

Nevertheless, despite our lack of the specific kind of 'proof' which a school reading-list might have supplied, there can surely be little serious doubt that Shakespeare read Chaucer if he read any English poetry at all. A quick look through Caroline Spurgeon's collection of Chaucer allusions for the period[6] reveals that almost every Elizabethan or Jacobean

2. 'Shakespeare's reading', *Shakespeare Survey 3* (Cambridge, 1950), 14–21.
3. San Marino, 1953.
4. *William Shakespeare's Petty School* (Urbana, Illinois, 1943).
5. A limited challenge is made to this assumption by W. Nelson in 'The teaching of English in Tudor grammar schools', *Studies in Philology [SP]*, xlix (1952), 119–45.
6. *Five Hundred Years of Chaucer Criticism and Allusion* (Cambridge, 1925).

writer we remember today referred to him at least once, and
that a wide cross-section of the educated Elizabethan public
at large either knew him at first hand or knew enough about
him to write as if they did. He enjoyed a very high reputation
as 'the father of English poetry' and 'our English Homer', and
he was readily available in handsome folio editions. He was
praised for his eloquence, his learning, and his sententious-
ness by poets, literary theorists, and theologians, and it is
evident that no-one with any serious interest in literature
would have been able to ignore him.

Yet at the same time there is an increasing amount of
criticism of Chaucer during this period. He is accused of
scurrility, his lines are said to be rough and irregular, and his
language becomes genuinely difficult to understand. Even
Spenser, his most fervent admirer and imitator, cannot really
convince us that he feels himself to be in a living tradition
which has Chaucer at its head, and later writers do not try.
There was in fact a gap between Chaucer's reputation and his
real influence, and this became more apparent as the Elizabethans' creation of their own vernacular tradition gave them
more confidence and relieved them of the necessity of trying
to relate themselves to a poet whom they really felt to be
remote and archaic. Since the ambiguity of Chaucer's position
in relation to the Elizabethans and their literature is of obvious importance to my subject, I shall consider the nature of
if briefly before returning to Shakespeare.[7]

At the beginning of the Elizabethan period, Chaucer was
almost the *only* English poet of any stature in the whole of
literary history, so that any writer in the native language who
wished to buttress his position by reference to a 'tradition'
was obliged to mention him. In an age of increasing national-
ism and literary self-consciousness this was regularly done,
though Chaucer sometimes shares the honours with Gower
and Lydgate, as when Francis Meres describes the native
tradition in his 'Comparative Discourse' of English and
foreign poets in *Palladis Tamia* (1598): 'As Greece had three
poets of great antiquity, Orpheus, Linus and Musaeus, and
Italy three other auncient poets, Livius Andronicus, Ennius

7. Further discussion of this subject can be found in Alice Miskimin's recent
book, *The Renaissance Chaucer* (Yale, 1975).

and Plautus: so hath England three auncient poets, Chaucer, Gower and Lydgate.'[8] This attempt to elevate the native tradition by giving it a respectable pantheon of poets is very common among critics at the time, but we often feel that the praise accorded to Chaucer is something of a formality, springing from the contemporary needs of the Elizabethan writers rather than from a sincere admiration for his actual work.

There is a similarly hollow ring about some of the extravagant praise for his style and language. References to his eloquence and 'golden pen' seem to have atrophied into mere cliché when we find them alongside criticisms of his 'rough' metres and complaints about the obscurity of his language. As early as 1550 we find Nicholas Udall commenting on the latter problem. Discussing the translation of literature in his version of Vermigli's *Discourse of Peter Martyr*, he asks 'What should Chaucer, Gower and Lydgate and others do abrode, whom some even of the learned sort do in some places scarcely take?'[9] That this difficulty increased during the period is apparent if we look ahead to 1635 when William Cartwright's prefatory poem hailed Sir Francis Kynaston's translation of *Troilus and Criseyde* into Latin with the lines

> Tis to your Happy cares we owe, that wee
> Read Chaucer now without a Dictionary.

As for the question of metre, we can understand the puzzled remarks of men like George Gascoigne[1] and John Bodenham[2] about Chaucer if we look at the printed texts which were available: the editors were unaware of the changes in pro-

8. Quoted by Spurgeon, vol. i, p. 159.

9. Quoted by R. F. Jones in *The Triumph of the English Language* (Stanford, 1953), p. 39.

1. '. . . although his lines are not alwayes of one selfe same number of syllables, yet being redde by one that hath understanding, the longest verse and that which hath most syllables in it will fall (to the eare) correspondent unto that whiche hath fewest sillables in it.' *Certayne Notes of Instruction* (1575), Spurgeon, i. 110.

2. 'I have omitted the sentences of Chaucer, Gower, Lidgate and other auncient Poets, because it was not knowne how their form would agree with these of ten syllables only, and that sometime they exceed the compasse herein observed, having none but lineall and complet sentences.' *Belvedere* (1600), Spurgeon, i. 161.

nunciation that had taken place in the last two hundred years, and their attempts to emend and correct Chaucer led to some very mangled lines indeed. (All my quotations from Chaucer in the later chapters of this book will be taken from sixteenth-century texts, so the reader will get some idea of this.) Particularly disastrous was their ignorance of the significance of final 'e' in Middle English; they add words and syllables in order to smooth out the lines, but rarely succeed in producing a satisfactory version for their readers.

While some writers found Chaucer a useful precedent to justify writing in the vernacular at all, and many cite him as one who had beautified and perfected his mother-tongue, it is abundantly obvious that linguistic changes had made his work irrelevant to the Elizabethans' real and immediate interest in poetic style and the use of the vernacular: if Chaucer had once perfected the language, things had changed so much by 1560 that the bulk of the work had to be done again. He was often admired for his practice of enriching the language by introducing foreign words, and many writers justified their own borrowings by reference to him,[3] while others less logically cited him as a precedent for the use of archaisms, but in both cases we feel that Chaucer became less necessary to the Elizabethans as their own confidence increased.

So much for the more technical and linguistic aspects of Chaucer's poetry, but what of his subject matter or content? How far did the Elizabethans admire him for what he said as well as for how he said it, and how sincere was this admiration? Their sense of the kind of poet Chaucer was seems very different from ours, and is another factor that should be taken into account when discussing questions of direct influence. Chaucer was a much more solemn, intellectual figure for the Elizabethans than he is in the popular mind today. He was often described as a 'moral' writer, and almost invariably as a 'learned' one. He was praised for his use of foreign authors, both ancient and modern, and there was some attempt to see him as a forerunner of both the Renaissance and the Reformation. The poem most frequently singled out for praise was *Troilus and Criseyde*, which was admired for its 'classical'

3. George Chapman, for example, in the preface to his translation of *Achilles' Shield* (*Iliad* xviii) in 1598.

setting, its formal ambitiousness and, of course, its senten-
tiousness. Again the grounds for admiration reflect the
Elizabethans' own literary attitudes and aspirations: it seems
inevitable that a man like Sidney, with a classical education
and neo-classical theories about literature, should feel happier
about *Troilus and Criseyde* than about *The Canterbury Tales*.
The latter often caused some embarrassment to those determined to admire Chaucer, who tended to be on the defensive
when they wrote about them,[4] and indeed it was during this
period that 'a Canterbury Tale' came to mean a bawdy story.

The contemporary editions encouraged readers to think of
Chaucer as a learned and moral writer, but some of their
reasons for this might come as a surprise to the modern critic.
There was considerable stress on the factual as well as the
didactic content of the works: Thomas Speght, the 1598
editor, introduced *The Astrolabe* with the remark, 'This
booke ... standeth so good at this day, especially for the
Horizon of Oxford, as in the opinion of the learned, it cannot
be amended.' His attitude was very similar to that of Gabriel
Harvey, who wrote,

Others commend Chaucer and Lidgate for their witt, pleasant
veine, varietie of poetical discourse, and all humanitie: I specially
note their Astronomie, philosophie, and other parts of profound
or cunning art. Wherein few of their time were more exactly
learned. It is not sufficient for poets to be superficial humanists:
but they must be exquisite artists and curious universal schollars.[5]

This emphasis on the sheer quantity of knowledge contained
in Chaucer made his reputation for 'learnedness' rather vulnerable at a time when great advances were being made in all
branches of knowledge.

His reputation as a 'moral' writer had a similarly surprising and insecure basis. It is one thing for Speght to
sprinkle the margins of his second edition with little hands
pointing to notable 'sentences', but another for John Foxe to
call Chaucer 'a right Wiclevian' in his *Ecclesiasticall History*
(1570)[6] and to see him as an outspoken critic of Rome. The

---

4. Francis Beaumont (the elder), for example, in his prefatory letter to
Speght's 1598 edition of Chaucer.
5. Manuscript notes in *Alexandrine* (1598), quoted by Spurgeon, i. 127.
6. Quoted by Spurgeon, i. 104.

reason for the latter opinion lies in the ascription to Chaucer of the large quantity of apocryphal material printed under his name, some of it, like *The Plowman's Tale* (first published in William Thynne's edition of 1542) and *Jack Upland* (first published by Speght in 1602) of a distinctly radical and anti-clerical nature. On the basis of such spurious works Speght indulged in the 'autobiographical fallacy', offering his readers a Chaucer who had to flee abroad after favouring 'some rashe attempt of the common people', and whose *Canterbury Tales* were of a distinctly political cast, showing 'with such Art and cunning . . . the state of the Church, the Court and Country' that the author was 'admired and feared' by all.

On the other hand, writers were becoming critical of Chaucer's morality, and the traditional defence of 'decorum' (i.e. appropriateness of tale to narrator) used by Chaucer himself was only grudgingly admitted, if at all. Sir John Harington accused Chaucer of 'flat scurrilitie' in his *Apologie for Poetrie* in 1591,[7] and *Greene's Vision* of 1592 opposed merry Chaucer to moral Gower by presenting the former giving encouragement to Greene with the words, 'If thou doubtest blame for thy wantonnes, let my selfe suffice for an instance, whose Canterburie tales are broad enough before, and written homely and pleasantly, yet who hath bin more canonised for his workes than Sir Geffrey Chaucer?'[8]

Thus Chaucer held, for the Elizabethans, the curious position of 'father' of a tradition which did not exist and perfector of a vernacular which was remote and archaic, while his reputation as a learned and moral writer rested on very shaky ground and was already subject to scepticism and challenge. Yet it is apparent from all the references to him that despite everything he was widely read and enjoyed; indeed the Elizabethans' admiration for him was increased by their feeling that his poetry was achieved in the face of enormous odds: Sidney was typical when he wrote, 'Chaucer, undoubtedly, did excellently in hys *Troylus and Cresseid*; of whom, truly, I know not whether to mervaile more, either that he in that mistie time could see so clearly, or that wee in

7. Reprinted in G. G. Smith (ed.), *Elizabethan Critical Essays* (Oxford, 1904), ii. 215.

8. Quoted by Spurgeon, i. 137–8.

this cleare age walke so stumblingly after him.'[9] That there
was felt to be such a wide gulf between 'that mistie time' and
'this cleare age' is perhaps one reason why comparatively little
work has been done on the influence of specific medieval
writers and texts in the Renaissance period. The Elizabethans
themselves were so sure that theirs was a new era, cut off
from the darkness and ignorance of the past by all sorts of
new discoveries and new attitudes, that we have taken them
at their word and directed our own attention towards the
emergence of the new rather than the continuity of the old.
Like them, we are puzzled by the strangeness and difficulty of
much of the literature of the earlier period and are relieved to
be able to dismiss it as irrelevant.

This has resulted in considerable distortion of medieval
literature by Renaissance-centred critics who have not really
troubled to study a text in itself before committing themselves
as to whether it influenced a later work or not. There are
several examples of this in the work done on Shakespeare's
Troilus and Cressida by critics who read Chaucer's *Troilus
and Criseyde* in the light of their own interpretation of Shakespeare's play. We are told such untruths as that Shakespeare
'adopts the character of Pandarus without change',[1] and that
Chaucer's affectionately drawn figure is 'Criseyde's elderly
uncle . . . frankly materialistic . . . a prototype of Falstaff'.[2]
The whole scheme of the poem becomes oversimplified when
critics like W. W. Lawrence[3] and Peter Ure[4] explain the
difference between it and the play by saying that the tradition
of 'courtly love' in which Chaucer wrote had been supplanted
by 'Christian marriage' by Shakespeare's time, implying that
Chaucer was unaware of any conflict between the two. One
becomes dubious about a critic's qualifications to assess the
influence of a poem when it seems that he has not read it carefully for himself.

9. *An Apologie for Poetrie* (c. 1583) reprinted in G. G. Smith (ed.), *Elizabethan
Critical Essays*, i. 196.
  1. R. A. Small, *The Stage-Quarrel between Ben Jonson and the so-called
Poetasters* (Breslau, 1899), p. 155.
  2. F. S. Boas, *Shakespeare and his Predecessors* (London, 1896), p. 369.
  3. 'The love-story in *Troilus and Cressida*', in B. Matthews and A. H.
Thorndike (eds), *Shakespearian Studies* (New York, 1916), p. 187.
  4. *Shakespeare's Problem Plays* (London, 1961), p. 35.

It is of course very difficult to be certain about the influence of Chaucer upon Shakespeare. There has been an alarming amount of contradiction and disagreement among the critics who have ventured into the field. *Troilus and Cressida* is again a good example, mainly because of the amount of attention it has received. From the very earliest comments on the source to the present day we find the critics radically divided. Several have argued for a fairly close connection between the two versions of the story, but we find a modern editor of the play saying there is 'no certainty of a debt at first-hand to Chaucer's tale'.[5] Frequently such statements are based on rather vague literary judgements: M. M. Reese remarked that 'one of the most surprising gaps in Shakespeare's reading is his comparative unfamiliarity with the works of Chaucer', revealing in a footnote that the evidence for this consisted in the difference in tone between *Troilus and Cressida* and Chaucer's poem.[6] Disagreements also occur when critics are concentrating on the evidence for the use of different sources, not just when their real interest is in making an evaluative comment on the later work. We find J. C. Maxwell, for example, believing that *The Rape of Lucrece* shows evidence of the use of Chaucer's *Legend of Good Women*,[7] when the considerable researches of T. W. Baldwin[8] had shown no such thing.

How is it possible for this kind of dispute to continue? Obviously there is something very strange and elusive about the kind of evidence that is being used when people flatly disagree about matters which seem as near to being simply factual as literary studies can get. One major problem is that Chaucer's stories are almost never original or exclusive, so that it is impossible to argue that Shakespeare must have taken a particular plot from him as the only available source: the story of Lucrece, for example, was readily available elsewhere, and that of Troilus and Criseyde had passed into common knowledge. Proof of a connection has then to be based on a

5. Alice Walker, New Cambridge edition (1957), p. xliii.
6. *Shakespeare's World and Work* (London, 1953), p. 392.
7. In his New Cambridge edition of *Shakespeare's Poems* (1966), p. xxi.
8. *The Literary Genetics of Shakespeare's Poems and Sonnets* (Urbana, Illinois, 1950), p. 106.

correspondence of more detailed aspects of the treatment of a subject, or on specific parallels in theme, idea, or image. Again one runs into difficulties: there is very little hope of finding close verbal similarity, perhaps the most convincing kind of evidence in a source-study, and when one does find a phrase or sentence which seems almost a quotation from Chaucer it invariably turns out to have been proverbial in the sixteenth century, as it probably was in the fourteenth. Chaucer's linguistic remoteness must have discouraged direct quotation, and he is not a poet who gives us many memorable 'purple passages' or startles us with completely new or distinctive thoughts and images. To an exceptional degree, his characteristics vanish when he is paraphrased, and his work becomes almost unrecognizable at second-hand.

Consequently, one can very rarely prove his influence beyond any doubt, but must frequently be satisfied with no more than a high degree of probability.[9] It is impossible to draw up a set of standards by which alleged parallels must be judged in a situation of such complex uncertainties, however desirable such fixed criteria might be. I hope one function of this book will be to provide a discussion of the kinds of evidence that are available in a source-study of this nature, as well as an attempt to judge their acceptability, and to differentiate between the degrees of certainty and amount of enlightenment we can expect to achieve from studying them. Basically one must establish a similarity between the stories or passages in question and then prove, as far as possible, that Chaucer is a more likely source than any other that can be suggested. It is often a case of carefully ruling out all other possible sources, paying special attention of course to any books or authors Shakespeare is known to have read. Then one must be sure one is not attributing to Chaucerian influence thoughts, phrases, and images which were in fact common-places or literary clichés. There are some good warnings here, such as H. Ord's attempt to prove the direct

9. Since writing this chapter I have read Göran Hermerén's book, *Influence in Art and Literature* (Princeton, 1975) which discusses the theoretical and methodological problems of influence studies. After considering a wide range of examples, he also concedes that it is almost impossible to be precise or conclusive in such matters.

influence of Chaucer's translation of *The Romaunt of the Rose* on Shakespeare's Sonnets without taking any notice of the high level of conventional content in both works.[1] A remark by Richard Farmer is again apposite: commenting on a somewhat abtruse 'plagiarism' from Anacreon noted by Dr Dodd, he says, 'Yet it may be alleged by those who imagine Shakespeare to have been generally able to think for himself, that the topicks are obvious, and their application is different.'[2]

I have said that the business of tracing and substantiating these Chaucerisms is a neglected task, but this has to be a relative description when one is talking about Shakespeare studies, and a certain amount of work has been done, much of it very valuable. It can be roughly divided into three categories. First, there are the large-scale surveys of Shakespeare's sources which take in the whole canon, and these range in scope and detail from H. R. D. Anders's one-volume *Shakespeare's Books*[3] to Geoffrey Bullough's eight-volume *Narrative and Dramatic Sources of Shakespeare*.[4] Then there are the more specialized works, including studies and editions of individual plays or groups of plays, essays, and contributions to periodicals. Finally there are books which consider medieval ideas or influences in a more general way, either limiting themselves to Shakespeare like E. C. Pettet's *Shakespeare and the Romance Tradition*[5] and Leo Salingar's *Shakespeare and the Traditions of Comedy*,[6] or taking a wider view of the period like W. Farnham's *The Medieval Heritage of Elizabethan Tragedy*.[7] The space devoted to Chaucer in most of these tends to be strictly limited, but there is a steady accumulation of evidence of the influence of the English vernacular tradition.[8]

1. *Chaucer and the Rival Poet in Shakespeare's Sonnets* (London, 1921).
2. 'Essay on the learning of Shakespeare', p. 163.
3. Berlin, 1904.
4. London, 1957–75.
5. London and New York, 1949.
6. Cambridge, 1974.
7. Cambridge, 1936.
8. G. C. Taylor's review of Farnham's book, 'The medieval elements in Shakespeare', *Shakespeare Association Bulletin*, xii (1937), 208–16, pointed out several more instances of medievalism in Shakespeare, and John Lawlor has considered medieval influences in *The Tragic Sense in Shakespeare* (London,

A fuller treatment of Chaucer's influence on Shakespeare was, I think, first attempted in 1873 in an anonymous article (later attributed to J. W. Hales) in the *Quarterly Review* called 'Chaucer and Shakespeare'.[9] After some discussion of the similarity between the two writers in general matters such as characterization, the use of pathos and irony, etc., Hales argued the probability of Shakespeare's knowledge of Chaucer by citing several specific instances of his borrowings, to which I shall return later when they are relevant to my more detailed argument. He marred his case by a somewhat too easy assumption of 'the profound congeniality that exists between the two minds' and some rather dubious parallels, such as the notion that *Venus and Adonis* is indebted to *Troilus and Criseyde* because both poems exhibit 'an extreme minuteness and fullness of description, an overbrimming abundance of imagery and illustration, an almost excessive display of poetical richness and power'.

English scholars let the matter rest for some time, but in Germany G. Sarrazin wrote a short article on 'Chaucer and Shakespeare' in 1897[1] which added a few parallels, and Otto Ballman produced a dissertation at Strassburg in 1901 called 'Chaucers Einfluss auf das Englische Drama in Zeitalter der Königen Elizabeth und der beiden ersten Stuart-Könige'. I have not been able to see this, but the author published a long article with the same title in *Anglia* the following year, and it seems reasonable to assume that the substance of the thesis is contained within these 85 pages.[2] His concern is to record references which prove that various dramatists, including

---

1960). There are a few relevant points in Glynne Wickham's *Shakespeare's Dramatic Heritage* (London, 1969), though reference to Chaucer here is naturally incidental. W. G. Meader in *Courtship in Shakespeare* (New York, 1954) and John Vyvyan in *Shakespeare and the Rose of Love* (London, 1960), have followed Pettet in studying 'courtly love' in Shakespeare, and articles by Nevill Coghill ('The basis of Shakespearean comedy', *Essays and Studies*, iii [1950], 1–28) and K. F. Thompson ('Shakespeare's romantic comedies', *Publications of the Modern Language Association of America* [PMLA], lxvii [1952], 1079–93) have related these ideas to the comedies. W. H. Schofield considers both Chaucer and Shakespeare in *Chivalry in English Literature* (Harvard, 1912), and C. B. Watson includes the medieval background in *Shakespeare and the Renaissance Concept of Honor* (Princeton, 1960).

9. *Quarterly Review*, cxxxiv (1873), 225–55.

1. *Anglia Beiblatt*, vii (1897), 265–9.

2. *Anglia*, xxv (1902), 1–85.

Shakespeare, did know Chaucer, and he makes no attempt, in the article at least, to discuss *how* the source was used. Most of his references are reliable, but sometimes he seems over-enthusiastic, as, for example, when he lists uses of the word 'chanticleer' as references to *The Nun's Priest's Tale*, when it would seem that it had passed into the common vocabulary and was no longer a literary allusion.

When Nevill Coghill came to review the state of research into the subject in his article on 'Shakespeare's reading in Chaucer' in 1959, he could find no comprehensive survey since that of Hales in 1873 which he describes as 'the only general assemblage [of details] as yet attempted'.[3] He does not refer to the German writers. Some general source-studies with passing references to Chaucer had been published, and a few articles on specific points. Coghill goes over the accumulated details carefully, adds some new ones from his own observation, and, most important, says he is not content merely to record these facts like his predecessors, but wishes to make more of an attempt to assess the significance of his findings. 'That Shakespeare really knew and loved Chaucer', he writes, 'would be a far more important affirmation to us— were we in a position to make it—than that he merely used him.' But we have to collect a reasonable number of basic factual details first, before going on to more interesting speculations, and this is the main emphasis of his article. It is also disappointing that he limits himself to the plays of the early 1590s and does not mention *Troilus and Cressida*.

One must return to Germany for the next and most recent contribution, another article entitled 'Chaucer und Shakespeare', written by M. Lehnert in 1967.[4] He is concerned less with noting allusions and parallels than with a general comparison of the two men as the fathers of English poetry, naturalistic observers of character, sharers of a common sense of humour and so on, rather in the same spirit as the opening of Hales's article. (A similar sort of thing had appeared again in English in 1950, when Marchette Chute's short article on 'Chaucer and Shakespeare' was published,

3. Coghill's article appears in *Elizabethan and Jacobean Studies presented to F. P. Wilson*, ed. H. Davis and H. Gardner (Oxford, 1959), pp. 86–99.
    4. Printed in *Shakespeare Jahrbuch*, ciii (1967), 3–39.

with its comparison of the two men on a personal level on the grounds that 'they resemble each other much more closely than they resemble any other poet or novelist or playwright in English literature'.)[5] Lehnert takes the personal parallel into the works with statements such as 'the appeal to humane mercy, forgiveness and goodness goes through all Shakespeare's plays and Chaucer's poems'. The trouble with these articles is that they do not provide enough solid evidence and detailed comparison to make one feel sure of the truth or value of such statements. Two recent books contain general remarks of a similar nature. In *The Renaissance Chaucer* Alice Miskimin briefly compares Chaucer and Shakespeare as ironists and as 'unoriginal' writers in terms of sheer invention of plot and substance,[6] and in *Poetic Freedom and Poetic Truth* Harriett Hawkins uses their work to illustrate the freedom of great artists to challenge the social and critical orthodoxies of their times.[7] These approaches are nearer to comparative literature (where it is quite legitimate to compare any artist with any other artist regardless of any known or supposed genetic connection between them) than to source-study.

Comparisons of this kind are certainly one of the rewards of conducting a close study of two such writers as Chaucer and Shakespeare. It is fascinating to compare their methods of characterization, their social and moral attitudes, their comic techniques, what they saw as the most tragic aspects of life, and so on. This is not strictly speaking my subject, but it is an area into which I shall venture occasionally as particular examples seem to demand it. My primary aim is to establish beyond doubt that Shakespeare not only read Chaucer but knew his work unusually well and was influenced by it in several different ways. It seems extraordinary that the longest and most ambitious treatment of the connection between the two writers should still be the thirty-page article written by Hales in 1873.

As Geoffrey Bullough remarks in the 'General Conclusion' to his *Narrative and Dramatic Sources*, source-studies have sometimes fallen into disrepute, being regarded as 'a form of

5. *College English*, xii (1950), 15–19.
6. Yale, 1975, pp. 4–5, 16–17.   7. Oxford, 1976.

truancy from the proper study of the plays, an occupation only suitable for pedants, outside the scope of true criticism'. This attitude is largely due to the shortcomings of the source-hunters themselves who have failed to realize that pin-pointing sources is not an end in itself:

their pursuit should be the first stage in an investigation of Shakespeare's methods of composition ... Above all, the comparative study of sources with the finished play often lets us glimpse the creative process in action as he took over, remade, rejected, adapted or added to chosen or given materials.[8]

This sort of insight into Shakespeare's craftsmanship should be possible in the case of the major 'Chaucerian' play, *Troilus and Cressida,* and, even more interestingly, in the case of *The Two Noble Kinsmen,* the play based on *The Knight's Tale* which he wrote in collaboration with John Fletcher at the very end of his career. Less substantial claims can be made for *Romeo and Juliet* and *A Midsummer Night's Dream,* but Chaucerian poems are important factors in the genesis of both these plays. Elsewhere Shakespeare's Chaucerian allusions are more incidental, passing references which do not make a substantial mark on the plays in which they appear. In such cases the interest of the source-study must be a more general one, as we learn from the accumulation of details not only how well Shakespeare knew his Chaucer but also what kind of character, incident, or image would spark off a Chaucerian association in his mind.

8. *Narrative and Dramatic Sources of Shakespeare* (London, 1957–75), viii. 341 ff.

2

The use of Chaucer by dramatists other than Shakespeare, 1558-1625

When investigation of Shakespeare's knowledge and use of Chaucer has been so piecemeal and uncertain, it comes as no surprise to find that investigation of other Elizabethan and Jacobean dramatists in this respect has been virtually non-existent. My own bias in this book is clearly towards Shakespeare and my work on other writers has been less intensive, but a short survey of the use of Chaucer in non-Shakespearian drama has its own rewards and constitutes a valuable context for the chapters on Shakespeare which are to follow. Any reader primarily interested in Shakespeare can omit this chapter without serious loss of continuity.

I have found evidence of a knowledge of Chaucer in the work of most of the dramatists of the period, including Lyly, Peele, Day, Marston, Jonson, Dekker, Chapman, Middleton, Beaumont, and Fletcher. Of these, Dekker, Chapman, and Fletcher seem particularly well acquainted with Chaucer, although any one of them would come a poor second to Shakespeare in any quantitative or qualitative measurement of allusions. This is interesting in itself, since it does not necessarily follow that because Shakespeare was the greatest dramatist of his time he should also have the best knowledge of Chaucer, although working on his sources does convince me that his combination of a highly retentive memory and unusually strong powers of association contributed significantly to the unique richness of his work.

Like Shakespeare, other dramatists used Chaucer in a wide variety of ways, ranging from single-line allusions to the poet himself, his characters or situations, to using his work as the basis for a whole plot or sub-plot. Many of the shorter allusions have been catalogued by Otto Ballman in the *Anglia* article I have already cited, so I shall concentrate here on the longer and more substantial examples, which are in any case more relevant to my argument about Shakespeare.

There would appear to have been at least thirteen plays based on Chaucerian poems written between 1558 and 1625, excluding Shakespeare's plays. Such a statement cannot be any more definitive for two reasons: first, there may have been more plays of which no record survives, and second, there is room for debate about some of these thirteen, since in the case of seven of them the play itself is lost and the evidence for believing in Chaucerian influence is entirely external. However, the plays, with their source-poems, are as follows:

1559	Grimald, N.	*Troilus ex Chaucero comoedia*	*Troilus and Criseyde*	Lost
1559	Radcliffe, R.	*De Patientia Griseldis*	*The Clerke's Tale*	Lost
1559	Radcliffe, R.	*De Meliboeo Chauceriano*	*The Tale of Melibee*	Lost
1559	Phillip, J.	*Patient Grissil*	*The Clerke's Tale*	
1564	B., R.	*Apius and Virginia*	*The Physician's Tale*	
1566	Edwardes, R.	*Palamon and Arcite*	*The Knight's Tale*	Lost
1594	Anon.	*Palamon and Arcite*	*The Knight's Tale*	Lost
1599	Dekker, T. et al.	*Troilus and Cressida*	*Troilus and Criseyde*	Lost
1600	Dekker, T.	*Patient Grissil*	*The Clerke's Tale*	
1600	Dekker, T. et al.	*Fair Constance of Rome*	*The Man of Law's Tale*	Lost
1602	Chapman, G.	*Sir Giles Goosecap*	*Troilus and Criseyde*	
1612	Beaumont, F. and Fletcher, J.	*The Triumph of Honor*	*The Franklin's Tale*	
1620	Fletcher, J.	*Women Pleased*	*The Wife of Bath's Tale*	

The first three plays, written apparently in the same year at the very beginning of the period, are all in Latin, and may well have been more directly Chaucerian than anything that was written later. Two of them refer to Chaucer in their titles as if they were closely based on his poems, and the third, Radcliffe's *De Patientia Griseldis*, seems almost certainly Chaucerian, since the same author acknowledges his source in his Melibee play, and the two stories are so similar: *The Tale of Melibee* has a male central character and treats the theme of 'patience' in a wider social context than the limited area of wife-testing in the Grissil story. Both tales were related by Chaucer to the higher subject of the 'vertuous suffraunce' of life itself and the acceptance of all that God sends, and our knowledge of the strong moral tone of much of the early Elizabethan drama makes it seem likely that Radcliffe followed him in this. The fact that Grimald calls his Troilus play a 'comoedia', as opposed to Chaucer's explicit 'litel myn tragedye' (v. 1786) may imply that he used only the first three books of the poem (as Chapman did later in *Sir Giles Goosecap*) and allowed the story to end happily. It is not surprising to find Chaucer being Latinized during this period; it implies a respect for his works and a desire to preserve them from the oblivion that might result from his having chosen to write them in the vernacular—a desire which appears again in Sir Francis Kynaston's translation of *Troilus* into Latin in 1635, mentioned above. (There was of course an academic tradition of Latin drama.)

The first extant Chaucerian play of the period is also the first one written in the vernacular, and it is another Grissil play: J. Phillip's *Commodye of pacient and meeke Grissil* of 1559. In their Malone Society reprint of the play in 1909, the editors, W. W. Greg and R. B. McKerrow, say 'The ultimate source of the play is of course the last novel of the *Decameron*, but whether the playwright drew his material direct from Boccaccio has not been ascertained.' The sources of the play have still to be investigated, but, in terms of general probability, it is unlikely that Phillip would have read the *Decameron* directly, either in Italian or in English, since it was by no means easily accessible at the time. E. Hutton, editor of the version of the *Decameron* published in 1909 in the Tudor

Translations series, records the lack of a complete translation of the work until 1620, and gives details of the isolated stories that had appeared in English before that date, including a *Patient Grissil* of 1619. Other scholars, such as W. Farnham[1] and H. G. Wright,[2] have considered the question of how and when Englishmen began to know the work, and they have not discovered any English version of this story apart from Chaucer's before that date either. This is mainly because Boccaccio became ashamed of the *Decameron* as a whole when, in later life, he spent his time writing serious Latin works under the influence of Petrarch—a literary friendship which did a great disservice to Italian vernacular literature. Consequently it became difficult to obtain the work, and it was very little known outside Italy. It is most likely that Chaucer did not know the vernacular *Decameron*, for example, though he certainly knew Boccaccio's *Teseide*, *Filostrato*, and perhaps *Filocolo*. For his own version of the Grissil story in *The Clerke's Tale* he used Petrarch's Latin translation of Boccaccio and a French version, as J. B. Severs has shown,[3] and the Clerk attributes the story to Petrarch. Chaucer may well have believed that the Latin version was the original, as many of his contemporaries did; none of them makes any mention of the *Decameron*, or of Boccaccio's connection with this or any of the other stories in it. This general ignorance continued in England until 1566 when William Painter included sixteen of the stories in his *Palace of Pleasure*, a work now famous as one of Shakespeare's sourcebooks.

Already we have an admirable illustration of the difficulties of tracing the influence of a writer who does not invent his own plots: it becomes necessary to define the origiynalit of Chaucer's version before we can judge whether Phillip used it rather than a version in Latin or French. Fortunately, Chaucer's version does have a number of distinctive details and effects which render the whole exercise possible. Since *Patient Grissil* was dramatized twice during this period and

1. 'England's Discovery of the Decameron', *PMLA*, xxxix (1924), 123–39.
2. *Boccaccio in England* (London, 1957).
3. *The Literary Relationships of Chaucer's 'Clerke's Tale'* (New Haven, 1942).

the same arguments will arise over the use of *The Clerke's Tale* it seems sensible to bring in the later play as well at this point and deal with both simultaneously.

Between October and December in 1599, Henslowe was paying Chettle and Haughton as well as Dekker for a *Patient Grissil* play.[4] Opinions as to the authorship of the different parts of the extant play have varied, but as Fredson Bowers says 'there is common agreement that the main plot is Dekker's'.[5] Boccaccio's original story had still not been translated into English and we have no evidence that Dekker knew Italian.[6] There is on the other hand considerable evidence scattered throughout his work that he knew Chaucer and he may have written as many as three plays based on Chaucer's works (including *Troilus and Cressida* and *Fair Constance of Rome*), although *Patient Grissil* is the only one extant. It is conceivable that Dekker may have known of the earlier play by Phillip, since there are several parallels between the two plays in the general methods of their adaptation to the stage, in the addition of new characters, comic material, and songs.

Both plays relate the somewhat unattractive story of the marriage of aristocratic Walter and low-born Grissil and the prolonged testing of the wife's patience which follows in a fairly traditional manner, without startling changes. Both fill out the story with additional materials which reflect the conventions and requirements of the stage at the different times of writing as well as the author's own interests and attitude to the story. The earlier play, for example, contains a 'Vice' figure called Politicke Perswasion who not only comments on the play and explains it to the audience (as was common in plays of this period) but also incites Walter to test his wife, thus externalizing the evil motivation and absolving this

4. *Henslowe's Diary*, ed. R. A. Foakes and R. T. Rickert (Cambridge, 1961), pp. 125, 128–9.

5. *The Dramatic Works of Thomas Dekker*, ed. Fredson Bowers (Cambridge, 1953–61), vol. i, p. 211. All quotations from Dekker's *Patient Grissil* and his other plays are from this edition.

6. In her book, *Thomas Dekker* (Columbia, 1911), M. L. Hunt comments, 'When one considers Dekker's general reading, what one misses, on the whole, is a knowledge of Italian literature and, in his plays, a dependence upon Italian motive' (p. 18).

problematic hero from some of his moral responsibility: a crude foreshadowing of the Othello/Iago relationship is in fact produced. Both dramatists provide Grissil with more of a family than the lone father she has in the medieval versions. Phillip invents a mother who appears early in the play solely in order to die and give Grissil occasion to display and discourse on filial piety, a theme much amplified and emphasized in this version. He also adds a Nurse as a speaking character in both the scenes in which Grissil is tested by being deprived of her children, presumably in order to provide adequate dramatic expression for the resentment and hostility the audience feel towards Walter at this point and which, from the very nature of the story, Grissil herself cannot express. Dekker writes in a brother for Grissil, a very Elizabethan discontented scholar called Laureo who fills exactly this role of railing against Walter at appropriate points. Similarly, both Phillip and Dekker provide some light relief in the form of music (each play contains a sprinkling of songs) and in the form of comedy: Phillip's 'Vice' character has some comic scenes (as for example in his search for a midwife for Grissil), while Dekker adds the clownish family servant Babulo and two comic sub-plots, though these may be the work of his collaborators. The sub-plots have superficially nothing to do with Chaucer, since they introduce new characters, the shrewish Gwenthyan and the cruel, aloof Julia, to contrast with Grissil, but this device is in itself a dramatic equivalent for the 'marriage group' of *The Canterbury Tales* where Chaucer gives us a small anthology of love and marriage relationships, balancing off the extremes of the *Wife of Bath's Prologue* and *The Clerke's Tale* against the 'golden mean' of *The Franklin's Tale*.

However, it is now time to look at the precise details in each play which make it possible to argue that Chaucer is the source for the main plot. In the earlier play the first indication of the possible influence of Chaucer comes before the story proper begins. Chaucer's Prologue for the Clerk, which has, of course, no parallel in any other version, emphasizes the problem of a choice of style for the Tale, with the Host requesting the Clerk to eschew rhetoric and speak simply:

> Your termes, your figures, and your coloures,
> Keepe hem in store tyl so be that ye endyte
> Hygh style, as whan men to kinges write.
> Speketh so playne at this time, I yow pray,
> That we may understonde what ye say.[7]
>
> (16–20)

The Clerk replies with a eulogy of his source, Petrarch 'whos rethorike sweete / Enlumined al Itallie of poetrie' (32–33), and describes how 'first with heigh stile he enditeth—A prohemie' (41–43) before getting down to the story, commenting on this long and ornate opening:

> And truely, as to my judgement,
> Me thinketh it a thinge impertinent,
> Save that him lyst convey his mateare.
>
> (53–55)

There is some discreet Chaucerian irony here, since in the Clerk's summary of Petrarch and in his own opening lines he gives at least as much scene-painting 'impertinence' as the Latin version, but on the surface he would seem to have acquiesced in the Host's desire, and the Tale is in fact related quite simply, though with the kind of evocative, lyrical simplicity that is paralleled in *The Prioress's Tale* and *The Man of Law's Tale* rather than the rougher, more colloquial kind of energy that we feel the Host might mean by a reference to Chaucer's 'plain style'.

There is a similar discussion of high and low style in the Preface to Phillip's play, where the speaker describes the search for suitably instructive 'histories' and says

Our Auctor found out one, wherein he tooke delight,
And moved therto by his frend, gave franke consent to wright:
So simplye as hee coulde, though wanting hawtie skill,
In that from *Helicons* fayre spring, the Muses him exile:
Ne would *Kay Citheria* seeme, Dame *Clio* to permit,
To garnishe him with Rethoricque, the Gods did frown at it:

7. All my Chaucer quotations are from the most recent edition at the time of a play's composition (see Bibliography for a list of sixteenth- and seventeenth-century editions). Line references, however, are taken from the edition of F. N. Robinson (London, 1957).

So pevish Pan possessed him, whose rusticke Pipes did carpe,
Whose concordes were far dissonant, to sweete *Apollois* Harpe.
                                        (8–15)[8]

Phillip uses a classical frame of reference which is not in
Chaucer, and there is of course a conventional element in an
apologetic prologue, but the emphasis on style is the same, as
well as the insistence that the story will be told simply rather
than rhetorically.

There are two significant moments in the unfolding of the
story itself where Phillip seems to follow Chaucer rather than
Petrarch or any close French or English translation of Boccaccio that might have been available to him. At the point
where Walter is sending Grissil back to her father and she
makes a pathetic request to keep one garment, partly in order
to preserve her modesty (and hence her husband's honour)
and partly as recompense for her virginity which she brought
with her but cannot take back, Boccaccio and his translators,
including Petrarch, show Walter weeping with pity for her
and having great difficulty in hiding his feelings. Chaucer
omits this as part of his general heightening of effects; in this
case he is emphasizing Walter's apparent heartlessness, as he
does elsewhere. Phillip seems to follow Chaucer in making no
mention of tears on Walter's part, nor giving him an aside in
which to express his feelings during the incident (ll. 1655–64),
which is surprising since his hero is more given to self-revela-
tion in general than Chaucer's, and is given several soliloquies
in which he thinks about his wife, and also conversations with
Politicke Perswasion, the Nurse, and some of his counsellors
in which he discusses his actions.

At the major climax of the story, Chaucer makes far more
of Grissil's reaction to the revelation that her children are still
alive than the other versions do. When Walter has explained
the truth, Petrarch says that Grissil almost died of joy as she
embraced her children, exhausting them with kisses. Chaucer
makes her lose consciousness entirely, a fact he stresses by
repetition (1079, 1099), and he spends much longer on the
description of Grissil embracing her children, giving us the
words she used to them, the reactions of the courtiers, the

8. All quotations from Phillip's *Patient Grissil* are from the Malone Society
text, edited by W. W. Greg and R. B. McKerrow (Oxford, 1909).

concern of Walter, etc., at some length (1079–120). Again Phillip appears to follow Chaucer in having Grissil faint (sd '*fall downe*' at l. 1956) and in making her address her children and praise God and her husband for their preservation. The other versions have no direct speech for her, and do not even say she spoke, although one presumes that she did. Even in a play as early as this I cannot find any Chaucerian verbal borrowings in the speech, and the parallel has a weakness in that it is obviously so much more effective dramatically to have Grissil both faint and speak to her children at this point that Phillip might have made the alterations by himself, even as Chaucer did.

However, these are the principle points on which Phillip coincides with Chaucer and diverges from the other versions. Combined with the general probability that he would have looked at what was not only the sole English translation available but also the work of the most admired English poet of the time, they do add up to a strong likelihood that Chaucer was indeed his primary source.[9] The resulting play is competent enough, but its literary merits are not such that a detailed investigation of the methods of dramatization on the assumption that Chaucer was used would be very rewarding. We have here a straightforward 'use' of Chaucer as a quarry for a plot, rather than the more complex and interesting type of influence we find in writers like Shakespeare and Chapman who were much more self-conscious (and often critical) about their source, allowing the critic greater insight into their creative processes.

Dekker, in these terms, is more a man who uses Chaucer than one who is creatively influenced by him, although the sheer quantity of his references makes him a significant 'Chaucerian'. There are many direct similarities between Chaucer's *Clerke's Tale* and his *Patient Grissil* although his adaptation of the story for the stage is altogether more sophisticated and thoroughgoing than that of Phillip.

Much of the detail of the opening scene of the play corresponds directly to that of the poem, although Dekker naturally

---

9. There is further evidence for Phillip's use of Chaucer in the several references to the character of Fame and to characters from *The Legend of Good Women*: see ll. 364, 695–7, 848, 858–9, 865, 986–9.

omits the description of the setting that opens the narrative, and he compresses the material for two 'scenes' in the poem into one: he begins *in medias res* by simply making the Marquis of Pavia, Gwalter's brother, recall the day on which Gwalter's subjects asked him to promise to choose a wife rather than depicting the situation itself as Chaucer does. Even so, we have the parallels of the offer and refusal of high-born wives (l. 22, cf. Chaucer 130–3), the discussion of marriage as a curtailing of freedom (ll. 60 ff., cf. 113 and 144 ff. in the poem), and Walter's declaration that he will make his own choice (l. 64, cf. 152 ff.). I am not quoting these passages as there are no verbal parallels: it is the details of the plot and the ideas mentioned in the dialogue that are similar rather than the actual words. In the exposition of the plot most of the ideas can be traced to Chaucer, although Dekker has rearranged and condensed things considerably, and this continues throughout the play. For example, both writers explicitly discuss the measurements for Grissil's new clothes in the subsequent proposal scene (I. ii. 61, cf. Chaucer's ll. 256 ff.), and both refer to the notion that virtue is often to be found dressed in poor garments (I. ii. 174, cf. ll. 425–6). Dekker adds a song to this scene, before the Marquis enters, like Phillip who also added short scenes concerning Grissil and her family in which she delivered songs expressing obedience, contentment, and piety (e.g. 218 ff., 495 ff.). The opening of the 'testing' theme, with Walter's criticism of Grissil, is closely comparable to Chaucer in substance, though Dekker makes Gwalter more harsh, telling his wife he hates her (II. ii. 50), while in the poem he stresses his continuing love (479). Both writers refer to the (mythical) hatred of Walter's people for Grissil, and go on to mention her low birth, a fact which is more relevant in Chaucer, since he has already mentioned the birth of a child. Dekker's Gwalter accuses his wife of forgetting her lowly origins at a slightly later point in the story (III. i. 89), while Chaucer's Walter does it here (469). Again, both writers use actual garments and references to them as a symbol of the change in Grissil's estate, an element which is not stressed by Phillip.

Later parallels can be found in the end of the story, when Walter sends for Grissil to attend his second marriage (end of

IV. iii, cf. 946 ff.), asks her opinion of his new wife (v. ii. 144, cf. 1030 ff.), and receives the same request to treat her more gently because she has not been used to hardship as Grissil herself was (v. ii. 147 ff., cf. 1037 ff.). At this point, the truth is revealed in both versions; Dekker does not follow Phillip in exaggerating Grissil's amazement and the general pathos of her situation by making her swoon more significant than it is in Chaucer, but passes on rather quickly to the resolution of the sub-plot.

Where Dekker's version differs from Chaucer's the changes can often be accounted for in terms of the necessities of dramatic adaptation, as was the case with Phillip. Dekker too compresses and rearranges, adds and omits in order to get the best stage effect. Sometimes he seems to be developing a hint in the poem and sometimes his work is entirely new. An example of the former might be the way in which Dekker expands Chaucer's brief but careful description of Walter's love for Grissil:

> He (not with wanton loking of folie)
> His eyen cast upon her, but in sade wise
> (236–7)

and his statement about Grissil herself that

> No likerous lust was in her hert ironne
> (214)

into the lengthy discussion on love and lust that takes place between Grissil and her father (I. ii. 25–74), in which her role is to defend her own virtue and the nature of her lover's intentions. Later in this scene the critical attitude of the Marquis's courtiers and their haughty behaviour may have been suggested by Chaucer's description of the ladies of the court who

> were nothing gladde
> To handle her clothes, in which she was clad.
> (375–6)

Frequently Dekker presents in dialogue or soliloquy what Chaucer does in narrative, as when in II. ii. the conversation with Furio gives us Gwalter's true feelings about his wife and reveals his intention to test her, information given us in direct authorial comment by Chaucer at 449 ff. Dekker is more like Chaucer in presenting the character apologetically than he is like Phillip, who introduces an external agent to motivate the plot. Similarly, we get the explanatory asides in the scene where the children are stolen (IV. i, e.g. 69–70, 128, 140, 153–5), as the parallel to Chaucer's narrative expositions (e.g. 512 ff., 579 ff.), and the words in which Furio and Gwalter praise Grissil at the end of the scene, after she has gone, are comparable to Chaucer's direct praise.

Like Phillip then, Dekker used Chaucer in a businesslike manner, if the evidence of this extant play is typical. Before looking at the reasons for believing that two lost plays with which Dekker was involved were based on Chaucer I shall however consider the other early Elizabethan play which is extant, 'R.B.''s *Apius and Virginia* of 1564, and the two lost *Palamon and Arcite* plays of 1566 and 1594.

Apius and Virginia (edited by W. W. Greg and R. B. McKerrow for the Malone Society in 1911) is in many ways similar to Phillip's *Patient Grissil* of 1559 both in source-problems and methods of dramatization. The alternative source would be Book iii of Livy's *History of Rome*, either in the original or in the translation given by Gower in *Confessio Amantis*, Book vii. Chaucer used Livy for his *Physician's Tale*, but his version is quite distinctive since he also used *The Romaunt of the Rose* (5589 ff.) and he cut the tale down to a mere 265 lines, ignoring the political and military context and turning it into a domestic tragedy with a straightforward emphasis on the martyrdom of Virginia. 'R.B.' similarly omits all the details given by Livy about the absence of Virginia's father on military duties, the conflicting letters sent to him, his journeys between the camp and Rome, the effect of the scandal on his soldiers and the subsequent march on Rome in support of the tragic family. Both Chaucer and 'R.B.' ignore Virginia's fiancé and her (admittedly ineffective) brothers: in all other known versions of the story she is an only daughter but not an only child.

Chaucer and 'R.B' further emphasize the importance of Virginia by stressing her age (14 in Chaucer, 16 in the play) and by adding a scene in which her father explains to her what he feels he must do and she accepts her fate. In Livy her father's action takes her by surprise: she is an unconscious victim rather than a conscious heroine. After her father has killed her (thereby saving her from being raped by Apius) he actually brings her head on stage in the play and shows it to the guilty judge, another incident which is not in Livy but is in Chaucer:

> Her father, with sorrowful hert and fell,
> Her heed of smote, and by the toppe it hente,
> And to the iudge he it yave in presente.
>
> (254-6)

Chaucer probably took this from *The Romaunt of the Rose* (5635-58), but if 'R.B.' is relying on a source rather than on his own instinct for a good dramatic effect Chaucer is the more likely of the two medieval sources, since he was so well-known. Finally, Chaucer's comment on his Tale at the end, with its sober moral 'Here may men se how sin hath his merite ... Forsake synne, or synne yow forsake' (277-86) could well have suggested the explicit judgements at the end of the play and the advice to repent in the Epilogue; there is certainly nothing comparable in Livy.

To what seems quite clearly a Chaucerian central core, 'R.B.' adds such early Elizabethan ingredients as a 'Vice' figure (Haphazard), a low-life sub-plot, some characters like Conscience, Memory, Reward, and Justice who hover between abstraction and naturalism, and a strong emphasis on piety and stability within the family. This method of adaptation is very similar to Phillip's treatment of the Patient Grissil story.

Like *Patient Grissil*, *Apius and Virginia* was dramatized twice during the period 1558-1625, but as F. L. Lucas has demonstrated in his edition,[1] the principle sources for John Webster's version in 1624 were classical, namely Livy and Dionysius of Halicarnassus. He finds no trace of Chaucer except perhaps in the introduction of an Advocate in v. i (the Host talks of 'thise iudges and hire advocates' at the end of the Tale), but Webster hardly needed encouragement from Chaucer to put an advocate into a play. A stronger point of comparison might be the fact that Webster again makes Virginia an only child (the Clown says to her at II. i. 5 'your

1. London, 1927.

father hath a fair revenue, and never a son to inherit'), though this is an obvious way of increasing her dramatic importance. We have so little other evidence that Webster knew Chaucer at all well that the case must remain very doubtful.[2]

Chronologically, the next two Chaucerian plays after 'R.B.''s *Apius and Virginia* are both *Palamon and Arcite* plays, and both lost. The earlier one, written by Richard Edwardes, was performed before the Queen at Oxford in two parts on 2 and 4 September 1566; the performance of Part I was unhappily marked as an occasion by the collapse of a wall which killed three of the crowd who were pressing to see the Queen. From accounts that survive it seems that the play followed Chaucer's *Knight's Tale* quite closely: Part I dealt with the story up to the point at which Palamon and Arcite are discovered by Theseus and his hunting party while they are fighting in the wood outside Athens, and Part II continued with the tournament, Arcite's victory and death, and the betrothal of Palamon and Emily.[3] The record of Elizabeth's reactions gives us some details about the play. We know, for example, that the sound-effects in the hunting scene were naturalistic from the following comment:

At ye crie of ye houndes in ye Quadrant uppon ye trayne of a foxe in ye huntinge of Theseus, when ye boyes in ye wyndowes cried 'nowe, nowe', 'O excellent' saide ye Queene, 'those boyes are readie to leape out at windowes to follow ye houndes'.

We know the play followed Chaucer in giving Arcite a funeral pyre (2933 ff.) because another spectator tried to stop an actor from throwing a cloak on to it (cf. 2948), causing the Queen to cry out 'Goo, foole, he knoweth his part'. Finally she rewarded the actor who took the part of Emily 'for gatheringe her flowers prettily in ye garden and singinge sweetlie in ye pryme of March',[4] which again sounds like a

2. R. W. Dent, in *John Webster's Borrowing* (Berkeley, 1960), pp. 294–5, has claimed a parallel between *The Physician's Tale* and *The Devil's Law Case* (1617), both of which mention the notion that the best park-keeper is a former poacher, but this is given as a proverb by M. P. Tilley, *A Dictionary of the Proverbs in England in the Sixteenth and Seventeenth Centuries* (Ann Arbor, 1950), (D191) and the other four Chaucerisms listed by Dent are equally doubtful.

3. See E. K. Chambers, *The Elizabethan Stage* (Oxford, 1923), i. 128.

4. Quoted by F. S. Boas in *An Introduction to Tudor Drama* (Oxford, 1933), pp. 47–48.

scene taken from Chaucer (1033 ff.), though it should be May.

We do not know if another *Palamon and Arcite* play recorded by Henslowe as performed by the Admiral's Men in 1594 has any connection with this earlier play. We do not even know the author(s), as Henslowe's records are only of receipts.[5] In so far as it is possible to speculate at all in these conditions it seems more likely that either Chaucer's poem or Edwardes's play was used than that the author(s) went back to Boccaccio's *Teseide*, but this can only be conjecture. A further conjecture could relate the play to Shakespeare: I claim below that *The Knight's Tale* had a considerable influence on *A Midsummer Night's Dream*, usually dated 1595–6, in which case this lost *Palamon and Arcite* play could have been a subsidiary source for Shakespeare or even (as in the case of *Troilus and Cressida*) the 'straight' version which inspired a slightly burlesqued reply.

There is an unusual cluster of Chaucerian plays around 1599–1602, which makes one wonder if Speght's new edition of Chaucer in 1598 (the first since 1561) was responsible. No less than five plays (including Shakespeare's *Troilus*) were produced during this period. It is clear from looking at their earlier work that the dramatists involved were not reading Chaucer for the first time in 1598, but the new edition may have refreshed their memories and drawn their attention to a new source of plots.

The least certain of this group of plays is the lost *Fair Constance of Rome*, though I believe the external evidence is strong enough to merit its inclusion. In June 1600, Henslowe's diary records payments made to 'An, Munday and the rest' for 'a booke Called the fayre Constance of Roome', and fortunately 'the rest' are soon specified as 'drayton, hathaway, (munday and) deckers'. We also discover that *Fair Constance of Rome* was in two parts, but the only other information we have about the play is to be found in a letter from Robert Shaw to Henslowe which discusses Robert Wilson's payment for his part in it and so adds him to the list of authors.[6] The story of Constance is related by Chaucer in

---

5. *Henslowe's Diary*, pp. 24, 25.   6. Ibid., pp. 135, 136, 294.

The Man of Law's Tale, and it has strong resemblances to the Patient Grissil story in its concentration on the testing and suffering of a virtuous heroine. It is possible that Dekker chose the subject, having been looking through the new edition of Chaucer for plots occasionally during the last two years; he may even have been attracted to the poem, which comes quite near to *The Clerke's Tale* in Speght's Chaucer, by an interest in the similarities and differences between it and the Patient Grissil story. It has what amounts to a duplication in its plot, since the heroine marries twice and in each case arouses the jealousy of her mother-in-law who plots to get rid of her and succeeds. The form of persecution is also repeated: on both occasions she is put into a rudderless boat and left to her fate. From this it seems that Chaucer's story would fit very well into a dramatic structure in two parts, as we know *Fair Constance of Rome* to have been. The first part might have dealt with the marriage to 'the Sowdan of Surrye', his mother's jealousy and plot, the first voyage of Constance, her reception by the constable and his wife, followed by the second plot against her which results in the dramatic moment when the voice of God himself clears her, and King Alla is converted to Christianity and marries the heroine. This would be an appropriate climax, and it is just over half-way through the poem (up to l. 693). The second part would then contain the jealousy of Alla's mother Donegild, her plot and its success, his despair and murder of his mother, Constance's second voyage, and the series of events which finally bring her back to Rome and reunite her with both her second husband and her father. The only rival source would seem to be the version given by Gower in his *Confessio Amantis*, Book ii, but this is comparatively pedestrian and uninspiring, and we have no evidence that any of the authors of *Fair Constance* had read Gower, whereas we have a respectable amount of evidence that Dekker at least had read Chaucer.

The *Troilus* play with which Dekker was involved in 1599 is also lost, but we know that Dekker's collaborator was Chettle,[7] and a fragmentary plot of the play survives. Like

7. Ibid., pp. 106–7.

Shakespeare's *Troilus*, it combined the love-story with that of
the siege, and it probably took the material for the former
from Chaucer and Henryson (whose *Testament of Cresseid*
had been appearing without acknowledgement in editions of
Chaucer since 1532). There are stage-directions reading
'Enter Tro(y)l(u)s and Pandarus . . . to them Cressida', and
later 'Enter Cressida with Beggars . . . to them Troylus', so
the play must have gone on after the point where Shakespeare
chose to end, and apparently took the story through to the
end of Henryson's sequel. Geoffrey Bullough has analysed
the fragment[8] and discussed its relation to Shakespeare's
play, which is almost certainly later, and which he therefore
suggests is a 'realistic answer to the unsophisticated mixture
of epic and didactic sentiment likely to have characterized
the piece by Dekker and Chettle'.[9]

The relationships between the various dramatic companies
during this 'war of the theatres' period are complex and
obscure, but it does seem certain that the Troilus and
Cressida story was the focus of more than one argument. It
was given a burlesque treatment in one of the most famous
'poetomachia' plays, Marston's *Histriomastrix* (1599), when
the characters representing 'the players' put on a scene from a
Troilus play with the following dialogue:

> TROY: Come *Cressida* my Cresset light,
>   Thy face doth shine both day and night,
>   Behold, behold, thy garter blue,
>   Thy knight his valiant elboe weares,
>   That When he shakes his furious Speare,
>   The foe in shivering fearefull sort,
>   May lay him downe in death to snort.
> CRES: O knight with vallour in thy face,
>   Here take my skreene, wear it for grace,
>   Within thy Helmet put the same,
>   Therewith to make thine enemies lame.[1]

This would also seem to be an attack on the Dekker play, in
all probability a sentimental piece, though the pun on

8. 'The lost *Troilus and Cressida*', *Essays and Studies*, xvii (1964), 24–40.
9. *Narrative and Dramatic Sources of Shakespeare*, vi. 100.
1. Quoted from *John Marston: Plays*, ed. H. H. Wood (Edinburgh, 1934–9),
p. 265.

Shakespeare's name in the fifth line here might imply that Marston knew the Lord Chamberlain's company were also preparing a *Troilus* play. However, Shakespeare's play is usually dated 1601-2, and it is not necessary to infer a connection between Shakespeare and the Troy story in order to make sense of a generalized attack on the public theatres.

The connection with Chaucer in the dialogue is not very specific: details such as the garter and 'skreene' (veil?) are not in his version, but are part of the general trappings of literary romance in a medieval setting. Possibly they occur in the Admiral's Men's play. Shakespeare uses a 'sleeve' which is similar, and is nearer to the objects mentioned here than it is to Chaucer's brooch. There may even have been something of a stage tradition: no other examples survive, but the story was so common that it is very likely to have been mentioned in plays of which we have no record. There is a 'show' of Troilus and Cressida in the popular *Rare Triumphs of Love and Fortune* (1582) which may have used the device, but it has neither dialogue nor description in the surviving text, so we cannot tell. For the same reasons we can do no more than speculate on the probable source; the lovers appear amongst a group of classical figures as they often do, but they are a strange mixture, the others being Alexander, Dido, Pompey, and Caesar, of whom Dido is the only remotely Chaucerian character, unless we take the others from *The Monke's Tale* as examples of the 'triumph of fortune'. They are all, however, so well-known that there need be no literary source at all.

A play which is also very concerned with literature and literary traditions and which contains some elaborate reference to *Troilus* is the first part of the Cambridge play, *The Return from Parnassus*. This was performed in 1600, so it falls into something of a peak period for references to *Troilus* in the drama: there are three plays which make substantial use of the poem, and we have already seen how Marston chose its characters for his satire, presumably because of their popularity. He was obviously well aware of the activities of the public theatres, and the author of the *Parnassus* plays was particularly sensitive to what was happening in the literary world, and where a career could be made in it.

The Return from Parnassus, however, does not use *Troilus* for a plot but refers to Chaucer and imitates his verses. A character called Gullio employs Ingenioso to write some verses for him 'in two or three divers vayns, in Chaucers, Gowers and Spencers and Mr. Shakespeares' (1027–8).[2] The Chaucerian stanzas are close to some in *Troilus*, though the actual poem to be imitated is not specified. This again attests to the fame of *Troilus* and its verse-form, which was thought to be particularly suitable for serious matters—in his *Short Treatise on Verse* in 1584, the future King James I had conformed with convention in advising his readers 'For tragicall materis, complaintis, or testamentis, use this kynde of verse following, callit Troilus verse —'.[3] Ingenioso's first stanza is a close copy. He has written

> Even as the flowers in the coulde of night
> Yclosed slepen in there stalkes lowe,
> Redressen them [against] the sunne bright,
> And spreaden in theire kinde course by rowe,
> Right soe mine eyne when I up to thee throwe,
> They bene y cleard; therfore, O Venus deare,
> Thy might, thye grace y heried be it here.
>
> (1146–52)

He found most of this in Chaucer:

> But right as floures through the cold of night,
> Iclosed, stoupen in her stalke lowe
> Redressen hem ayen the Sunne bright
> And spreden in her kinde course by rowe
> Right so gan tho his eyen up to throwe
> This Troilus, and saied, 'O Venus dere,
> Thy might, thy grace, yheried be it here!'
>
> (ii. 967–73)

The next stanza has slightly more originality. Ingenioso has

> Nor scrivenly nor craftilie I write;
> Blott I a litell the paper with my teares,
> Nought might mee gladden while I [did] endite
> But this poor scrowle, that thy name y bears.
> Go blessed scrowle, a blisfull destinie
> Is shapen thee, my lady shalt thou see. (1153–8)

2. Quoted from *The Parnassus Plays*, ed. J. B. Leishman (London, 1949).
3. Reprinted in G. G. Smith (ed.), *Elizabethan Critical Essays* (Oxford, 1904), i. 222.

Nevertheless, four lines are paralleled in Chaucer:

> Ne scriveinishe or craftely thou it write
> Beblotte it with thy teares eke a lite
> (ii. 1026–7)

> And said, 'Lettre, a blisful destine
> The shapen is: my lady shal the se'.
> (ii. 1091–2)

The last stanza in the play is even less directly derivative:

> Nought fitteth me in this sad thinge I feare
> To usen iolly tearmes of meriment;
> Solemne tearmes better fitten this mattere
> Than to usen tearmes of good content:
> For if a painter a pike woulde painte
> With Asses feet, and headed like an Ape,
> It cordeth not, soe were it but a iape.
> (1159–65)

But the last notion is taken from Book ii of *Troilus* again:

> For if a painter would painte a pike
> With asses feet, and hedded as an ape,
> It cordeth not, so were it but a iape.
> (ii. 1041–3)

This last stanza gives us an example of a change of meaning that has taken place since the fourteenth century: Gullio objects to the word 'iape' on the grounds that 'my chaste ladye will never endure the reading of it', whereupon Ingenioso explains that 'the word as Chaucer useth it hath noe unhonest meaninge in it, for it signifieth a ieste'. Gullio also picks up an alleged obscenity in Spenser, so his blind prejudice for Shakespeare is triumphantly confirmed. This is the only example I have found of direct imitation of Chaucer in the drama of the period, and I am indebted to J. B. Leishman who notes the parallels in his edition of the Parnassus plays. The stanzas are interesting in that they show a basic appreciation of Chaucer's metre alongside an ignorance of Middle English grammar and of the use of final 'e'.

The last of the turn-of-the-century *Troilus* plays is the most surprising of them all, Chapman's *Sir Giles Goosecap* (1602), which makes extensive use of plot, dialogue, ideas, and images from the first three books of Chaucer's poem but assimilates them so well into a typical Renaissance comedy that they hardly betray their medieval origins at all. This play is about contemporary with Shakespeare's *Troilus*, but there is a sufficiently wide margin for the dates of both that we cannot say certainly which came first. There could be a link between Chapman's play and the lost Troilus play written by Dekker and others for the Admiral's Men in 1599, since Chapman was writing for that company until 1599 or 1600 and the use of Chaucer's poem for this play may have encouraged him to look at it when writing *Sir Giles Goosecap*, which T. M. Parrot thinks was his first play for the Chapel Children.[4] Chapman may have been particularly attracted to *Troilus* because of his current preoccupation with the Homeric Troy material (the first seven books of the *Iliad* and 'Achilles' Shield' from Book xviii were published in 1598, and twelve more in 1609), though his play has nothing whatever to do with Troy.

Miller Maclure has called *Sir Giles Goosecap* a 'serious, pedantic, neoplatonic allegory of the Troilus–Cressida story',[5] which sums up many of the changes. Troilus is transformed from a medieval courtly lover into Clarence, a Renaissance gentleman and scholar, with priggishness as his weakness rather than sentimentality, and Cressida becomes Eugenia, a self-possessed Elizabethan widow who is likely to yield, her uncle tells Clarence, not through compassion like Criseyde, but because 'she is a good scholar and like enough to bite at the rightest reason' (I. iv. 139). This uncle, unlike Shakespeare's Pandarus or any other current conception of the character, is a thoroughly sympathetic figure, the nobleman Lord Momford. He uses the tact and humour of his predecessor to bring about the union of the young pair, but his office can be presented in a favourable light to the audience because the final aim is marriage in this case. The play is set in England and the Sir Giles Goosecap of the title, like the name-parts of some of Chapman's other comedies such as *The Gentleman Usher* (1602) and *Monsieur D'Olive* (1604),

4. In his edition of *Chapman: The Comedies* (London, 1912), p. 893. All quotations from the play are from this edition.
5. *George Chapman* (Toronto, 1966), p. 91.

is something of a character-part, involved in a nebulous and uneventful sub-plot and having only a tenuous connection with the central romantic story.

Parallels to *Troilus and Criseyde* were first noticed by G. L. Kittredge in 1898,[6] and O. Ballmann also listed a few, but there are many more detailed resemblances that no-one has yet described. From Clarence's confession of his love through the writing and delivery of his letter, the reply, the uncle's plan to invite his niece to supper at his house and to have Clarence feign illness, right up to the happy union of lovers at the end, the plot is simply the first half of Chaucer's poem translated into Elizabethan terms. And not only the plot, but many small details have been used: in II. i, for example, Momford visits his niece in order to tell her of Clarence's love, realizing he must be careful how he does it. First, Chapman uses Chaucer's introductory talk about dancing. In the poem Pandarus finds Criseyde reading, and he begins by encouraging her to stop behaving like a widow:

> Do way your barbe, and shew your face bare
> Do way your boke, rise up and let us daunce,
> (ii. 110–11)

Momford also comments on his niece's clothes:

> Why alas, niece, y'are so smeared with this wilful-
> widow's-three-years black weed, that I never come
> to you but I dream of corses and sepulchres and
> epitaphs all the night after—   (II. i. 56–59)

and shortly afterwards we have for him the stage direction *he danceth speaking* (l. 75). Eugenia comments 'Your lordship is very dancitive, methinks' (l. 80), to which Momford's reply, 'Ay, and I could tell you a thing would make your ladyship very dancitive' (l. 81) is very close to Pandarus's

> Yet could I tel a thing, to don you play.
> (ii. 121)

Chaucer's characters move into a general discussion of the war that surrounds them, and Pandarus turns the conversation to praise of Troilus with transparent simplicity when

6. 'Notes on Elizabethan plays', *Journal of English and Germanic Philology* [*JEGP*], ii (1898), 7–13.

Criseyde 'gan axen hym how Ector ferde' (ii. 153):

> 'Ful wel, I thanke it God', said Pandarus,
> 'Save in his arme he hath a little wound;
> And eke his fresh brother Troilus,
> The wise, worthy Hector the secound,
> In whom that every vertue list habound—'
> (ii. 155-9)

Similarly, Momford begins talking about Clarence in reply to an inquiry from Eugenia about his own health:

> Why, well, very well, niece; and so is my
> friend Clarence well, too; and then is there
> a worthy gentleman well, as any is in England,
> I can tell ye.   (ll. 73-75)

In both works the uncle examines the niece's appearance solemnly and then tells her a piece of good fortune is about to befall her (Chaucer ii. 274 ff., Chapman II. i. 108 ff.). Criseyde and Eugenia react to the examination in exactly the same way:

> Saw ye me never ere now—What sey ye, no?
> (II. 277)

> Why, how now, uncle, did you never see me before?
> (113)

and they have the same reaction to the news itself when it finally comes out: a mixture of distress for themselves, regret at not being able to trust anyone, and irony about the 'good fortune'.
Criseyde says:

> Alas for wo! Why nere I deed?
> For of this world the faith is al agone
> Alas what sholden straunge unto me done,
> When he, that for my best frend I wend,
> Rate me to love, and should it me defend.

> —What! is this al the joy and al the fest?
> Is this your rede? Is this my blisful cas?
> Is this the very mede of your behest?
> (ii. 409-13, 421-3)

Eugenia is briefer:

> Ay me, poor dame! O you amaze me, uncle!
> Is this the wondrous fortune you presage?
> What man may miserable women trust?
>
> (II. i. 143–5)

This scene is typical of Chapman's use of Chaucer in this play, in that he is able to use so much, while his purposes are really entirely different. We are completely on Momford's side in *Sir Giles Goosecap* because his aim is to bring about a marriage for his niece which we believe she should consider. We know already that Clarence is eminently worthy, but Chapman reminds us early in this scene by an aside from Momford while he dances:

> My head must devise something while my feet are
> piddling thus, that may bring her to some fit
> consideration of my friend, who, indeed, is only
> a great scholar, and all his honours and riches lie
> in his mind.   (ll. 67–70)

This echoes Pandarus's concern to make the approach carefully (267 ff.), but the different motives which determine the sympathy of the audience become clear as, after the initial delivery of the news and the woman's reaction, each writer goes into the arguments as to why this love should be accepted. Momford is in a very strong position, opposing his friend's intellectual and moral qualities against 'the judgement of the world' which will censure Eugenia for marrying 'a poor gentleman' (166 ff.). Pandarus is on more ambiguous grounds; he can extol his friend's virtues quite sincerely, but his main argument has to rest on the 'cruelty' of his niece and the danger of Troilus (and perhaps himself) dying if she will not yield (ii. 323 ff.). Both writers mention the concept of 'honour', and in this respect Chapman's use of Chaucer amounts to a conscious critique of the earlier work. Pandarus and Criseyde agree in defining 'honour' in terms of public opinion, and Eugenia assumes the same when she says she will lose 'honour' by this match, but Momford quickly demonstrates how external and superficial this kind of 'honour' is, and argues that Clarence can offer his niece a more essential kind of honour, beseeching her to repair her judgement 'for your own honour's sake'.

The next scene which affords a considerable number of parallels is IV. i, in which Momford delivers Clarence's letter to Eugenia. When she first sees him she says

> What wind blows you hither, trow?
>
> (66)

which was surely suggested by Criseyde's words in exactly the same situation, when Pandarus brings the first letter from Troilus:

> What maner winds gideth you now here?
>
> (ii. 1104)

Both women refuse to take the letter, and Momford's line

> Kind bosom, do thou take it then
>
> (71)

shows that he takes the same action as Pandarus:

> And in her bosome the letter doune he thrast.
>
> (ii. 1155)

They both take advantage of the presence of other people, before whom Criseyde and Eugenia will not make a scene, and shortly afterwards they both guess that the woman has read the letter (Chaucer ii. 1196, Chapman iv. i. 97). Criseyde and Eugenia then refuse to reply (Chaucer ii. 1161, Chapman 109), and Pandarus, as usual, paints an affecting picture of the drastic consequences Criseyde's cruelty will have. This becomes a joke in Chapman:

MOMFORD: What, will you have my friend and I perish? Do you thirst our bloods?

EUGENIA: O y'are in a mighty danger, no doubt on't!

MOMFORD: If you have our bloods, beware our ghosts, I can tell ye—   (110–14)

He goes on to offer to dictate the letter as Pandarus does in Chaucer at this point (1162) but Criseyde refuses and this scene (in which Eugenia accepts help) is more nearly comparable to the way in which Pandarus had advised Troilus on *his* letter and fussed over him (ii. 1023 ff.)—a passage

Chapman has not yet used, since Clarence has composed his letter in soliloquy (III. ii). Chapman may also have used this idea for the letter-writing scene in III. ii of *The Gentleman Usher*, written about the same time as this play. It is the more likely here because Chapman does not follow one sequence in Chaucer through as he did in II. i, but combines elements scattered through Chaucer's second and third books in this scene.

Earlier Momford had invited the whole company to supper (93–94), and he repeats his invitation to his niece when they are alone and after she has written the letter (213 ff.), but she says

> No, no, my lord; you will have Clarence there.
>
> (222)

This is jumping ahead in Chaucer to Book iii, where Pandarus invites Criseyde to supper (560) and

> Soone after this, she to him gan rowne,
> And asked him if Troilus were there.
>
> (568–9)

She is put off by Pandarus's reply that Troilus is 'out of towne' (570), though Chaucer is careful to admit some doubt about whether she believed this or not (575–8). Eugenia is told that Clarence is 'extreme sick' (223–6), an idea which also comes from Chaucer but on a different occasion: Chapman conflates the meeting at Deiphobus's house for which Troilus *does* pretend to be sick, with the later incident of the supper with Pandarus when he is supposed to be out of town. We find details of plot and scraps of dialogue from both used here and in IV. iii, when Momford returns to Clarence and, after a discussion about love and women, tells him

> I have invited her to supper here,
> And told her thou art most extremely sick,
> Which thou shalt counterfeit with all thy skill.
>
> (IV. iii. 82–84)

whereupon Clarence ruefully continues

> Which is exceeding small to counterfeit
>
> (85)

This comes from Book ii of *Troilus and Criseyde*, where
Pandarus tells Troilus to pretend to be sick (1511 ff.) and he
replies

> —Iwis, thou nedelesse
> Conseilest me that sickelich I me faine,
> For I am sike in ernest doutlesse,
> So that wel nigh I sterve for the paine.
> (ii. 1527–30)

But Chapman is leading up to the supper at Momford's
house while Chaucer is preparing for the first meeting of his
young couple at the house of Deiphobus, for the sake of
which Pandarus is ready to set up a fairly complex deception
about Criseyde being persecuted and seeking help. Momford's plans are not nearly so elaborate but, unlike Pandarus,
he feels a need to justify the deceit, and explains

> Ladies whom true worth cannot move to ruth
> True lovers must deceive to show their truth.
> (IV. iii. 96–97)

In the event, Eugenia takes the initiative (v. ii.) and reveals
that she has been in sympathy with her uncle all along. She
decides to go and see Clarence before his plan takes effect,
and Momford is surprised and delighted to find them together. Now that Eugenia has made her decision on the
ground of personal merit, he reveals that he has made
Clarence his heir so they will be rich after all. None of this
ending is taken from Chaucer, of course, nor is the stress put
by Eugenia on the intellectual aspect of the match:

> I could give passion all her blackest rites,
> And make a thousand vows to thy deserts;
> But these are common; knowledge is the bond,
> The seal, and crown of our united minds,
> And that is rare and constant.   (v. ii. 213–17)

This is more in accordance with Chapman's independent
conception of his characters: Clarence is a Renaissance neoplatonic philosopher whose meditations are far more central
to our conception of him, as well as being comparatively
longer and more important, than the Boethian reflections of

Troilus. In one sense Chapman has translated the philosophy as well as the characters into contemporary terms, but he has gone further than this, particularly in the characterization of his hero. There are several long soliloquies (e.g. I. iv. 1 ff., II. i. 1 ff., III. ii. 1 ff.) in which Clarence talks of the debate between the will and the reason, and the subjection of idealism to physical desire. Such subjects are also discussed by him and Momford, and they sometimes remind us more of Shakespeare's *Troilus and Cressida* than of Chaucer, especially when Clarence is trying to describe his love in rhetorical terms and is struggling with the problems of the subjectivity of judgement and the conquest made by love over reason (particularly in I. iv and III. ii).

With all its differences, there is no doubt that parts of *Sir Giles Goosecap* are based very closely upon *Troilus and Criseyde*. This is perhaps the only play in the whole period for which we can say definitely that its author must have had a copy of Chaucer open beside him as he wrote. Others may show a very good memory for Chaucer, but there are never such closely paralleled sequences of words and ideas. One of the most interesting things about the play apart from this is the complete transformation the material has undergone. It would be very easy to read it without suspecting its source at all, although the details, once suggested, are so convincing. I think the nature of the poem itself helped to make this possible. We can easily feel that Chaucer would have preferred to treat this story as Chapman does and give it a happy ending. He would have liked the courtship of Criseyde to end in marriage, and he writes long stretches of his first three books in a purely 'comic' vein as if this were indeed the prospect. Of course we are not really allowed to pretend it is: the poem is weighted with ironies, warnings, and direct authorial references to the impending tragedy. Nevertheless, the parts of the poem which deal with successful courtship and requited love have an independent validity which is not completely destroyed by our knowledge of the tragedy to come. Indeed the very painfulness of the tragedy is a result of the degree of credibility of the happiness that preceded it—an effect Shakespeare denies himself. So Chapman can draw on these 'comic' aspects of the poem and produce something quite different from our over-all appreciation of *Troilus and Criseyde*, though closely founded on the text. By doing this he can exploit Chaucer's skill in good-natured humour, an element in *Troilus* which is almost completely lacking in any other reference to it I have found. In both the scenes I have described, II. i and IV. i, he makes good use of the comedy he found in Chaucer's scenes between Pandarus and Criseyde. Finally, despite all the charges that Chaucer was difficult and obsolete in language being made by so many of his contemporaries, Chapman shows his appreciation of the straightforward, lively, and remarkably realistic dialogue of *Troilus* by founding so much of his own upon it. The play is one of the most interesting 'Chaucerian' ones in the period because, while not using Chaucer's names or following Chaucer's story right through, the author gives us considerable insights into how he read the poem and how he saw it could easily be adapted to his own brand of realistic-romantic comedy.[7]

After this group of plays around the turn of the century, there are no more plays substantially based on Chaucer except for the ones by Beaumont and Fletcher in 1612 and 1620. This may reflect a general decline of interest in Chaucer during the period, partly attributable to the fact that as the Elizabethans' own output of literature increased the need to struggle with medieval writers either for poetic excellence or plot-material became less evident. Beaumont and Fletcher are unusual representatives of the second generation of playwrights in this respect—if indeed it is possible to claim that both of them were familiar with Chaucer. For Fletcher we have the internal evidence of *The Two Noble Kinsmen*, as well as the two plays I am about to discuss, and for Beaumont the external evidence that his father was a Chaucer enthusiast who wrote a preface for Speght's 1598 edition of the poems.

There seems little doubt that these playwrights used Chaucer as a source for *The Triumph of Honor*, one of the

7. In the same year, 1602, Chapman wrote *May-Day*, a comedy about an old husband/young wife situation which has several echoes of Chaucer's *Merchant's Tale*, in particular the boasting of Lorenzo in I. i (cf. *Canterbury Tales*, E 1249, 1403, 1457 ff.) and the suggestion that 'Cupid will hoodwink the old buzzard' in II. iv.

short plays in *Four Plays or Moral Representations in One* of
1612. The plays depict the triumphs of Honor, Love, Death,
and Time by means of short exemplary episodes. *The
Triumph of Honor* uses the Lucrece theme of the attempted
seduction or rape of a virtuous wife,[8] but although the setting
is ancient Athens and the would-be seducer a Roman general,
the heroine's name is Dorigen and the details of the story are
closely comparable to Chaucer's *Franklin's Tale*.

At the beginning of *The Triumph of Honor*, the Roman
general Martius has just conquered Athens and is, we pre-
sume, about to kill its Duke Sophocles. However, the courage
and nobility of this man and the beauty and virtue of his wife
Dorigen dissuade Martius from this course of action, and we
soon discover that he has in fact fallen in love with Dorigen.
He is presented as a basically virtuous character and he
strives against his desire for her but finally feels impelled to
tell her about it, saying he must die if she will not help him.
She is duly horrified, tells him how much she values her
chastity, and finishes with

> Perish *Martius* then;
> For I here vow unto the gods, These rocks,
> These rocks we see so fix'd shall be remov'd,
> Made champion field, ere I so impious prove,
> To stain my Lords bed with adulterous love.
> (p. 304)[9]

This condition is the same as that given by Chaucer's
Dorigen to her pathetic lover Aurelius:

> Looke what day that end long in Britaine
> Ye remeve all the rockes, stone by stone,
> —Then woll I love yow best of any man.
> (992–3 and 997)

but it is introduced quite arbitrarily in the play, while in the
poem we have already heard about 'these grisly fiendly rockes
blake' (868), and how Dorigen hates and fears them because
of the damage they may do to her husband Arveragus's ship

8. This theme is also used in *The Triumph of Death*. In neither case is it
possible to claim a specific source.

9. Quotations from A. Glover and A. R. Waller (eds), *The Works of Francis
Beaumont and John Fletcher* (Cambridge, 1905–12), vol. x.

when he returns from his voyage, so that the seemingly impossible task she sets for her lover is something she has previously desired on her husband's account:

> And would God that all these rockes blake
> Were sonken into hell for his sake!
> These rockes doe slee mine heart for feare.
> (891–3)

Their marriage has been presented as an ideal one, and we feel that the choice of this condition and the very illogicality of it illustrate how firmly Dorigen's mind is fixed on her husband and how much she cares for his safety.

Of course neither woman believes for a moment that the rocks can be removed, but both Martius and Aurelius are helped by their brothers to produce at least an appearance of the necessary achievement. Martius's brother Valerius also loves Dorigen, but gives his brother almost immediate comfort by saying

> by my skill
> Learn'd from the Old *Caldean* was my Tutor,
> Who train'd me in the *Mathematicks*, I will
> So dazzle and delude her sight, that she
> Shall think this great impossibilitie
> Effected by some supernatural means. (p. 307)

The relief is delayed much longer in Chaucer: Aurelius lies sick on Dorigen's account for two years until his brother remembers reading in Orleans when he was a student about 'magyk natureel—By which men make diverse appearances', and, thinking his brother may be assisted by such a practice, prevails on him to go to Orleans where they do indeed fall in with a magician, apparently by fate (1171 ff.), who shows them various apparitions and finally undertakes

> to make illusion,
> By such an apparence of iogglerie—
> —That she and every wight should wene and say
> That of Britaine the rockes were away.
> (1264–5, 1267–8)

Both writers are careful to stress that it will only be an illusion, and Chaucer's Aurelius recklessly promises a

thousand pounds if it can be done. There is no reward promised for Valerius, but he soon appears 'as Mercury' to fulfil
his words in a scene suggestive of masque-like spectacle. We
have the stage directions *Solemn musick. A mist ariseth, the
rocks remove*, and 'Mercury' sings

> Martius rejoice, Jove sends me from above.
> His Messenger, to cure thy desperate love;
> To shew rash vows cannot binde destinie:
> Lady behold, the rocks transplanted be.
> Hard-hearted Dorigen, yield, lest for contempt,
> They fix thee here a rock, whence they're exempt.
>
> (p. 307)

Aurelius's magician waits for the right astrological moment,
and we have no public display but a private scene between
Dorigen and Aurelius in which he tells her quite gently that
she is now obliged to honour her promise (1297 ff.).

The public scene in the play is something of an anti-
climax as nothing can actually happen before Dorigen has
discussed things with her husband. He is distraught but
decides she should keep her word:

> Come weep no more, I have ponder'd
> This miracle: the anger of the gods
> Thy vow, my love to thee, and *Martius*:
> He must not perish, nor thou be forsworn,
> Lest worse fates follow us; Go, keep thy oath:
> For chaste and whore are words of equal length:
> But let not *Martius* know that I consent.
> O! I'm pull'd in pieces.   (pp. 308–9)

At this point Dorigen tells him she loves Martius before going
off to keep her vow, which naturally makes him even more
distracted. Chaucer's Dorigen worries about her position and
considers many precedents in legend and history which lead
her to decide that she should kill herself rather than be un-
faithful to her husband. She tells him everything, and he
takes it all remarkably calmly:

> This housbond, with glad chere, in sundry wyse
> Answerd and saied as I shal you devyse:
> 'Is ther ought els Dorigene but this?'   (1467–9)

He also insists that she should keep her word, but like Sophocles, he is deeply moved and stipulates secrecy, though he is
concerned about the deed itself rather than his own part in it:

> 'Trouth is the hiest thing that men may kepe'—
> But with that word he brast anone to wepe,
> And saied, 'I yow forbid, on paine of death,
> That never, whiles you lasteth life or breath,
> To no wight tell of this misaventure'.   (1479–83)

Chaucer is uncomfortable about why Arveragus should make
this decision, as he shows by his aside to his readers:

> Paraventure an heep of yow, yuis,
> Wol holden hym a lewed man in this
> That he wol put his wife in jupartie.
> Herkneth the tale er ye upon her crie,
> She may have bettre fortune than yow semeth;
> And whan that ye han herd the tale, demeth.
> (1493–8)

It does not really help to justify the decision by the happy outcome, on which Arveragus could have no influence, and
Chaucer only succeeds in pointing out for us the main weakness of his tale. These lines are not in the 1602 edition and it
does not seem to worry Beaumont and Fletcher so much, perhaps because they are so much more at home in situations
where different kinds of 'honour' are in conflict, so used to
setting their works in what John Danby has described as 'a
world of clashing absolutes'.[1] It is typical of their dramatic
techniques to arouse shock and suspense by Dorigen's
declaration of love for Martius. This is not in Chaucer at all
of course, where the heroine goes off sadly to keep her appointment.

Equally typical of Beaumont and Fletcher is the complete
reversal that happens as soon as Dorigen is in the presence of
Martius. She disobeys her husband's stricture and almost
dares Martius to go ahead:

> For *Sophocles* commands me to obey.
> Come, violate all rules of holiness,
> And rend the consecrated knot of love.
> (p. 309)

1. *Poets on Fortune's Hill* (London, 1952), p. 161.

She then threatens to commit suicide if he does, the notion probably having been suggested by the decision Chaucer's heroine came to in private. Martius repents at this point, and falls to admiring her virtue even more than her beauty; then Sophocles appears and offers to fight with him, but is diverted from his purpose when Martius agrees that he deserves to die. The play ends with explanations and forgiveness all round, and we discover that Dorigen's strange behaviour was partly a test of her husband and partly revenge for his willingness to let Martius violate her honour.

Though Dorigen is disobeying Sophocles when she tells the would-be seducer that she has her husband's permission and even command to come to him, she is following the example of her predecessor in Chaucer who meets Aurelius and tells him that she is going

> Unto the garden, as my husbond bad,
> My trouth for to hold, alas! alas!
>
> (1512–13)

Aurelius, who has always been presented as a sympathetic character, unable to help his luckless passion, is so impressed by her sorrow and by the 'gentillesse' of Arveragus in sending her to him that he finally says

> I have well lever ever to suffer wo
> Than depart the love betwixt you two.
> I you release madame into youre hond
> Quite every surement and every bond
> That ye have made to me as herebeforne.
>
> (1531–5)

She thanks him on her knees and rushes joyfully back to her husband. Aurelius, however, is left with a debt of a thousand pounds to the magician, but when he relates his story, the magician appreciates the nobility of Arveragus in telling his wife to keep her vow and that of Aurelius in releasing her, and says that a 'clerk' like himself knows how to do a 'gentil' deed as well as a knight or a squire, so he refuses to take any money. The tale ends with an invitation to the audience to decide which of the three behaved most nobly.

I think there is no doubt that the story comes from Chaucer. Boccaccio does tell a similar tale twice, in *The*

Decameron, x. 5, and *Filocolo*, iv. 4, but the names and details are different. The differences between the poem and the play are nevertheless very striking. Beaumont and Fletcher have not brought Chaucer up to date as Chapman did in *Sir Giles Goosecap*, but have relegated him to their own peculiar variety of classical setting. The play has been claimed for Beaumont and Field, but there are so many similarities with *Valentinian*, written by Fletcher alone in 1614, that it seems likely he had a hand in it. Compared with *The Franklin's Tale*, the plot and characters of *The Triumph of Honor* are very crude and bare, though of course this is partly because the dramatic form cannot go into the wealth of detail and background we find in the narrative. Also, Beaumont and Fletcher are not trying to write a naturalistic play here but a short 'moral representation'. They are quite consciously using Chaucer's story as a quarry from which to abstract a moral argument about honour, and, if the characterization fails, the abstract ideas are more important anyway.

Chaucer is however far more successful than the dramatists in portraying the moral conflict as well as in making the characters convincing. To some extent the two go together, since moral problems are just not particularly interesting in literature when they are cut off from individualized human beings as they so often are in Beaumont and Fletcher. We know so much about the marriage of Chaucer's Dorigen and Arveragus and about her feelings throughout this narrative that we really care about the outcome and understand the motives and decisions of the participants. Comparatively, we know nothing about the Greek Dorigen and Sophocles and we are confused by their sudden, violent, and apparently arbitrary behaviour (which is so typical of Beaumont and Fletcher it can hardly be dismissed as an inevitable effect in a short play). Likewise, we have learnt to understand and sympathize with Aurelius, apart from the fact that we have quite different and much warmer feelings about the lover when he is a poor scholar than when he is a conquering general. (Boccaccio's Baron Ansaldo is more comparable to Martius.) This is one change which also impoverishes the moral content of the story, since Martius can obviously use force against Dorigen in the play if he wants to (he is after all the leader of the occupying army), whereas the only force operating on the heroine of the poem is the concept of honour she shares with her husband. It is true that Dorigen's honour in the play defeats Martius's force, but the conflict has become a cruder affair altogether. Beaumont and Fletcher omit Chaucer's delicate balancing of different kinds of honour almost entirely, and reduce the argument to a dull and predictable opposition between lust and chastity, thus fitting the story quite neatly into their own repetitive pattern of themes. Like Chapman, they have adapted Chaucer to their own purposes rather than retold one of his stories directly, but while Chapman appreciated the characteristic ways in which Chaucer treated his material and took something of the actual spirit of *Troilus and Criseyde* over into his play, Beaumont and Fletcher ignore everything that is unique in Chaucer's handling of the story (though this gave it the power that presumably impressed them) and borrow only the plot.[2]

Something similar happens in the last Chaucerian play in the period, Fletcher's *Women Pleased* of 1620. In this tragi-comedy of courtship and marriage, Fletcher draws on the folklore plot of *The Wife of Bath's Tale* to fill out his story but omits to pay much attention to the ways in which Chaucer makes the bare plot more interesting. As in his parts of *The Two Noble Kinsmen*, Fletcher's method is to take an outline from Chaucer and adapt it to his own successful dramatic pattern rather than to attempt anything like a full presentation or interpretation of the poem itself. In so far as he does this, it does not really matter if he is using Chaucer or someone else, since the first thing he does is to reduce the source to its most basic elements (which are common to many versions) and borrow only those. However, it is generally agreed that Chaucer's version *is* the source for this play, so one should consider exactly what this means.

The main plot of *Women Pleased* is concerned with the love of Silvio, 'A Gentleman of quality', for the Princess Belvidere, daughter of the Duchess of Florence. Belvidere is in love with Silvio, but her mother wants her to marry the

2. This plot was used again by 'I.C.' in Act II of *The Two Merry Milk-Maids*, first printed in 1620. The author used Boccaccio as well, but his brief version of the story is closer in spirit to Chaucer than that of Beaumont and Fletcher.

Duke of Sienna, so keeps her away from him, and when she
finds them together in II. v says Silvio must die. However, pity
for her daughter so affects her that she changes the sentence
to banishment and even mitigates that by saying he need go

> But for a year: and then again in this place
> To make your full appearance: yet more pitty,
> If in that time you can absolve a question,
> Writ down within this scrowl, absolve it rightly,
> This lady is your wife, and shall live with ye;
> If not you lose your head.[3]   (p. 258)

These words remind us at once of *The Wife of Bath's Tale*,
though the circumstances are different. Silvio has not raped
anyone, and he is promised a possible reward as well as a
punishment, though this is incredible in the naturalistic
scheme of the play: one wonders what happens to the betrothal of Belvidere to the Duke of Sienna which is so important
to the Duchess? In the Tale, the hero is condemned to death
for his rape of a nameless girl, but the queen, like the
Duchess, pities him and says

> I graunt thee thy life, if thou canst tell me
> What thing is it that wommen most desiren.
> —And if thou canst nat tell it me anon,
> Yet woll I yeve thee leve for to gon
> A twelvemonth and a day, to seeke and lere
> An answere suffisant in this matere;
>   (904-5, 907-10)

We are not told the question in the play, and it seems odd
that the Duchess, who has been behaving so arbitrarily,
should suddenly produce a 'scrowl' which has obviously
been prepared in advance. The nature of the question is not
in fact revealed until just before it is answered in v. i, so
naturally there is no search for the answer in the play.

Much of the central part of the play is filled up with a pro-
fusion of other plots and characters, while in the main plot
Belvidere is duly betrothed to the Duke of Sienna, but she
runs away, so he declares war. Silvio wanders around the
countryside and in IV. i meets a band of rustics who are
preparing a morris dance and entertainment 'for the honour

3. Quotations from Glover and Waller, op. cit., vol. vii.

of our Town' (this is very like Arcite's encounter with the rustics in *The Two Noble Kinsmen*), but their sports are interrupted by the arrival of a captain trying to raise an army against the Duke of Sienna. Silvio heroically volunteers to serve in place of the man who has been chosen, but before he goes he hears a strange song encouraging him to fight bravely, and an old hag appears (sd *Enter Belvidere deformed*). This scene is based on Chaucer again, with the morris dance taking the place of the 'daunce' of four and twenty ladies the hero finds in the forest, and the disguised Belvidere appearing for the 'olde wyf' who is left behind when they vanish (Chaucer 989–98). In the poem, the old woman says she will save the hero's life by returning to court with him and giving the right answer to the question if he will promise

> The next thing that I require of thee,
> Thou shalt it do . . .   (1010–11)

The knight complies, but the request is not specified yet and they set out for the court.

In the play (IV. ii), the hag proclaims her love for Silvio and gives a brief account of her powers which is reminiscent of Shakespeare's Puck (p. 268). She advises him to single out the Duke of Sienna and fight him alone, and she reveals her knowledge of his love for Belvidere (p. 287), promising him 'For every precious thought of her, I'll lend thine honor a new spurre'. No other promise is made or requested at this point, but the pair arrange to meet after the battle. This second meeting takes place in IV. iv, and Silvio describes how he overcame the Duke, presented him as a prisoner to the Duchess while remaining himself unknown, and took from him in token of his conquest a 'jewel' which turns out to contain a miniature portrait of Belvidere. While he is rhapsodizing over this discovery, the old woman reminds him that it is time for him to return to court with his answer. He is ready to despair, but she tells him to rely on her, though

> The good old woman for her pain, when everything
>   stands fair again,
> Must ask a poor Boon, and that granting, there's
>   nothing to thy journey wanting.   (p. 296)

As in the poem, the knight gives the promise freely.

The next scene (v. i) takes place at the court, where every-one is wondering at the deeds of the 'stranger knight' (rather as they do in *Cymbeline*) until Silvio appears to claim his victory and receive acknowledgement and gratitude, before he reveals his identity and is threatened with prison and death if he cannot answer the question. There is a tense moment before he can do this (sd *Enter* Belvidere, *and secretly gives him a paper, and Exit*), but then he reads out the question (which we hear now for the first time) and the answer to-gether:

Question

Tell me what is that only thing,
　For which all women long;
Yet having what they most desire,
　To have it do's them wrong.

Answer

Tis not to be chaste, nor fair,
　Such gifts malice may impair;
Richly trimm'd to walk or ride,
　Or to wanton unespy'd;
To preserve an honest name,
　And so to give it up to fame;
These are toys. In good or ill
　They desire to have their Will;
Yet when they have it, they abuse it,
　For they know not how to use it.

(p. 300)

The Duchess confesses that this is the right answer and Silvio claims Belvidere, only to learn that she is 'stol'n from Court' and no-one knows where she is. He is ready to despair again when the hag enters to claim her promise and says

The boon I crave for all my service to thee,
Is now to be thy wife, to grant me marriage.

(p. 301)

The courtiers make jokes and Silvio asks her to choose again, but she insists and the Duchess says he must keep his word.

This is all close to Chaucer, although in *The Wife of Bath's Tale* the hag seems to have revealed the answer to the knight previously and we are not aware of her presence in the court until she rises to claim her promise (1046). Like Silvio, he asks her to 'chese a new request' (1060) when she asks 'that thou take me unto thy wyf' (1055), but he has to keep his promise.

After a sub-plot scene, the play moves on to a moment just before the wedding (v. iii) when the Duchess and courtiers are ridiculing Silvio with references to his 'young fair Bride' which specify her physical defects. They are busy mocking his grief when music is unexpectedly heard and a masque of spirits appear who say they are

> From the good old Beldam sent,
> Cares and sorrows to prevent.
> (p. 308)

Then Belvidere appears in her own shape and asks Silvio if he loves her like this or as she has been. He must choose:

> If thou wilt have me young and bright,
> Pleasing to thine eye and sight,
> Courtly and admir'd of all,
> Take heed lest thy fame do fall,
> I shall then be full of scorn,
> Wanton, proud, beware the horn,
> Hating what I lov'd before,
> Flattery apt to fall before,
> All consuming, nothing getting,
> Thus thy fair name comes to setting.
> But if old, and free from these
> Thou shalt chuse me, I shall please:
> I shall then maintain thee still,
> With my virtue and my skill
> Still increase and build thy name,
> Chuse now *Silvio*, here I am.
> (pp. 308–9)

Silvio is unable to decide:

> I know not what to say, which way to turn me,
> Into thy Soveraign will I put my answer.

Belvidere tells him she will be 'your old Love', and explains how she has been disguised and how she has now come 'to make ye laughing sport at this mad marriage', which of course turns into a real marriage. One of the play's loose ends is tied up when the Duchess and the Duke of Sienna also agree to marry.

There are considerable alterations from the source here. Chaucer tells us wryly that he is not going to give us any details about the wedding celebrations because 'ther was no joye no feeste at al' (1978). The wedding takes place privately and, significantly, it is not until after it has happened that the wife begins the conversation that ends

> 'Chese now', quod she, 'oon of these things twey:
> To have me foul and old till that I dey,
> And be to you a true humble wife,
> And never you displese in all my life,
> Or els woll you have me yong and faire,
> And take your aventure of the repaire
> That shall come to your house because of me,
> Or in some other place may well be.
> Now chese yourselve wheither that yow liketh'.
>
> (1219–27)

This is similar to what happens in the play, but the lengthy discussion preceding it is quite omitted by Fletcher. Chaucer's 'wife' goes through the reasons why the knight should not despise her because of her apparent low rank, since true nobility consists in personal virtue rather than heredity and

> he is gentil that doth gentil deedis.
>
> (1170)

There is also a serious argument as to why he should esteem poverty, and a less serious one about the respect due to age. All this gives the knight good reason to be ashamed of himself and to admire his wife's wisdom, so that we appreciate his true meaning when he says

> My lady and my love, and wife so dere,
> I put me in your wise governance;
> Cheseth yourselfe which may bee most plesance,
> And moost honour to you and me also. (1230–3)

It is a more exciting moment in some ways than it is in the play, as we have no reason to believe that the old woman really can be young and beautiful, and the result is even more satisfying, as she says

I wol be to you both,
This is to say, to be, both fair and good.
(1240–1)

There is no explicit statement that Belvidere in the play will be both. More important perhaps, there is no moral debate and no correction of the scorn and ridicule poured on the old woman by Silvio, the Duchess, and the courtiers. In fact Belvidere herself seems to admit that the match would have been unworthy and ludicrous. The debate, such as it is, takes place before Silvio is fully committed by marriage, and though Chaucer's opposition of qualities is used, Fletcher is obviously far more interested in beauty than in virtue, since he does not discuss the latter at all or bother to make it clear that Belvidere will have the virtue of the old woman as well as her own youthful beauty.

The play also suffers from the way in which it introduces the Duchess's question so late, and without the solid context of a discussion of female desires and marital situations we find in *The Wife of Bath's Prologue* and *Tale*. It is strange that Fletcher does not tell us this earlier, since it would both have a bearing on Belvidere's actions and help to integrate some elements in the sub-plot, as well as allowing more scope for a discussion of possible answers than is afforded by the brief list given in the reply.[4] Much of the suspense of Chaucer's poem is dissipated by the treatment of Belvidere, and even if we do not know all along that she is only disguised as the old woman (which would depend on the acting and staging), this character is so firmly linked with Silvio's love for the princess from her first appearance in IV. ii that we have at least a strong suspicion that all will be well. Fletcher, then, is simply using parts of the Tale for his own quite different purposes. While a comparison of the two has a rather negative bearing on the play, it does serve to illustrate quite how remote Fletcher's moral and artistic world is from Chaucer's, a point which will be relevant again in my study of *The Two Noble Kinsmen*.

Thus the non-Shakespearian drama of the period yields a

4. The examples of wrong answers given in Fletcher's rhyme are comparable to the findings of the poem's hero during his quest (919 ff.) and to some of the feminine desires described in the Prologue to this Tale.

total of six extant plays based on Chaucer which provide us with a variety of examples of how he could be used, ranging from simple plot-borrowing to the mixture of affectionate re-creation and implied criticism in Chapman. The type of story that attracted the dramatists' attention is significant, since it shows an interest in the serious, romantic side of Chaucer rather than in the comic naturalism for which he is perhaps best known today. No-one dramatized *The Miller's Tale* or *The Reeve's Tale* for example, which might seem more stage-worthy to a modern writer than *The Knight's Tale* and *The Clerk's Tale*. The comic treatment of alchemy in *The Canon's Yeoman's Tale* was exploited by two dramatists, Lyly in *Gallathea* and Jonson in *The Alchemist*, but it is not a substantial element in either play.[5] A reading of the wealth of references from non-dramatic works in Caroline Spurgeon's *Five Hundred Years of Chaucer Criticism and Allusion* reveals that the dramatists were not unusual in the view of Chaucer that their use of him implies, but it remains to be seen whether Shakespeare also fits into this pattern.

5. Both plays are discussed in this respect by C. M. Hathaway in his edition of *The Alchemist* (New York, 1903).

3

Shakespeare's use of Chaucer outside *Troilus and Cressida* and *The Two Noble Kinsmen*

Reserving the two most important plays for subsequent chapters, I shall present here a survey of the references to Chaucer scattered through the rest of the canon. They vary enormously in kind, from single-line allusions or images to the use of a Chaucerian poem as a subsidiary source for a whole play, as in the case of *Romeo and Juliet*. The sheer quantity of the material involved implies that Shakespeare did not merely use Chaucer for a plot or two (as he did some authors) but knew him so well that he recalled his work (often unconsciously, one would imagine) in virtually every play. Since the references are not spread equally throughout the canon but are concentrated in particular plays it is also possible to speculate on questions such as when Shakespeare read or re-read Chaucer, what sort of subject-matter reminded him of Chaucer and indeed what sort of poet he thought Chaucer was.

It is necessary to examine the nature of various claims that have been made (or could be made) for Chaucerian influence with some care, bringing in all sorts of different criteria: Is the alleged parallel a proverbial saying? Is it so obvious or well-known that no literary source is necessary? Is it to be found in Shakespeare's other non-Chaucerian sources? And so on. Some of the arguments which arise are of interest in themselves while others can only be justified as a means to an end. I have classified the references and arranged them, more or less, in an ascending order of critical interest, from 'parallels' which may be merely proverbial sayings to the pervasive influence of Chaucer on an entire play. This classification cuts across the chronological development of Shakespeare's use of Chaucer during his career, but that can be seen in the table given as an Appendix at the end of the book, which also shows the number of different poems used in any one play.

1. Proverbial sayings

For the sake of completeness I include here some lines in Shakespeare which have been claimed as Chaucerisms by various critics but could be evidence of the continuity of proverbial tradition rather than of the direct influence of one writer upon another. Nevill Coghill cites two possible references to *The Canterbury Tales* in *Romeo and Juliet* which are of this type, first Mercutio's words to Romeo:

> If thou art Dun, we'll draw thee from the mire
> Of—save your reverence—love, wherein thou stick'st.
> (I. iv. 41–42)

which may recall the Host's exclamation when he notices that the cook has fallen asleep on his horse:

> Sirs: what! Dunne is in the mire.
> (*Manciple's Prologue*, H 5)

but Tilley lists 'To draw Dun out of the mire' as a proverb throughout the sixteenth century (D 643). Secondly, Coghill quotes the shocked Juliet's description of Romeo after the murder of Tybalt

> O serpent heart, hid with a flowering face,
> (III. ii. 73)

as well as Lady Macbeth's instruction to her husband

> Look like the innocent flower,
> But be the serpent under it.
> (I. v. 62)

as references to Chaucer's image of the terclet as described by the falcon in *The Squire's Tale*:

> Right as a serpent hideth him under flours
> Till he may see his time for to bite . . .
>
> (F 512–13)

but he admits the image is 'as old as Eve' and overlooks the fact that it occurs in Shakespeare's primary source, Arthur Brooke's *Romeus and Juliet,* though at an earlier point in the narrative, when Juliet first discovers Romeus is a Montague and wonders

> What if his suttel brayne to fayne have taught his tong,
> And so the snake that lurkes in grasse thy tender hart hath stong?
>
> (385–6)

The snake here is hiding in grass rather than flowers but the application of the image is very like Shakespeare's.[1]

Coghill also suggests Chaucer's description of Arcite in love, 'Now up now doune, as boket in a well' (1533) as the source of Richard II's words to Bolingbroke:

> Now is this golden crown like a deep well
> That owes two buckets, filling one another,
> The emptier ever dancing in the air,
> The other down, unseen and full of water.
> That bucket down and full of tears am I,
> Drinking my griefs, whilst you mount up on high.
>
> (IV. i. 184–9)

The contexts are so different that this does not seem very convincing, especially when Peter Ure points out that Fortune's buckets were a very common medieval and Elizabethan figure, rated as proverbial by Tilley.[2] The use of the same image in John Day's *The Isle of Gulls* (1606) appears more arguably Chaucerian to me. This play adapts its plot from Sidney's *Arcadia,* changing the names of the two heroes to Lysander and Demetrius: an interesting echo of *A Midsummer Night's Dream* which itself shows considerable use of *The Knight's Tale.* Commenting on the fact that the heroes have gained favour with the king and his family but are no

1. Spenser also uses the image of a snake hiding in grass in *The Faerie Queene,* Book III, canto xi, stanza 28, though he is describing gold thread in a tapestry rather than the practice of deceit.

2. See his note on this passage in the New Arden edition of *Richard II* (London, 1956).

further forward with their suits to his daughters, the page says

I can compare my lord and his friend to nothing in the world so
fitly as to a couple of water buckets; for whilst hope winds the one
up dispaire plunges the other downe, whilst I, like a Harlekene in
an Italian comedy, stand making faces at both their follies.

(II. iii. 19)

This coincides with Chaucer's use of the image in mockery of
a lover which seems to make it a much more likely parallel
than Shakespeare's use of it to illustrate the deposition of a
king.

Two quasi-proverbial lines in *The Winter's Tale* have also
been related to Chaucer. S. R. Maveety found a parallel
between Leontes's description of himself as a child with

> my dagger muzzled,
> Lest it should bite its master, and so prove,
> As ornaments oft do, too dangerous.
>
> (I. ii. 156–8)

and January's words in the *Merchant's Tale*

> A man may do no sin with his wife
> Ne yet hurt himself with his owne knife.
>
> (E 1839–40)

This is not listed as a proverb by Tilley, and Maveety
emphasizes the significance of the context, with a wife as the
'dangerous ornament' in both cases (though the *Winter's
Tale* reference is indirect).[3] The fact that Speght marks the
lines as a 'notable sentence' in his 1602 edition of Chaucer
might strengthen the case, but Shakespeare also uses the
image in *1 Henry IV* in quite a different context when at the
very beginning of the play the king says optimistically

> The edge of war, like an ill-sheathed knife,
> No more shall cut his master.   (I. i. 17–18)

In the same scene of *The Winter's Tale*, J. H. P. Pafford gives
Chaucer's description of Aurelius in *The Franklin's Tale*,
'Anon for ioy his heart gan to daunce' (F 1136), as a possible
source for Leontes's

3. S. R. Maveety, 'Hermione, a dangerous ornament', *Shakespeare Quarterly*,
xiv (1963), 485–6.

> I have tremor cordis on me: my heart dances,
> But not for joy—not joy.   (II. ii. 110-11)

But he admits it was a common phrase.[4]

Finally, Rosalind's spirited lines on the audacity and ingenuity of feminine wit in IV. i of *As You Like It*, building to the climax 'You shall never take her without her answer, unless you take her without her tongue', echo the promise made by Proserpine to all women in *The Merchant's Tale*

> That though they ben in any gilte itake
> With face bolde they shullen hemselve excuse
> And bere hem doun that wold hem accuse
> For lacke of answere non of hem shull dien.
>   (E 2268-71)

The Wife of Bath's Prologue also describes how women avoid recriminations for their faults by getting in a false counter-accusation first (D 387-95), and her 'play hard to get' axiom

> . . . togreat c heap is hold at to litel pris,
> This knoweth every woman that is wise.
>   (D 523-4)

is repeated by Shakespeare's Cressida:

> That she beloved knows nought that knows not this:
> Men prize the thing ungained more than it is.
>   (I. ii. 280-1)

As with the other examples, the similarity is undeniably there, but the sentiments seem so familiar that one would hesitate to claim a direct source relationship.

2. Mere names

It is usually very difficult to tell whether a reference to the mere name of a character who appears in one of Chaucer's poems should be counted as an allusion to Chaucer or not, since so many of the stories he tells can be found in other authors or else they are so well known that it is not necessary to posit a literary source at all. The story of Troilus and Cressida, for example, seems to have been accepted by the

4. See his note on this passage in the New Arden edition (London, 1963).

Elizabethans as a 'pattern of love' alongside stories of considerably greater antiquity (Hero and Leander, Dido and Aeneas) without any differentiation between the classical and medieval traditions. Chaucer is the ultimate source for the details of this story, and most subsequent medieval and Renaissance writers on the theme refer to him as their own principle source, but casual references to the characters could easily be at third or fourth hand. Chaucer's story was not even absorbed into the tradition as he left it, but was distorted by the way that Henryson's *Testament of Cresseid* became from 1532 onwards an inseparable (and anonymous) sequel.

Hence, despite the reputation of Chaucer's *Troilus* as a serious tragic work, it is rare to find allusions in which the characters are treated 'straight'. As Sidney tells us, the word 'pandar' had passed into common usage,[5] and it had done so in such a way as to reflect little glory on the Chaucerian character who defended his role thus:

> But God, that al woteh, take I to witnesse,
> That never I this for covetise wrought,
> But only for to abredge that distresse
> For which welnie thou didest.   (iii. 260–3)

Chapman's Ludovico in *May-Day* (1602) justifies his own action in bringing Aemilia and Aurelio together in a similar way, though denying the defence to its very originator:

> . . . this is no Pandarisme, is it? No for there
> is neither money nor credit propos'd or expected.
> (III. iii. 114)

Shakespeare shares the common conception of 'pandarism' as a mercenary activity when Benedict refers to Troilus as 'the first employer of Pandars' in *Much Ado About Nothing* (v. ii. 28), and implies it again in *Twelfth Night* when Feste tries to persuade Viola to double his pecuniary reward by saying 'I would play Lord Pandarus of Phrygia, sir, to bring a Cressida to this Troilus' (III. i. 48–50). Feste also comments 'Cressida was a begger' (III. i. 53). Even Pistol says contemptuously 'Shall I Sir Pandarus of Troy become?' taking offence

---

5. *An Apologie for Poetrie* (as cited), p. 166.

at Falstaff's request that he deliver love-letters to Mistress
Page and Mistress Ford in *The Merry Wives of Windsor*
(I. iii. 72). This play has several examples of the use of 'pandar' as noun, verb, and even adjective (panderly rascals'), but
it is arguable that a distinction can be made between this sort
of common use and references to 'Sir Pandarus' as a character. The kindest reference I have found in Shakespeare to the
character is in *All's Well* when Lafeu brings Helena to the
king and departs with the remark 'I am Cressid's uncle, That
dare leave two together' (II. i. 96).

Cressida's reputation had declined as much as that of her
uncle by Elizabethan times. (To be fair, it is really Chaucer
who is out of step in providing such an unusually sympathetic
portrait.) Shakespeare is again typical in having Pistol refer to
Doll Tearsheet as a 'lazar kite of Cressid's kind' in *Henry V*
(II. i. 74), showing his knowledge of the Henryson sequel.
Given such company, even Troilus cannot remain uncon-
taminated, but is subjected to ridicule, as in Petruchio's use
of the name for his spaniel (*Taming of the Shrew*, IV. i. 134)
and in Rosalind's jocular reference:

> Troilus had his brains dashed out with a
> Grecian club; yet he did what he could to
> die before, and he is one of the patterns
> of love.   (*As You Like It*, IV. i. 87–90)

Occasionally, however, the story was treated seriously as
one of the archetypes of romantic tragedy, and it is interesting
to find that when this happens the other 'patterns of love'
referred to are often from Chaucer's own *Legend of Good
Women*. This is certainly true of Shakespeare, whose
Merchant of Venice provides the only explicit reference to
Troilus and Cressida in the whole canon which is not comic
or satirical. It occurs in Act V, when Lorenzo begins the
opening scene by evoking a setting from Chaucer's *Troilus*:

> The moon shines bright. In such a night as this
> When the sweet wind did gently kiss the trees,
> And they did make no noise, in such a night
> Troilus methinks mounted the Trojan walls,
> And sigh'd his soul toward the Grecian tents
> Where Cressid lay that night.   (V. i. 1–6)

The reference is to Chaucer's description of Troilus in Book v:

> And every night, as was his wont to doone
> He stood the bright moone to behold . . .
>
> Upon the walles faste eek would he walke
> And on the Grekes host he would se
> And to himself right thus he would talke
> Lo, yonder is mine own lady fre
> Or els yonder, there the tentes be
> And thence cometh this ayre, that is so soote
> That in my soule I fele it doth me boote.
>
> And hardly this winde that more and more
> Thus stoundmele encreaseth in my face
> Is of my ladies depe sighes sore . . .
>
> (v. 647–8, 666–75)

Shakespeare's recollection of the passage is not strictly accurate, since it is Criseyde who is sighing out her soul in Chaucer. R. K. Root has pointed out a more serious 'misreading' in that the moon in Chaucer is quite explicitly and necessarily a new one, since Troilus is asking Lucina to 'ren faste about thy sphere' so that Criseyde's promise to return 'Er Phebus suster, Lucina the shene, The Leoun passe out of this Ariete' (iv. 1591–2) will soon be fulfilled.[6] Shakespeare can here be accused of turning a precise set of astronomical references into a conventional piece of moonshine. He goes on to mention three heroines from *The Legend of Good Women*, starting with Thisbe:

> In such a night
> Did Thisbe fearfully o'ertrip the dew,
> And saw the lion's shadow ere himself,
> And ran dismayed away.   (v. i. 6–9)

This is not really long enough to enable us to say whether Chaucer or Ovid's *Heroides* is the source, taken in isolation. Chaucer mentions the 'dew of herbes wete' but Golding's Ovid has 'dewie grasse', though Chaucer and Shakespeare both have a lion, compared with Ovid's lioness. Chaucer

---

6. 'Shakespeare misreads Chaucer', *Modern Language Notes* [MLN], xxxviii (1923), 346–8.

speaks of the moon twice (ll. 812, 825), and Shakespeare had exploited the moonlit setting in his own *Midsummer Night's Dream* of course. Malone in his 1790 edition suggested that the details given in the next lines about Dido:

> In such a night
> Stood Dido with a willow in her hand
> Upon the wild sea-banks, and waft her love
> To come again to Carthage.   (9–12)

come from Chaucer's *Legend of Ariadne*, since his Dido does nothing like this, but of Ariadne he says:

> And to the stronde barefote fast she wente
> And cryed: Theseus myn hert swete
> No man she sawe, and yet shone the mone
> Her kerchefe on a pole stycked she,
> Ascaunce he should it wele yse.   (2189 ff.)

I cannot find any other source suggested for this, and the fusion of the two is not uncharacteristic of Shakespeare. When we come to Medea, her story is in Chaucer but the particular incident mentioned by Shakespeare

> In such a night,
> Medea gathered the enchanted herbs
> That did renew old Æson.   (12–14)

is not, and it seems from verbal details that he was recalling Golding's Ovid. None of these references is decisive in itself, but, given the Chaucerian setting, it is likely that J. Hunter is right in suggesting that Shakespeare merely turned over the pages of his edition and found the Legends of Thisbe, Dido, and Medea (in that order) following *Troilus*, and used the characters, though he did not reread the poems for actual details but relied on his general knowledge.[7]

Several other playwrights combined reference to *Troilus and Cressida* with reference to one or more of the stories in the *Legend of Good Women*, a connection first made by Chaucer himself who presented the *Legends* as a penance for the libel on female constancy he had perpetrated in *Troilus*. The most interesting of these is in the anonymous play *Common Conditions* of 1576 where two characters

7. *New Illustrations* (London, 1845), vol. i, pp. 309–15.

argue about the relative faithfulness of men and women as follows:

NOMIDES: What constancy in Cressida did rest in anything?
  What love, I pray you, bear Phaedra unto her Theseus,
  When in his absence she desired his son Hippolytus?
  What true love eke bare Medea unto Duke Jason, he?
  Tush, lady! in vain it is to talk; they all deceitful be.
  And therefore, lady! you must yield to me in that respect:
  Men still are just, though women must their plighted vows
    neglect.
SABIA: Then, sir knight! how faithful was Aeneas to Dido's grace?
  To whom he plighted faith by vow, none other to embrace.
  How faithful was Duke Jason, he, whom Medea did aid
  When he, to win the golden fleece, by Otus was dismayed?
  And Theseus, I pray you, also, how faithful did he bide
  When that the vow he once had made to Ariadne he denied?
  How faithful was Diomedes, one of the Greekish crew?
  Though Troilus therein was just, yet was he found untrue:
  And so between those twain and fortune's luckless hap,
  She was, like Lazar, fain to sit and beg, with dish and clap.[8]

Apart from Troilus and Cressida all the characters here are from Chaucer's *Legends*, and the context of the debate is also obviously Chaucerian. It is notable that the dramatist uses the same examples on each side, indicating that he had appreciated the ambiguity of the original poems—a subject still disputed by critics. The introduction of Troilus and Cressida into the group and the use of the title 'Duke' for Jason confirm Chaucer as the source rather than Ovid.[9]

Shakespeare's attitude to the Troilus story, then, and the ways in which he referred to it, are fairly typical of the age. He does not refer to the characters at all after writing his own play on the subject, and this would appear to coincide with a general decline in allusions by other writers: I have not found any definite references to Chaucer's poem from 1608 to 1625. It is possible that Shakespeare's play adversely affected other people's reading of the poem (as it still does today), but this would depend on its having been well known and there is

8. Edited by J. S. Farmer in *Five Anonymous Plays*, Fourth Series (London, 1908), pp. 212–13.
9. There are also references combining *Troilus* and figures from the *Legends* in Dekker's *Westward Hoe* (v. i. 232–7) and *The Roaring Girl* (III. ii. 52).

still some doubt about whether it was ever performed publicly.

Shakespeare does refer briefly elsewhere to characters from *The Legend of Good Women*, mostly in the early plays. In *Titus Andronicus* the body of Bassianus is compared with that of Pyramus:

> So pale did shine the moon on Pyramus
> When he by night lay bathed in maiden blood.
> (II. iii. 231–2)

In *The Two Gentlemen of Verona* Julia indirectly relates her own experience when she pretends to describe to Silvia how she acted at a Pentecost pageant.:

> For I did play a lamentable part.
> Madam, 'twas Ariadne passioning
> For Theseus' perjury and unjust flight.
> (IV. iv. 162–4)

And in *A Midsummer Night's Dream* Hermia swears to meet Lysander

> . . . by that flame that burned the Carthage queen,
> When the false Troyan under sail was seen,
> By all the vows that men have ever broke—
> In number more than women ever spoke.
> (I. i. 173–6)

In this last instance the context of a comparison between the fidelity of men and women supports the claim for Chaucer as a source rather than a classical version of the story of Dido, but otherwise each claim has to rest on external evidence, such as further instances of use of Chaucer within the same play or more definitive use of the same reference elsewhere. For example, strong evidence of the use of Chaucer elsewhere in *A Midsummer Night's Dream* would support the claim for the *Legend* as a source here, and strong evidence of the use of Chaucer's poem in *Troilus and Cressida* would make it possible to claim that Chaucer was also the direct source for other less substantial references.

Further examples of Shakespeare's use of 'mere names' which might be Chaucerian include Petruchio's optimistic (or ominous) prediction concerning Kate

For patience she will prove a second Grissel,
(*Taming of the Shrew*, II. i. 287)

and Theseus's words to one of the kneeling queens in the opening scene of *The Two Noble Kinsmen*:

O no knees, none, widow:
Unto the helmeted Bellona use them
And pray for me, your soldier.
(I. i. 74–76)[1]

At I. iii. 13 Emilia echoes him: 'The great Bellona I'll solicit.' Bellona is not mentioned at all in the primary source for this play (Chaucer's *Knight's Tale*) but another poem by Chaucer, *Anelida and Arcite*, introduces her in the opening invocation to Mars

That in thy frostie countrey called Thrace,
Within thy grisly temples full of drede
Honoured art as patrone of that place,
With thy Bellona Pallas full of grace. (2–5)

This poem is apparently about the same Arcite as *The Knight's Tale* and could easily have attracted Shakespeare's attention for that reason. It uses the rule of Creon in Thebes and the campaign of Theseus against him as its narrative context, but Shakespeare could have drawn all that material from his primary source. Bellona is however a relatively uncommon reference and was very probably suggested by *Anelida and Arcite*.[2]

More doubtful is a reference to the story of Apius and Virginia (Chaucer's *Physician's Tale*) in *Titus Andronicus* when Titus asks Saturnine

Was it well done of rash Virginius
To slay his daughter with his own right hand,
Because she was enforc'd, stain'd and deflow'r'd?
(V. iii. 36–38)

Although Chaucer was the most easily available English source, these facts do not agree with his version of the story,

1. Quotations from this play are from the Regent's Renaissance edition by G. R. Proudfoot (London and Nebraska, 1970).
2. Shakespeare's only reference to Bellona elsewhere is when Macbeth is described as 'Bellona's bridegroom' (I. ii. 55).

in which Virginia is killed by her father in order to prevent
Apius from raping her, not because he has done so. This may
be a mistake on the part of the compositor of Shakespeare's
play, who could have set 'Because' for 'Before', since 'Because'
is in the same position seven lines before and three lines after,
or it may be a mistake or a deliberate alteration by Shakespeare, as it turns the story into a much closer parallel for the
immediate situation of Titus and Lavinia. J. C. Maxwell, however, in his edition of this play, cites examples of references
to a version of the story in which the rape did happen.[3]

It has been claimed that Shakespeare was relying on Chaucer as his source for other classical narratives, or at least had
Chaucer's version in mind as well as classical ones. F. E.
Budd has considered all the references to Nero in the plays
and concludes that they can be accounted for adequately by
the information in Chaucer's *Monk's Tale*.[4] This does not
seem to be strictly true. There are five references, three of
which give a very common character-sketch of Nero which
is indeed to be found in Chaucer amongst other sources, but
which was part of popular tradition then as it still is today.
Shakespeare probably did not need to read Chaucer before he
mentioned Nero as a type of unfeeling cruelty in *3 Henry VI*
(III. i. 40), or referred to his famous matricide in *King John*
(v. ii. 152) and again in *Hamlet* (III. ii. 384). One of his
allusions gives the detail of Nero playing his lute while Rome
burnt (*1 Henry VI*, I. iv. 95) which was equally well-known,
but does not occur in Chaucer's account. I find it is only the
allusion in *King Lear* which carries any conviction as a
Chaucerism (and thus, perhaps, gives weight to the rest). This
is in one of Edgar's mad speeches, where we find the line

> Nero is an angler in the lake of darkness.
>
> (III. vi. 7)

Budd relates this convincingly to Chaucer's

> Nettles of gold threde had he great plente,
> To fish in Tiber when him list to play.
>
> (B 3665–6)

3. New Arden edition (London, 1953), p. 119.
4. 'Chaucer, Shakespeare and Harsnett', *Review of English Studies* [RES], xi
(1935), 421–9.

It is certainly an unusual association, and therefore a more likely borrowing. Budd suggested a further link between *King Lear* and *The Monk's Tale*, or rather *The Monk's Prologue*, in which the Host gives examples of his wife's dominating attitude:

> False coward . . . I woll have thy knife,
> And thou shalt have my distaffe, and go spin.
> Alas, she saith, that ever she was shape
> To wed a milkesop, or a coward ape,
> That woll be overleide with every wight.
>
> (B 3095–4001)

This is like the relationship between Goneril and Albany which is described in the same terms in iv. ii. of the play in which Goneril calls her husband a 'milk-livered man' (l. 50) and declares

> I must change arms at home, and give the distaff
> Into my husband's hands.   (17–18)

Returning to classical figures, there may be a reminiscence of *The Monk's Tale* in *Julius Caesar* in the fact that both Chaucer and Shakespeare make the mistake of locating the murder of Caesar in the Capitol, rather than the Senate House as in Plutarch. Shakespeare apparently equated the two, since Decius Brutus says to the conspirators 'And I will bring him to the Capitol' (ii. i. 211), but to Caesar himself 'I come to fetch you to the Senate House' (ii. ii. 59), and Portia inquires anxiously 'Is Caesar yet gone to the Capitol?' (ii. iv. 23). References to the Capitol in other plays repeat this error, which enables Hamlet to make his pun to Polonius, 'It was a brute part of [Brutus] to kill so capital a calf there' (iii. ii. 102). Chaucer's version of the death of Caesar in *The Monk's Tale* runs

> This Julius unto the Capitoll went
> Upon a day, as he was wont to gone,
> And in the Capitoll anon him hent
> This false Brutus and his other fone.
>
> (3893–6)

This mistake occurs elsewhere in medieval versions, but Renaissance writers such as William Alexander and Ben

Jonson refer consistently and correctly to the Senate House, leaving Shakespeare somewhat isolated in his allegiance to the medieval tradition, which is as likely to have been transmitted to him by Chaucer as by any other writer.[5]

A similarly significant mistake was noted by Ernest Schanzer in *Antony and Cleopatra* where Shakespeare refers three times to Cleopatra as having been previously married to Ptolemy (I. iv. 6 and 17, II. i. 37), which is not in his classical sources, Plutarch and Appian, nor in the plays by Samuel Daniel, the Countess of Pembroke, and Fletcher and Massinger on the theme, but is in Chaucer whose life of Cleopatra in *The Legend of Good Women* opens thus:

> After the death of Ptholome the king,
> That all Egipt had in his governing,
> Reigned his Queene Cleopatras.
>
> (580–2)

Chaucer and Shakespeare both assume that Ptolemy was Cleopatra's husband rather than her brother, in fact.[6] There do not seem to be any other specific links between the two versions, though Chaucer's very sympathetic treatment of both the principal characters may have had a general influence on Shakespeare.

Finally, some brief references to stock characters such as Dame Partlet, Patience, and Fame are worth mentioning. Otto Ballmann listed instances of the use of the name 'Chanticleer' as Chaucerian borrowings, but I think the name was too common in non-literary material for this to be valid. The name of Chanticleer's wife in *The Nun's Priest's Tale*, however, was less common, so when Falstaff addresses Mistress Quickly with 'How now, Dame Partlet the hen!' (*I Henry IV*, III. iii. 51) and Leontes speaks of Paulina to Antigonus as 'thy dame Partlet' (*The Winter's Tale*, II. iii. 75) Shakespeare may have been recalling Chaucer.

Similarly, there could be a passing reference to Chaucer in *Twelfth Night*, where Viola's pathetic fiction about her sister who concealed her love and

---

5. See L. A. Fisher, 'Shakespere and the Capitol', *MLN*, xxii (1907), 177–82.
6. E. Schanzer, '*Antony and Cleopatra* and *The Legend of Good Women*', *Notes and Queries* [*N & Q*], vii (1960), 335–6.

> . . . with a green and yellow melancholy,
> . . . sat like Patience on a monument,
> Smiling at grief.   (II. iv. 112–14)

seems to recall Chaucer's *Parlement of Foules*:

> Dame Pacience sittyng there I fond,
> With face pale, upon an hill sonde.
>   (242–3)

Lewis Theobald noted this as a Chaucerism in his 1733 edition of Shakespeare, though other editors have referred the reader to traditions in the visual arts. Patience comes up again in *Pericles* when the king says to Marina

> . . . thou dost look
> Like Patience gazing on king's graves, and smiling
> Extremity out of act.   (V. i. 136–8)

Chaucer's Patience does not smile, which weakens the parallel.

Visual tradition must also be remembered when dealing with references to the character of Fame, though when Inigo Jones designed a 'House of Fame' set for Jonson's *Masque of Queens* in 1609 he relied on Chaucer's description rather than on any picture.[7] Fame is a very popular figure, both as a reference and as a stage personification, in Elizabethan and Jacobean drama, so the source can rarely be pinpointed. Virgil had described the person of Fame in Book iv of the *Aeneid* and Ovid had written of her House in Book xii of the *Metamorphoses*, but Chaucer was original in combining these two and in devoting an entire poem exclusively to the subject of Fame, so it may be his version Shakespeare has in mind when Aaron says

> The emperor's court is like the house of Fame,
> The palace full of tongues, of eyes and ears.
>   (*Titus Andronicus*, II. i. 126–7)

and again when Rumour 'painted full of tongues' appears as the Prologue for 2 *Henry IV*. As one of the very few medieval

---

7. See *The Masque of Queenes* in *Ben Jonson: Complete Masques*, ed. S. Orgel (New Haven and London, 1969), ll. 450–8.

poets still read in Elizabethan times, Chaucer's role as a hander-down of many stories, characters, and concepts must have been considerable even when we cannot prove a direct link.

3. Non-proverbial ideas, images, verbal borrowings

The references included in this group may seem arbitrarily defined, overlapping at times with both the previous categories especially the first, since some of the ideas and images are familiar if not exactly (on documentary evidence) proverbial. I can only say that I do not hold a strong brief for my categories as anything other than one possible way of organizing this somewhat intractable material, and I hope the reader will perceive the problem, while not necessarily agreeing with my solution. To take an immediate example of the difficulty, Otto Ballmann noticed a parallel between a speech by Valentine in *The Two Gentlemen of Verona*,

> O gentle Proteus, Love's a mighty Lord,
> And hath so humbled me, as I confess
> There is no woe to his correction,
> Nor to his service no such joy on earth . . .
> (II. iv. 132–5)

and one by Theseus in *The Knight's Tale* beginning

> The God of love, ah benedicite
> How mighty and how greate a lorde is he
> Again his might there gaineth no obstacles.
> (1785–7)

It does not seem as if 'Love's a mighty Lord' actually was proverbial, but it is very close. Certainly one could not claim that the idea is so unusual that Shakespeare must have found it in Chaucer! The fact that *The Two Gentlemen of Verona* is very much a play on the theme of love and friendship and Chaucer's *Knight's Tale* was one of the most famous examples of that genre must be brought in to support the parallel. Similarity of context as well as of idea or phrasing is often important, as in another *Knight's Tale* notion:

> Thou wist it nat or now
> Whether she be woman or goddesse
> Thyne is affection of holinesse
> And mine is love, as to a creature,
>
> (1156–9)

repeated by Longaville in *Love's Labour's Lost*:

> A woman I forswore; but I will prove,
> Thou being a goddess, I forswore not thee:
> My vow was earthly, thou a heavenly love;
> Thy grace being gain'd cures all disgrace in me.
>
> (IV. iii. 60–63)

In both cases the speaker is using the quibble to persuade himself that he is not forsworn, Longaville by breaking his vow not to see ladies (let alone love them) and Arcite by breaking the vow he and Palamon have sworn, 'Neither of us in love to hindre other' (1135).

This similarity of context argument can also be used to strengthen a verbal parallel between *The Franklin's Tale* and *The Tempest*. In the Tale, the brother of Aurelius, the love-sick clerk, takes him to Orleans to visit a magician who may be able to help him fulfil Dorigen's impossible conditions. As they sit in his room before their meal he demonstrates his ability to conjure up illusions by showing them a forest with animals and a hunt, a river with falconers, a tournament with knights jousting, and even Dorigen dancing. When all these things have appeared, Chaucer describes how the illusion was broken:

> And when this master that this magike wrought
> Saw it was time, he clapped his honds to,
> And farewell our revel, all was ago. (F 1202–4)

This is similar to a passage in Act IV, scene i of *The Tempest*. Prospero is also demonstrating his art, in this case for Miranda and Ferdinand, and when the spirits have appeared and blessed the couple, he 'starts suddenly' (sd), remembering Caliban's conspiracy, and dismisses them, explaining in the famous speech beginning

> Our revels now are ended.
>
> (IV. i. 148)

Conversely, we also find some convincing echoes of Chaucer scattered through Shakespeare's plays (especially the earlier ones) in places where the context is entirely different. One of the most familiar and frequently noted of all such echoes comes in *Richard II* when Bolingbroke asks

> O who can hold a fire in his hand
> By thinking on the frosty Caucasus?
>
> (I. iii. 294–5)

Critics from Sarrazin in 1897 to A. Freeman in 1963 have pointed out the similarity with a metaphor used to describe true virtue in *The Wife of Bath's Tale*:

> Take fire and beare it into the derkest hous
> Betwixt this and the mount Caucasus,
> And let men shut the dores, and go then,
> Yet will the fire as faire lie and brenne
> As twenty thousand men might it behold.
>
> (D 1139–43)

The context is quite different, but Chaucer does seem to be the only other author to combine references to fire and to the Caucasus in this particular way, so the probability of a direct allusion is strong.[8] Equally surprising and at first sight unlikely is an echo of *The Parson's Tale* spotted by T. M. Pearce in *Troilus and Cressida*. He quotes part of Troilus's cry of despair and disgust after watching Cressida and Diomede:

> And with another knot, five-finger-tied,
> The fractions of her faith, orts of her love,
> The fragments, scraps, the bits, and greasy relics
> Of her o'ereaten faith, are bound to Diomed.
>
> (v. ii. 155–8)

and relates the phrase 'five-finger-tied' to the *De Luxuria* section of the Tale (paragraph 76) in which the parson says 'the fifth finger of the Divels hond, is the stinking deed of lecherie', having given looking, touching, foul words, and kissing for the other four fingers to make an extended metaphor on the subject, elaborating his statement that 'this is

---

8. See A. Freeman, '*Richard II* I. iii.294–5', *Shakespeare Quarterly*, xiv (1963), 89–90, and the arguments quoted by Peter Ure in the New Arden *Richard II* (London, 1956), p. 38.

that other hond of the devill, with five fingers, to catch the people to his villanie'. This seems a convincing explanation of a somewhat obscure half-line, especially as Thersites has mentioned 'the devil luxury, with his fat rump and potato-finger' earlier in the scene. Chaucer may well be the source, if it was not a common analogy in sermons.[9]

A similar sort of allusion crops up in *Hamlet* according to J. W. Hales who thought that the lines Chaucer addresses to the daisy in the Prologue to *The Legend of Good Women*:

> My word, my workes is knit so in your bonde
> That, as an harpe obeieth to the honde,
> And make it soune after his fingering,
> Right so mowe ye out of mine hart bring
> Soch voice, right as you list, to laugh or pain.
>
> (89–93)

were in Shakespeare's mind when he made Hamlet praise Horatio for being one of those

> Whose blood and judgement are so well commeddled
> That they are not a pipe for Fortune's finger
> To sound what stop she please.   (III. ii. 67–69)

and later in the same scene, he offers Guildenstern a pipe, saying

> You would play upon me; you would seem to
> know my stops; . . . do you think I am easier
> to be played upon than a pipe? (III. ii. 355–60)

If there is a direct link here it would be good evidence that Shakespeare knew Chaucer very well indeed, since otherwise the connection between *Hamlet* and *The Legend of Good Women* is very unlikely. However, this parallel also seems open to the familiar charge that 'the topicks are obvious and their application is different'.

Two parallels with *The Parlement of Foules* are more detailed and less obvious if equally unpredictable. Shake-speare appears to have drawn upon Chaucer's discussion of dreams for Mercutio's 'Queen Mab' speech in *Romeo and Juliet*. The relevant stanza of the poem runs

9. T. M. Pearce, 'Another knot, five-finger-tied', *N & Q*, vii (1960), 18–19.

> The wearie hunter, slepyng in his bedde
> To wodde ayein his minde goeth anone
> The Judge dremeth how his plees be spedde
> The Carter dremeth how his cartes gone
> The rich of gold, the knight fight with his fone
> The sicke mette he drinketh of the tonne
> The lover mette he hath his ladie wonne.
>
> (99–105)

Shakespeare discards the logic of *somnium animale* by making Queen Mab responsible for all the dreams:

> —And in this state she gallops night by night
> Through lovers' brains, and then they dream of love;
> O'er courtiers' knees, that dream on curtsies straight;
> O'er lawyers fingers, who straight dream on fees;
> —Sometime she driveth o'er a soldier's neck,
> And then he dreams of cutting foreign throats—
> Of breaches, ambuscadoes, Spanish blades,
> Of healths five fathom deep;   (I. iv. 70–86)

We have the additional element of the association of the dream with an appropriate part of the body, but Shakespeare's lover, lawyer, and soldier correspond with Chaucer's lover, judge, and knight. He omits the hunter, carter, the rich man, and the sick man, and adds courtiers, ladies, and a parson, though his soldier's dream of 'healths five fathom deep' may be a reminiscence of the dream of Chaucer's sick man. J. W. Hales first noted this parallel in 1873, and J. C. Maxwell substantiated the claim recently when he compared the rival claims of Chaucer and Claudian (Chaucer's source) for this passage and concluded that the English writer was the more likely direct source.[1]

Hales also noticed a parallel between *The Parlement* and *Measure for Measure* (in most respects a singularly un-Chaucerian play) in the matter of a description of the pains of the afterworld. Claudio's horror of being

> imprisoned in the viewless winds
> And blown with restless violence round about
> The pendant world   (III. i. 125–7)

perhaps derives from Chaucer's lines

1. 'Chaucer in the Queen Mab speech', N & Q, vii (1960), 16.

> And breakers of the law, soth to saine
> And likerous folke, after that they ben dede,
> Shull whirle about the world, alway in paine.
>
> (78–80)

The thought is obviously similar, and Chaucer's reference to 'likerous folke' may be the link. The main rival is Chaucer's own source, the *Somnium Scipionis*, and again the English version is more likely.[2]

A more familiar theme treated by both Chaucer and Shakespeare is the idea that personal merit is more important than hereditary 'nobility'. The obvious example in Shakespeare is in *All's Well* when the King tells Bertram not to despise Helena for her low birth:

> From lowest place when virtuous things proceed,
> The place is dignified by the doer's deed.
> Where great additions swells and virtue none,
> It is a dropsied honour . . .
>   . . . honours thrive
> When rather from our acts we them derive
> Than our foregoers.   (ii. iii. 123–35)

This is very like the speech made by the 'olde wyf' in *The Wife of Bath's Tale*, which has a similar admonitory function:

> Here may ye see well how that gentrie
> Is nat annexed to possessioun, . . .
> For God it wot, men may full often find
> A lords sonne done shame and villany
> And he that woll have prise of his gentry . . .
> And nill himselfe don no gentil deedes, . . .
> He nis not gentle, be he duke or erle,
> For villaines sinfull deeds maketh a cherl. . . .
> Thy gentleness cometh fro God allone,
> Then cometh our very gentleness of grace,
> It was nothing bequeath us with our place.
>
> (D 1146–64)

This parallel was noted by Nevill Coghill, who also pointed out that the probability of Chaucerian borrowing was in-

---

2. See also J. E. Hankins, 'Pains of the afterworld in Milton and Shakespeare', *PMLA*, lxxi (1956), 482–95.

creased by a further parallel with the same Tale in I. i where
Parolles's mocking attack on virginity,

It is not politic in the commonwealth of nature to preserve
virginity. Loss of virginity is rational increase, and there was never
virgin got till virginity was first lost . . .   (I. i. 120 ff.)

can be compared with the Wife's own words in her Prologue:

> For had God commaunded maidenhead,
> Then had he damned wedding out of dread,
> And certes, if ther were no seed ysow,
> Virginity then whereof should it grow?
>   (D 69–72)[3]

Finally we come to Shakespeare's longest and most precise
verbal borrowing from any Chaucer edition, which is ironically not from Chaucer at all but from the apocryphal passage
known as 'Merlin's prophecy' which was first printed as a
space-filler in Caxton's Chaucer and dutifully reprinted by all
subsequent editors. In Speght's editions of 1598 and 1602 it
appears amongst the prefatory matter just before *The
Canterbury Tales* and runs:

> When faith faileth in Priestes sawes
> And lordes hests are holden for lawes
> And robberie is holden purchace
> And lechery is holden solace
> Then shall the lond of Albion
> Be brought to great confusion.

This is of course familiar to us from *King Lear*, where the
Fool speaks it:

> When priests are more in word than matter;
> When brewers mar their malt with water;
> When nobles are their tailors' tutors;
> No heretics burned, but wenches' suitors;
> When every case in law is right;
> No squire in debt, nor no poor knight;
> When slanders do not live in tongues;
> Nor cut purses come not to throngs;
> When usurers tell their gold i'the field;
> And bawds and whores do churches build;

3. There is a similar tirade against virginity in William Rowley's *All's Lost by
Lust* (1619), II. i. 72–79, but he may be depending on *All's Well* itself.

Then shall the realm of Albion
Come to great confusion:
Then comes the time, who lives to see't,
That going shall be used with feet.

(III. ii. 81–94)

And he adds 'This prophecy Merlin shall make; for I live before his time'. It may be important as further evidence that Shakespeare was familiar with printed editions of Chaucer, but the lines are quoted quite frequently during the period.[4]

4. General influence, plots, and sub-plots

There are several broad parallels between the plots of Chaucer and Shakespeare, especially in the areas of courtly romance and comedy. Both writers begin their careers by writing remarkably sophisticated and somewhat artificial works (*The Book of the Duchess* and *Love's Labour's Lost* for example) and move towards a greater degree of naturalism (*The Canterbury Tales* and the mature comedies and tragedies) though without of course abandoning various sorts of stylization. Shakespeare adds a third phase to the cycle by returning to a more artificial style in his last plays. It would be possible (though an oversimplification) to make out a case for a development in Shakespeare's use of Chaucer which corresponds to this chronological development from artificiality to naturalism and back again. Certainly the atmosphere and ideas of courtly romance as epitomized by *The Romaunt of the Rose*, Chaucer's dream visions and more artificial romances are more evident in Shakespeare's earlier plays (from *The Two Gentlemen of Verona* to *Romeo and Juliet*) and in the late Romances than they are in the plays of the middle period.

What is most interesting about this pattern is that Shakespeare seems to have thought of Chaucer *primarily* as a writer of romantic and courtly poetry rather than as a comic naturalist. M. C. Bradbrook has called *The Canterbury Tales* 'the nearest analogue' in our literature to the naturalism of

4. See Spurgeon's collection of Chaucer allusions and later supplements to this work.

Shakespeare's mature comedies,[5] but the parallel has to remain on a very generalized level: the sort of fabliau material Chaucer handles so well is quite unlike Shakespeare's low-life comedy which usually depends on the exposure of ignorance and self-importance and on sheer verbal effects rather than on marital difficulties and sexual farce. We are more likely to find Chaucer as a serious source for the main plots of the comedies than as a comic source for the sub-plots, despite our twentieth-century reading of him and the attempts of some critics to draw comparisons between such figures as Falstaff and the Wife of Bath as 'rich comic characters'. It is the Tales of the Knight and the Man of Law which are analogous with the comedies, not those of the Miller and the Reeve.

I have already mentioned *The Knight's Tale* as a general source for the love and friendship theme of *The Two Gentlemen of Verona* and I shall be discussing its more specific influence on *A Midsummer Night's Dream* and *The Two Noble Kinsmen* below. Nevill Coghill has suggested that *The Man of Law's Tale* has a bearing on 'the whole metaphysical scheme' of *Romeo and Juliet*, quoting the lines about the 'Sowdan of Surrye':

> Paraventure in that thilke large booke
> Which that cleped is the heven, iwriten was
> With sterres, whan that he his birth tooke
> That he for love should han his death, alas.
>
> (B 190–3)

There is the individual parallel between Romeo and the Sowdan as well as the more general parallel between two works which attempt to combine a sense of astral destiny with orthodox Christian belief. The story of Constance in *The Man of Law's Tale* with her simple, shining virtues, arousing the jealousy of her mothers-in-law, twice consigned to the sea to take her fortune, twice surviving to bring others to virtue through her own goodness, and finally miraculously reunited with her husband and father, provides a strong analogy with Shakespeare's Romances, especially *Pericles*. Shakespeare's use of Gower in that particular play might have encouraged a general recollection of his poetically

---

5. *Shakespeare and Elizabethan Poetry* (London, 1951), pp. 168–9.

superior contemporary, and the Man of Law even refers to
the story of 'Tyro Appollonius' and 'the cursed King Antio-
chus' (80 ff.). The quantity and quality of attention Shakespeare gives to his heroine as compared with his primary
sources is very like Chaucer's treatment of Constance.

The theme of patience in the Romances, and especially the
patience necessary to endure separation from a loved one, is
is of course to be found in *The Clerke's Tale* as well as *The
Man of Law's Tale*. There are two specific points of comparison with *The Winter's Tale* here, first the pathos of the
woman's separation from her children, and then the extraordinary joy of the final reunion of husband and wife—as
Chaucer says

> For more solemne in every mans sight
> This feast was, and greater of costage,
> Than was the revell of her mariage.
>
> (E 1125–7)

Such analogies illustrate how close Shakespeare was to the
serious, romantic side of Chaucer. Even the Wife of Bath
seems to have provided him with serious rather than comic
material. The theme of sovereignty in marriage is the subject
of both her long Prologue and her short Tale, but David M.
Bergeron has claimed that it is the Tale which has close parallels with Shakespeare's *Taming of the Shrew*.[6] He finds in
both works the serious theme of the transformation of an out-
cast through human acceptance, with marriage as a climax
paradoxically providing freedom and happiness through sub-
mission. Katherine's shrewishness is seen as a parallel to the
age of Chaucer's 'wyf' as a deterrent to normal acceptability,
neither wedding is celebrated with the proper festivities, each
bride is transformed after the ceremony and each falls into a
didactic role at the end. Outside this and Luciana's attitude
in *The Comedy of Errors* (II. i) Shakespeare's comedies carry
the same 'message' about relationships as the 'marriage
group' of *The Canterbury Tales*, namely that a balanced
relationship based on love is the only comfortable solution to
the battle of the sexes.

6. 'The Wife of Bath and Shakespeare's *Taming of the Shrew*', *University
Review*, xxxv (1969), 279–86.

A more precise plot suggestion derived from Chaucer has been found by two critics at the end of *Love's Labour's Lost* where the lovers are dismissed, like the birds at the end of *The Parlement of Foules*, to spend a year in the service of love before they can marry.[7] This is an attractive parallel but not a close one since in the poem we have rival suitors performing their year's service in a competitive spirit while they await their lady's choice, but in the play the choices have all been made and have only to be confirmed. Another moment towards the end of *Love's Labour's Lost*, the appearance of Marcade in v. ii which brings the shock of death into the pastoral sports, is similar to the appearance of the 'man in black' in *The Book of the Duchess* who also brings news of death. The whole play is close to the atmosphere of Chaucer's dream-visions in such a way as to make these parallels more probable.

It was once hoped that the mysteries of *The Phoenix and the Turtle* could be solved by relating the poem to the tradition of allegorical treatments of the Court of Love, and specifically to Chaucer's *Parlement of Foules*.[8] J. C. Maxwell takes a more cautious view in his recent edition where he says

There is enough to suggest—in conjunction with the evidence from other works that he knew the poem [he refers to articles on the Queen Mab speech and the ending of *Love's Labour's Lost*]— that Shakespeare took a few hints from *The Parlement of Foules*, but there is nothing in Chaucer that really throws much light on what is distinctive in *The Phoenix and the Turtle*.[9]

The 'hints' are mostly parallels between the lists of birds (e.g. Shakespeare's 'bird of loudest lay' may be Chaucer's 'crane, the geaunt with his trompes soun') which are almost inevitable in the context and, as Maxwell says, not particularly enlightening as far as the poem is concerned, though they do contribute their mite to the current argument.

A poem which does use Chaucer more extensively is *The Rape of Lucrece*, which derives several of its details from the

7. See Nevill Coghill (as cited) and R. K. Presson, 'The conclusion of *Love's Labour's Lost*', N & Q, vii (1960), 17–18.

8. A. H. R. Fairchild, '*The Phoenix and the Turtle*', *Englische Studien*, xxxiii (1904), 337–84.

9. New Cambridge edition (Cambridge, 1966), p. xxviii.

version given in *The Legend of Good Women*, according to at least two modern editors.[1] The parallels range from the general tenor of an extended passage to the odd verbal echo. A good example of the first might be Chaucer's reproach to Tarquin:

> Tarquinius, that arte a kynges heyre
> And shuldest, as by linage and by right
> Done as a lorde and a very knight
> Why hast thou done despite to chivalrye
> Whi hast thou done thy lady vilanie?
> Alas, of the this was a vilainous dede.
>
> (1819–24)

which Maxwell finds to be used twice by Shakespeare, first when Tarquin argues with himself before the deed:

> O shame to knighthood and to shining arms!
> O foul dishonour to my household's grave!
> —Then my digression is so vile, so base—
>
> (197 ff.)

and again in the words of Lucrece herself:

> In Tarquin's likeness I did entertain thee;
> Hast thou put on his shape to do him shame?
> To all the host of heaven I complain me
> Thou wrong'st his honour, wound'st his princely name.
> Thou art not what thou seem'st; and if the same,
>   Thou seem'st not what thou art, a god, a king;
>
> (596 ff.)

On the other hand, a single line which seems to have impressed itself upon Shakespeare is Chaucer's

> And in the night ful thefely gan he stalke,
>
> (1781)

which appears in his description of Tarquin as a 'creeping thief' at l. 305, and in the line

> Into the chamber wickedly he stalks.
>
> (365)

There are a few details in the narrative where Shakespeare

1. J. C. Maxwell again for the New Cambridge (Cambridge, 1966), and J. W. Lever for the New Penguin (Harmondsworth, 1971).

seems to follow Chaucer, as when Tarquin threatens to kill one of Lucrece's own slaves to impute the rape to him (515), which is paralleled in the *Legend* (1807), while Ovid and Livy do not specify the ownership of the slave. Similarly, the physical helplessness of Lucrece—

> That dying fear through all her body spread;
> And who cannot abuse a body dead?
>
> (1266–7)

recalls the actual swoon of Chaucer's heroine (1814–18), since this does not happen in other versions. And there is a final parallel in the treatment of the body:

> They did conclude to bear dead Lucrece thence,
> To show her bleeding body thorough Rome,
> And so to publish Tarquin's foul offence;
>
> (1850–2)

This follows Chaucer's account

> And openly let cary her on a bere
> Through al the towne, that men may se and here
> The horrible dede of her oppressyoun.   (1866–7)

In Livy she is just brought into the market-place.

The story of Lucrece is also analogous to that of Lavinia in *Titus Andronicus*, though Philomel (also one of Chaucer's *Good Women*) is the more obvious and explicit reference. One of the most important scenes in this play, Act II, scene iii, which contains the love-scene between Aaron and Tamora, the murder of Bassianus, the rape and mutilation of Lavinia and the trapping and accusation of her brothers, has three references to figures in Chaucer's *Legend of Good Women*, namely Dido (l. 22), Philomel (43), and Pyramus (231). Also the threat of death in a pit of snakes invented here by Tamora (98 ff.) is not in the immediate sources (in so far as we know them) but recalls Chaucer's version of the death of Cleopatra in her *Legend* (678 ff.) which seems to have been his own invention. If Shakespeare had recently read Chaucer for *The Rape of Lucrece*, probably written very close in time to *Titus Andronicus*, it is very likely that the influence was carried over into the play.

Finally we come to the two plays which, apart from *Troilus
and Cressida* and *The Two Noble Kinsmen*, show the most
substantial and pervasive influence of Chaucer in the whole
canon, *A Midsummer Night's Dream* and *Romeo and Juliet*.

A Midsummer Night's Dream is the play which has
received most critical attention in respect of its Chaucerian
borrowings which are primarily from *The Knight's Tale* but
also from *The Merchant's Tale, The Legend of Good Women*,
and (perhaps) *The Parlement of Foules*. The borrowings are
of every kind, from substantial parallels of plot to the briefest
of one-line references. The most obvious parallels with *The
Knight's Tale* are in the play's framing action of the wedding
of Theseus and Hippolyta, the setting in Athens and the near-
by woods (in which two rivals intend to fight over a girl), the
hunting scenes, and the final wedding celebrations. All these
were noted in 1873 by Hales who also commented on Shakespeare's use of the name Philostrate for the Master of the
Revels, since that is the name assumed by Chaucer's Arcite
when he returns to Theseus's court in disguise and is promoted to the position of squire of the duke's chamber
(1428 ff.). It was H. R. D. Anders who first remarked that
Shakespeare also calls Theseus a Duke, and F. Sidgwick
suggested in 1908 that Hermia's father Egeus might have got
his name from the father of Theseus in the poem, although
this could come from other sources for the Theseus story
such as Plutarch. He also thought that the names of the kings
who come to the tournament in support of Palamon and
Arcite, Lygurge and Emetreus, might have suggested Shakespeare's Lysander and Demetrius.[2]

Apart from these parallels of plot and nomenclature,
A Midsummer Night's Dream is somewhat exceptional
amongst Shakespeare's works in having a couple of close
verbal borrowings from Chaucer. In the opening scene,
Hippolyta refers to the coming celebrations as 'solemnities'
(i. i. 11) and Theseus says he will wed her

> With pomp, with triumph, and with revelling.
> (i. i. 19)

2. See Hales and Anders (as cited) and F. Sidgwick, *Sources and Analogues of
'A Midsummer Night's Dream'* (London, 1908).

This may recall the poet's description of how Theseus brought his bride home

> With mykell glory and solempnyte.
>
> (870)

Later Shakespeare's Theseus says to the lovers

> We'll hold a feast in great solemnity
>
> (IV. i. 182)

and at the very end of the play he uses the word again:

> A fortnight hold we this solemnity.
>
> (V. i. 358)

Returning to the first scene, there may be a reminiscence of Chaucer in Lysander's words to Hermia about a wood

> Where I did meet thee once with Helena
> To do observance to a morn of May.
>
> (I. i. 166–7)

Chaucer's Arcite also goes out in to a wood near Athens

> —for to doen his observaunce to Maie.
>
> (1500)

and we first meet Emily, the heroine of *The Knight's Tale*, on 'A morne of May', when she too has arisen to 'do observaunce' (1034 ff.). Shakespeare refers to May rather more than we might otherwise expect in a play ostensibly set on midsummer night: in IV. i, Theseus even hazards an explanation of the presence of the lovers asleep in the wood by saying

> No doubt they rose up early to observe
> The rite of May;   (IV. i. 129–30)

All this seems to suggest the influence of Chaucer.

Shakespeare's Theseus is very like his predecessor in *The Knight's Tale*, not only in his current situation and the things we are told about him such as his love of hunting and his recent conquest of Thebes (V. i. 51 in the play, and of course the subject of the early part of Chaucer's poem) but also in his role as the slightly aloof spectator, judge, and figure of authority *vis-à-vis* the lovers. He is less remote from them in the play in so far as his marriage remains uncelebrated until the end, whereas it is over near the beginning of Chaucer's poem, but the characters still complement each other quite well in that Shakespeare allows his Theseus to speak as one slightly above common passion (as in his famous dismissal from the point of view of 'cool reason' of the 'shaping fantasies' of lovers and poets in v. i) while Chaucer's Theseus, though theoretically above the fray, ruefully recalls his subjection to the god of love:

> A man mote bene a foole other yong or olde
> I wotte it by my selfe ful yore agone
> For in my tyme, a servaunt was I one.
>
> (1812–14)

The Theseus of the *Dream* is much closer to Chaucer's character than the Theseus of *The Two Noble Kinsmen*, Shakespeare's second dramatization of *The Knight's Tale*, in which he is much less in control and more worried.

I think it is hardly an exaggeration to call *A Midsummer Night's Dream* Shakespeare's first dramatization of the Tale in some respects. In 1908, Sidgwick said rather tentatively 'It is conceivable that the story of Palamon and Arcite affected, but did not supply, the plot of the four lovers' (for which there is no other known source), and this idea has been taken up by later critics, notably Dorothy Bethurum and L. S. Champion. Bethurum thought that Shakespeare found in Chaucer the hint for making the love-story a comic satire on human folly, and that the fairies in the play might be a lighter version of the supernatural influences in the poem.[3] L. S. Champion went further in suggesting that

In *A Midsummer Night's Dream* Shakespeare was not creating a structural masterpiece by fusing three or four disparate strands of action but was, rather, adapting *The Knight's Tale*—the prototype of these narative lines—to the purposes of romantic comedy.[4]

He analyses the two works in order to demonstrate that 'the basic structure and sequence of events run parallel from

---

3. 'Shakespeare's comment on medieval romance in *A Midsummer Night's Dream*', MLN, lx (1945), 85–94.

4. '*A Midsummer Night's Dream*: the problem of source', *Papers on Language and Literature*, vol. 4 (Southern Illinois University, 1968), pp. 13–19.

beginning to end'. In each we have the wedding-scene followed by a quite separate story of love and rivalry, the latter plot leads to conflict and somewhat arbitrary supernatural intervention, and both works end with attempts at explanation and another wedding-scene. However, this distorts Chaucer's narrative somewhat: the part of his poem which deals with the love, rivalry, and conflict of Palamon and Arcite is much longer, more detailed, and more serious than Shakespeare's single night in the wood, and it *is* the main substance of the poem, whereas the lovers in *A Midsummer Night's Dream*, though technically central, seem in practice not much more important than the three 'disparate strands' of the mechanicals and their play, Oberon, Titania, and the fairies, and the 'framing' plot itself.

Nevertheless, I think it can be argued that Shakespeare was using Chaucer quite extensively in this play without setting up such rigid parallels. It is more a matter of variations on a number of themes than a close echoing of the poem's structure. The symmetry which is such a remarkable feature of *The Knight's Tale* might well have invited Shakespeare to vary and elaborate the plot as he did. He had already used the two men/one girl story, perhaps not entirely to his own satisfaction, in *The Two Gentlemen of Verona*, and he knew it would be difficult to resolve without actually killing one of the heroes, which he would hardly want to do in a comedy, perhaps written for a wedding. He was not at this point interested in the strange stylized effect of Chaucer's symmetry as a thing in itself (as he seems to have been later in *The Two Noble Kinsmen*), so the obvious procedure would be to add another heroine, thus clearing the way for a happy ending (as Julia theoretically does in *The Two Gentlemen of Verona*) and increasing the potential number of comic triangular situations. The single, passive heroine is comparatively poor material dramatically (as both Shakespeare and Fletcher were to find later), so she is not only doubled but activated: Shakespeare can get twice as much anguish and laughter out of the situations if the women are allowed to have desires as well as the men. Even so I believe Shakespeare does not sacrifice the powerful conception of chastity and the single life associated with Chaucer's Emily, but uses it in I. i when

Theseus tells Hermia that she must either accept her father's choice of a husband or

> . . . live a barren sister all your life,
> Chanting faint hymns to the cold fruitless moon.
> . . . on Diana's altar to protest
> For aye austerity and single life.   (I. i. 70–90)

This passage evokes in an awesome and rather repellent manner (Hermia is to be a rose 'withering on the virgin thorn') the single life so desired by the heroine of the poem and for which she prays, also at Diana's altar (2297 ff.). Titania, too, is associated with the moon (and hence with Diana) though being a 'votaress' of her order clearly does not demand virginity.

All these parallels add up to a strong case for the influence of *The Knight's Tale* on *A Midsummer Night's Dream*. One snag however that critics have usually overlooked is the possibility that Shakespeare might have drawn his 'Chaucerian' material from the lost *Palamon and Arcite* play put on by the Admiral's Men in 1594 which I mentioned in the previous chapter. Clearly we cannot be sure, but since Shakespeare's usual habit seems to have been to look up several available versions of any single story it is likely that he would have used the play and the poem together if he used the play at all. It would be fascinating to know if the *Dream* is in any way a parody of a more serious treatment of the material by a less sophisticated dramatist but we shall discover this only if the play or an account of it comes to light.

The use of *The Knight's Tale* in *A Midsummer Night's Dream* provides support for less incontrovertible references to Chaucer within the same play. In 1902 Otto Ballmann suggested *The Merchant's Tale* as a source for the Oberon–Titania quarrel, although Chaucer's Pluto and Proserpine conduct a debate rather than a serious argument. Dorothy Bethurum rediscovered the parallel and elaborated it in her article on *A Midsummer Night's Dream* by commenting on the way in which, in both works, the fairies reveal mortal folly by 'opening the eyes' of the people concerned. She also noticed that Chaucer mentions the story of Pyramus and Thisbe in *The Merchant's Tale* (2128–31), which may be another link. Without supporting evidence I think the parallel is weak, but the number of other Chaucerian references in this play makes it more convincing. We know that, for a play like *Cymbeline*, Shakespeare took names and incidents that were widely scattered in Holinshed and used them in a single work, so it seems likely that, having decided to use *The Knight's Tale*, he turned over the pages of his Chaucer in search of further material.

Kenneth Muir has made a thorough investigation of the astonishing number of sources used for the Pyramus and Thisbe episode and concludes that 'Shakespeare took very little from Chaucer's version, presumably because it is not naturally ludicrous'.[5] He assumes Shakespeare knew the poem, but finds only two specific examples of influence: Chaucer's line

> Thus wolde they saine, Alas, thou wicked wal—
> (756)

seems to be echoed in Shakespeare's

> O wicked wall, through whom I see no bliss.
> (v. i. 178)

and the lion is depicted 'with bloody mouth' by both writers (Chaucer 807, Shakespeare v. i. 142).

I am not quite so sure that Chaucer's version is 'not naturally ludicrous': there is something tongue-in-cheek about most of the Legends, and Chaucer seems to be over-doing things deliberately here. There is a great deal too much exclamation, which makes me think that Chaucer's constant reiteration of 'allas' may have influenced Shakespeare's ludicrous exclamatory style. The ironic interpretation is not only a modern one: the author of *Common Conditions* in 1576 showed awareness of irony on Chaucer's part, and anyone who knew the stories of characters like Cleopatra, Medea, and Philomela from other sources must have doubted Chaucer's seriousness in setting them up as wholly admirable 'martyrs'. As I have said above Shakespeare also refers to the Legend of Dido in the *Dream* (I. i. 173 ff.).

5. 'Pyramus and Thisbe: a study in Shakespeare's method', *Shakespeare Quarterly*, v (1954), 141–53.

Finally, I would suggest a fleeting reference to Chaucer in
IV. i when Theseus and his hunting party come upon the
lovers in the woods and he greets them

> Good morrow, friends. Saint Valentine is past:
> Begin these wood-birds but to couple now?
>
> (IV. i. 136–7)

The coupling of birds on St Valentine's day is of course the
central theme of *The Parlement of Foules*.

The most interesting and significant of all the examples of
Chaucerian influence covered in this chapter comes last, with
the case of *Romeo and Juliet*. Geoffrey Bullough says of this
play that 'Undoubtedly Shakespeare's main and perhaps sole
source was Arthur Brooke's long poem *The Tragicall
Historye of Romeus and Juliet*'.[6] No-one would deny that
Brooke was the main source, but several critics have noted
hints of Chaucer's *Troilus and Criseyde* in the play and I
think a case can be made for a general and pervasive use of
Chaucer as at least a subsidiary source. In this particular case
I have been especially aware of the gap between the source-
study as such and a more speculative critical interest in a
comparison between the two works. It is both possible and
rewarding to compare them regardless of any genetic connection. The chain of proof required by the source-study is
on a different level and might even be said to be irrelevant to
the critical comparison. Nevertheless the two approaches can
be seen as complementary in so far as the source-study might
add to the critical comparison the extra interest of being able
to assume that Shakespeare himself was conscious of the
many links.

There are obvious reasons for grouping the two works
together as similar kinds of narrative. Before Shakespeare
wrote *Romeo and Juliet* the principal characters had been
placed alongside Troilus and Criseyde as 'patterns' of love,
as for example in the lover's speech in praise of his mistress
Aurelia in Brian Melbancke's *Philotimus* published in 1583:

Fye, pleasure, fye, thou cloyest me withe delyghte. Nowe Priam's
sone, give place; thy Helen's hewe is stainde! O Troylus, weepe no

---

6. *Narrative and Dramatic Sources of Shakespeare* (London, 1957–75), i. 274.

more, faire Cressed thyne is lothely foul. Nor Hercules thou haste cause to vaunt for thy swete Omphale; nor Romeo thou hast cause to weepe for Juliet's losse, if ever Aurelia had saluted your sight, whose bright eyes beam like the precious carbuncle.[7]

The two pairs are alike in being not only patterns of love but patterns of tragic love—indeed one might say that Shakespeare's *Romeo and Juliet* succeeded Chaucer's *Troilus and Criseyde* as the single most important and influential love-tragedy in English poetry, the archetype to which situations in both life and literature were referred. This coincidence in itself encourages the modern critic to make a comparison of the two works, but one should perhaps begin by attempting to establish whether it was a coincidence of which Shakespeare himself might have been aware. Shakespeare is typical of his age in referring to Troy more frequently than to any other topic in classical history or mythology.[8] The fall of Troy was to the Elizabethans, as it had been to Chaucer, the great symbol of the precariousness and mutability of organized society, and one of the reasons for the success of *Troilus and Criseyde* must have been that Chaucer managed to set an archetypal personal tragedy against the familiar background of an archetypal social tragedy.

That Chaucer's poem was sufficiently well known and respected to spring automatically to the mind of an Elizabethan writing a love-tragedy is conveniently illustrated by an examination of Shakespeare's main source for *Romeo and Juliet*. When Arthur Brooke was writing *The Tragicall Historye of Romeus and Juliet* in 1562 he must have noticed similarities between the narrative he was working on and Chaucer's *Troilus and Criseyde*, for he drew upon the latter to amplify *his* source in Boaistuau, as J. J. Munro was the first to demonstrate.[9] Contrary to what one might expect from the emphasis on the didactic potential of the tale in Brooke's 'Address to the Reader', where the passion of the

7. Quoted in the Variorum *Romeo and Juliet*, ed. H. H. Furness (Philadelphia, 1874), p. 407.

8. See Dougas Bush, 'Classical myths in Shakespeare's plays' in *Elizabethan and Jacobean Studies presented to F. P. Wilson*, ed. H. Davis and H. Gardner (Oxford, 1959), pp. 65–85.

9. See his edition of *Romeus and Juliet* for *The Shakespeare Classics* series (London, 1908).

lovers is condemned as an example of 'the hedlong fall of loose dishonestie', his additions seems to have been chosen in order to intensify the emotional impact of the poem rather than to give it a better grounding in moral philosophy. He borrows, for example, the strong image of the lover waiting for his friend's help as the sick man waits for the doctor (l. 613, cf. Chaucer i. 1086), the extravagant emotional behaviour of the hero on being told bad news (1291, cf. Chaucer iv. 293), and his extreme grief on being parted from his lady (1755, cf. v. 659). He seems also to use Chaucer's scene of the parting of the lovers at dawn (1701, cf. iii. 1515), and is probably influenced by him in his stress on the concept of 'false Fortune'. It would however be difficult to argue that Brooke's use of *Troilus* adds very much by way of depth or subtlety to his poem, or that he shows himself to be aware of the peculiar and superior qualities of the poem he is raiding.

If Brooke turned automatically to Chaucer it is *a priori* conceivable that Shakespeare may have done so too, and quite possible that he might have taken a more self-conscious and positive interest in the nature of the work's greatness. At all events he wrote a play which contains a number of very interesting parallels to Chaucer's poem, whether one attributes this to direct influence or to the coincidence whereby two independent versions of a sort of ideal love-tragedy will resemble each other.

It has often been remarked that *Romeo and Juliet* is untypical of Shakespearian tragedy on the general grounds that it does not set up strong causal relationships between the nature of its central characters and the nature of the events which befall them. In other words it has been seen as a tragedy of external fate (or sheer bad luck) rather than a tragedy of character, and for some critics this has been a proof of its inferiority. John Lawlor, however, in a spirited defence against this position, has argued that the tragedy of fate is not necessarily inferior, but simply a different kind of tragedy, and one which the Elizabethans had inherited from the Middle Ages.[1] *Romeo and Juliet* is very close to this

---

1. '*Romeo and Juliet*' in *Early Shakespeare*, ed. J. R. Brown and B. Harris (Stratford-upon-Avon Studies 3, London, 1961), pp. 123–43. See also his book *The Tragic Sense in Shakespeare* (London, 1960), pp. 77–87.

medieval conception of tragedy whose 'central truth is that Fortune knows nothing of human deserving'. Such a view of life is of course saved from pessimistic absurdity by religion: '[Fortune's] activities are not, in the end, inscrutable; for those who are minded to learn, a greater good is in prospect.' Not surprisingly, Chaucer's *Troilus* is cited as an outstanding example of this genre: the exalted vision of the hero at the end of the poem has the effect of taking us beyond the immediate disaster to a deeper understanding of life. In a similar way, the catastrophe that overtakes Romeo and Juliet leads directly to the recreation of order and love in a disordered society.

But neither story should be seen as merely exemplary in this sense. They are particularly powerful because of the way in which they present their central situations as well as through the philosophical context in which they place them. Both express what has been felt by many people to be essentially true about a certain kind of love. They confirm both our hopes and our fears about the nature of intense passion, which is shown to be positive and resplendent at the same time as it is vulnerable and even reprehensible. Both authors were writing for Christian audiences which ought in theory to have condemned as excessive the value placed by the protagonists upon earthly felicity, and this can still be seen as a moral problem today, though the lovers would be accused simply of self-indulgence rather than blasphemy. The subtlety of what both Chaucer and Shakespeare achieve in this area is a major reason for their over-all success. Chaucer has the simpler task in that his characters are pagans and his narrative format allows him to indicate a Christian commentary without undermining the sympathetic nature of the story. Shakespeare has a more difficult time reconciling the religion of Christ and the religion of Cupid, but there is no doubt that he achieves a more delicate blend than the crude mixture of glorification and condemnation of passion we find in Brooke.[2] Both Chaucer and Shakespeare require a double response from their audience: we need simultaneously to sympathize with the lovers who are irresistibly swayed by

2. Paul N. Siegel compares Shakespeare with Brooke and other Elizabethan adaptors of Italian *novelle* in this respect in his essay on 'Christianity and the religion of love in Romeo and Juliet', *Shakespeare Quarterly*, xii (1961), 371–92.

their passion and to acknowledge that such a neglect of the traditional teachings about the need for man to be governed by the higher faculties can lead only to disaster.

It seems particularly appropriate to the subject-matter that both stories should depend so much on Fortune and chance since this is indicative of the nature of love. One would not expect such a degree of external opposition and bad luck to accompany every love story but it conveys very forcefully the central perception that love is irrational, unpredictable, and undeserved. Even when Chaucer has the opportunity to root the tragedy more firmly in his heroine's character he prefers to put the emphasis on the general frailty of human beings and the vulnerability of love to all kinds of circumstances. This kind of love is indeed not only vulnerable but almost suicidal. In both works our attention is drawn to the intensity of the love as an ominous sign: Criseyde warns herself that 'Full sharpe beginning breaketh oft at ende' (ii. 791), and Friar Lawrence tells Romeo, 'These violent delights have violent ends' (II. vi. 9).

These lines figured as part of a more strict source-study when they were claimed as a direct parallel by J. W. Hales, and it is true that there is no parallel in Brooke, but Tilley's dictionary of proverbs for the period lists 'Such beginning, such end' as a common saying (B 262). On the positive side, the proverb is vague while the lines from Chaucer and Shakespeare are more specific and are applied to very similar situations. Incidentally if this _is_ Chaucerian it comes up again in _Othello_ when Iago assures Roderigo that Desdemona's love for the hero 'was a violent commencement in her, and thou shalt see an answerable sequestration' (I. iii. 45–46). However, the important point seems to be that the lines illustrate a basically similar perception about passion rather than that they prove a particular borrowing. Without of course being an explicit part of the plot (as it is for example in the story of Tristan and Isolde), the death-wish is an important underlying theme in both works.

Troilus and Romeo are both very ready to see love as the direct cause of despair and death. This occurs very early in _Troilus and Criseyde_, where Troilus is ready to give up before he has even spoken to Criseyde:

God would I were arrived in the port
Of death, to which my sorrowe woll me lede
Ah Lorde, to me it were a greate comfort
Than were I quite of languishing in drede.
(i. 526–9)

This mood recurs when he hears that Criseyde must leave him (e.g. iv. 501 ff.), and is of course prevalent during the last book of the poem. Romeo is similarly desperate on hearing of his banishment and of Juliet's death. The near-suicide of Troilus on thinking Criseyde has died of grief (iv. 1156 ff.) is closely paralleled in Romeo's death, but the ending of *Romeo and Juliet* adds a dimension to the love-and-death theme which is not possible in *Troilus and Criseyde*, in so far as it presents death as not only an escape from earthly difficulties but also a positive fulfilment and continuation of love. The reason for Criseyde's failure was that she 'forsoke him er that she deide' (i. 56), the choice of words implying that she should have chosen to die first. The drive towards death is in fact a consequence of the mutability Criseyde's action illustrates: only in death can love become completely stable and invulnerable, a theme Shakespeare was to repeat even more powerfully in *Antony and Cleopatra*. Even Juliet is not free from the tendency to associate love with death. As Nicholas Brooke points out, her speech anticipating the night ('Gallop apace, you fiery-footed steeds,') in iii. ii. is remarkable for its omission of any reference to fertility or growth (associations which are also completely absent from the portrayal of Criseyde) and for the way it can lead straight into the suicidal

Come cords; come nurse; I'll to my wedding-bed;
And death, not Romeo, take my maidenhead!
(iii. ii. 136–7)[3]

But alongside this solemnity and sadness in both works there is a surprisingly large amount of comedy. It is one of the most striking resemblances between the two works that (unlike the somewhat heavy-handed Brooke) they are able to maintain a comic or affirmative tone much of the time. They both begin by revealing their tragic outcome before the narrative proper has even begun, Chaucer referring to 'The

3. *Shakespeare's Early Tragedies* (London, 1968), pp. 99 ff.

double sorow of Troilus' in his opening lines and Shakespeare providing a Chorus to forecast 'The fearful passage of their death-marked love' before his lovers are introduced. This 'framing' device allows for a certain poignancy and irony in any subsequent happiness, but neither poet takes it to preclude utterly any sense of joy or optimism. Both present the love itself as a kind of affirmation, however doomed and fragile, and both underline that affirmation with passages of very splendid verse unalloyed by hints of the tragedy to come.

A major problem for both writers is the familiar and conventional nature of the material, which calls for a careful avoidance of cliché and a positive attempt to prevent the story from over-balancing into melodrama or farce. Chaucer is able to give his story a degree of depth and solidity by the weight of detailed context surrounding it, and Shakespeare achieves a similar effect by his depiction of the feuding families and by giving us scenes with minor characters such as the household servants or the musicians. But principally both writers protect their central theme from ridicule by the bold device of including within the work itself a controlled element of comedy to deflect our laughter. Chaucer stops us from laughing at the idealistic attitudes of Troilus and Criseyde by providing the down-to-earth attitude of Pandarus as a contrast, and it is arguable that Shakespeare does a very similar thing with Juliet's Nurse. Her role in the affair is of course comparable in terms of the plot, but this need not imply thematic similarity.

The nurse is present in a sketchy form in Brooke's version, but her wider role as an important centre of contrast and a lightning-conductor for laughter may well have been developed with the help of Chaucer's Pandarus. This is an area where the general comparison overlaps with the source-study, since it seems to me there are at least two scenes which indicate specific borrowing or reminiscence. The extended and exasperating delay on the part of the Nurse in passing on vital news to Juliet in II. v has a general similarity to the long preamble Pandarus gives to the announcement of Troilus's love when he visits Criseyde at the beginning of Chaucer's Book ii (a comparable point structurally), but there is a closer parallel in the exhibition of what Professor Bullough calls the Nurse's 'weathercock dishonesty' in III. v, which is very like the advice Pandarus gives to Troilus when they hear that Criseyde is to be exchanged for Antenor. In both cases the crisis causes a clash between the idealistic and potentially tragic attitude towards love held by the protagonists and the 'practical' and hitherto comic attitude of their companions. Pandarus encourages his friend by telling him

> This toune is ful of ladies al aboute
> And to my dome, fairer than suche twelve
> As ever she was, shall I finden in some route . . .
> If she be lost, we shal recover an other.
>
> (iv. 401–6)

'The newe love out chaseth oft the old' he says cheerfully, just as Juliet's Nurse encourages her to think of Paris and assures her of his superior attractions:

> O, he's a lovely gentleman!
> Romeo's a dish-clout to him; an eagle, madam,
> Hath not so green, so quick, so fair an eye
> As Paris hath.   (III. v. 219–22)

Neither receives much gratitude for this comfort. Juliet is horrified and asks incredulously 'Speak'st thou from thy heart?' On being assured that her Nurse is sincere she immediately begins to deceive her former confidante, pretending to fall in with her opinion but calling her 'most wicked fiend' when she has gone. The formerly comic character has become 'ancient damnation' and has lost much of the audience's sympathy too. Pandarus fares better as he is shown *not* to be speaking from the heart.

Chaucer explains his attitude:

> These wordes saied he for the nones all
> To helpe his friende, lest he for sorowe deide
> For doubtlesse to doen his wo to fall
> He raught nat what unthrift that he seide.
>
> (iv. 428–31)

And Troilus knows that his friend sympathizes with his feelings, as he shows by asking Pandarus

> But tel me now, sens that the thinketh so light
> To chaungen so in love, aie to and fro
> Why hast thou nat doen bisily thy might
> To chaungen her that doeth thee al thy wo?
>
> (iv. 484–7)

Pandarus is a lover himself and is closer to Juliet than to her
Nurse in his ability to appreciate the finality and pathos of
Troilus's statement that he cannot alter his love:

> It lithe nat in my power, leve brother,
> And though I might, yet would I nat doe so.
>
> (iv. 458–9)

The whole incident is of course outlined in Brooke, but he
does not convey the sense of shock achieved by both Chaucer
and Shakespeare in their dramatic presentations of conflicting
attitudes here. Brooke's Juliet comes back from her visit to
the Friar already determined to deceive her Nurse as well as
her parents (2288 ff.), and although she is 'diseased' by the
woman's flattery of Paris we do not feel she had expected
anything different. If Shakespeare is using Chaucer here the
argument would depend partly on the superior quality and
effectiveness of Chaucer's incident over Brooke's. It is
interesting that Pandarus and the Nurse trace almost complementary trajectories in terms of audience sympathy:
having taken a somewhat dubious view of Pandarus during
the early stages of *Troilus and Criseyde* we retain a surprising
amount of sympathy for him at the end (especially at v. 1723
ff.), while the Nurse begins by delighting us and ends somewhat abruptly beyond the pale.[4]

Given a conventional 'courtly-love' romance, both Chaucer
and Shakespeare seem to acknowledge that there is not a
great deal one can do with the hero. Romeo can be contrasted
with Troilus in that he is actually a lover (though of someone
else) when the story begins. It has in fact been claimed by
Hales that Mercutio is modelled on Troilus in his flagrant
mockery of love, but figures of this kind are common and it

---

4. In *Shakespeare's Tragedies of Love* (London, 1970), H. A. Mason says as
part of his argument for 'Shakespeare the Opportunist' that the Nurse is not a
naturalistically consistent character anyway, but a 'vehicle for various
"moments" ' which exist independently of each other (p. 35).

might be argued that Proteus in *The Two Gentlemen of Verona*, Berowne in *Love's Labour's Lost*, and Benedick in *Much Ado About Nothing* are all closer to Troilus than Mercutio is in that after mocking love they are shown to fall victim to it themselves.

The obvious way of adding novelty and interest to such a story is to strengthen the role of the heroine. Both Chaucer and Shakespeare had previously written works which included conventionally passive heroines (Emily in *The Knight's Tale*, Silvia in *The Two Gentlemen of Verona*) and both must have realized that the whole set of conventions could be given a new twist by bringing the heroine firmly into the action, comparing her experience with that of her lover at every stage. Moreover the heroine's role is by nature a more dignified and less ludicrous one than the hero's. His role is to suffer and implore while hers is to decide. He runs the risk of seeming self-absorbed in his desires while she has to weigh up the situation and choose how to mingle compassion with wisdom. Both Criseyde and Juliet come off rather well in a comparison with their lovers. In both works there is a striking point at which we realize that the man is still ensnared in the rhetorical flummery of 'courtly love' while the woman has passed beyond this to a straightforward and therefore moving declaration of affection. In *Troilus and Criseyde* this point comes just before the consummation of the love in Book iii. Troilus has sunk rather low in our estimation by conniving with Pandarus to produce a completely trumped-up tale of being jealous of a rival so that he can demand reassurance from Criseyde in the middle of the night. After a lot of lying the device succeeds in gaining him entrance to her bedroom, but when he cries ('Now be ye caught,—Now yeldeth yow, for other boote is none' (iii. 1207–8) in his excitement she replies calmly

> Ne had I er now, my swete herte dere,
> Been yolde, iwis, I were now not here!
> (iii. 1210–11)

Her sincerity and touch of humour at this point are very powerful in arousing our sympathy despite our knowledge of the end of the story. The comparable point in *Romeo and*

Juliet is the balcony scene, where the contrast between Juliet's
straightforward concern for Romeo's safety and his indul-
gence in conventional hyperbole is almost comic:

JULIET: How cam'st thou hither, tell me, and wherefore?
  The orchard walls are high and hard to climb;
  And the place death, considering who thou art,
  If any of my kinsmen find thee here.
ROMEO: With love's light wings did I o'erperch these walls,
  For stony limits cannot hold love out;
  And what love can do, that dares love attempt.
  Therefore thy kinsmen are no stop to me.
JULIET: If they do see thee, they will murder thee.
ROMEO: Alack, there lies more peril in thine eye
  Than twenty of their swords; look thou but sweet,
  And I am proof against their enmity.   (II. ii. 62–73)

We remember Juliet's earlier admonition 'You kiss by
th'book' (I. v. 108), and indeed the whole sequence fits into
the typical Shakespearian pattern (most obvious in *As You
Like It* and *Twelfth Night*) whereby the heroine appears to
lead her lover out of his adolescent romanticizing into
mature love. One would obviously not want to claim a direct
source-relationship here, but one *would* want to point out
the similarity in the ways in which conventional material is
transcended.

    J. W. Hales did claim direct influence of Chaucer on Shake-
speare's scene depicting the parting of the lovers at dawn
(III. v.), but the resemblance seems to me a very general one.
It is certainly an instance of the medieval 'aubade' tradition
in Shakespeare but there are no unusual touches which would
link these two particular examples and nothing that Shakespeare could not have found in Brooke, who is, as I have said,
using Chaucer here himself. Hales seems on much firmer
ground when he compares two incidents later on in their
respective narratives, namely the illusion of hope experienced
by Troilus waiting for Criseyde on the walls of Troy towards
the end of the poem and the similar experience of Romeo in
Mantua in v. i of the play. This is by no means a conventional
element in such a story and there is nothing like it in Brooke.
In Chaucer, Troilus is combating the implied scepticism of
Pandarus over whether Criseyde will keep her word to

return by telling him of a strange sense of comfort he feels

> But hardely, it is not all for nought
> That in mine harte I now rejoice thus
> It is ayeinst some good I have a thought
> Not I not how, but sens that I was wrought
> Ne felte I soche a comfort, dare I seye
> She cometh tonight, my life, that durst I leye.
>   (v. 1164–9)

This is followed not by an immediate announcement of disaster but by Chaucer's first direct indication of the cynicism that Pandarus, the author, and the readers now begin to feel:

> Pandarus answerde, 'it maie be well inough'
> And helde with him of all that ever he saied
> But in his harte he thought, and soft lough
> And to himself full soberly he saied
> 'From hasel-wodde, there Joly Robin plaied
> Shall come all that thou abidest there
> Ye, farewell all the snowe of ferne yere!'
>   (v. 1170–6)

And it has been preceded by Chaucer's description of how Criseyde gave her love to Diomede, so the reader cannot fail to see Troilus's optimism as tragic irony.

Similarly in the play we already know that events have taken a fairly desperate turn for Romeo (Juliet has just faked her own death in order to avoid being married to Paris), though it is not until after Balthasar has spoken (reporting that she is truly dead) that we realize quite how disastrously things are going to go wrong. Before his servant arrives, Romeo, like Troilus, is wondering at the strange sense of comfort he is experiencing:

> If I may trust the flattering truth of sleep,
> My dreams presage some joyful news at hand.
> My bosom's lord sits lightly on his throne,
> And all this day an unaccustomed spirit
> Lifts me above the ground with cheerful thoughts.
>   (v. i. 1–5)

There is a strong similarity of situation and thought here, and the same effect of tragic irony, though nothing by way of a verbal parallel.

As usual, verbal parallels are rare and somewhat flimsy. G. Sarrazin did claim in 1897 that Juliet's exclamation in the balcony scene,

> O! for a falc'ner's voice,
> To lure this tassel-gentle back again.
>   (II. ii. 158–9)

derived from the following lines in Chaucer:

> And whan that [Troilus] come riding into the toun
> Ful oft his lady from her window doun
> As fresh as faucon, comen out of mue
> Ful redely was him goodly to salue.   (iii. 1782–5)

He was presumably impressed by the location of the scene at a window as well as by the falcon-image (the parallel is given in a list with no comment), but the case is still weakened by the fact that it is such a common image. Shakespeare himself uses it in the context of love-making elsewhere at least three times, in *The Taming of the Shrew* (IV. i. 174 ff.), *Troilus and Cressida* (III. ii. 51–52), and *Othello* (III. iii. 264–7), and all these instances are closer both to Chaucer and to convention in that they see the man as the falconer and the woman as the falcon, unlike the reversal made by Juliet.

Brooke does not use the falcon-image, which may have given the parallel with Chaucer a specious attractiveness. He does employ the image of love as a dangerous voyage quite frequently, but nevertheless this seems to me both a stronger and a more interesting parallel between Shakespeare and Chaucer. The issue is a complicated one and two important speeches by Romeo are involved, each of them coming just before a critical moment in his career. The first comes when Benvolio is hurrying Romeo towards the feast at which he is destined to meet Juliet and warns him they may be too late. Romeo replies

> I fear, too early; for my mind misgives
> Some consequence, yet hanging in the stars,
> Shall bitterly begin his fearful date
> With this night's revels and expire the term
> Of a despised life clos'd in my breast,
> By some vile forfeit of untimely death.
> But he that hath the steerage of my course
> Direct my sail!   (I. iv. 106–13)

A similar complex of images involving the stars, the ship, and death as a kind of financial transaction with a fixed date, occurs in Romeo's final speech in the play as he takes the poison:

> O! here
> Will I set up my everlasting rest,
> And shake the yoke of inauspicious stars
> From this world-wearied flesh. Eyes, look your last.
> Arms, take your last embrace. And, lips, O you
> The doors of breath, seal with a righteous kiss
> A dateless bargain to engrossing death!
> Come, bitter conduct, come, unsavoury guide.
> Thou desperate pilot, now at once run on
> The dashing rocks thy sea-sick weary bark.
>
> (v. iii. 109–18)[5]

There are other short references to love as a voyage in the Prologue ('The fearful passage of their death-mark'd love') and in the balcony scene when Romeo tells Juliet

> I am no pilot; yet, wert thou as far
> As that vast shore wash'd with the farthest sea
> I should adventure for such merchandise.
>
> (ii. ii. 82–84)

The most striking occurrences of the image in Brooke come when he gives us, three times, a detailed description of a threatened shipwreck (799–808, 1359–78, 1513–26), but on each occasion the ship comes safely to port as it were, and the lovers are reconciled. The last time he uses it is to describe the state of both lovers after the death of Tybalt and the news of Romeo's banishment; he does not use it at all in the second half of his poem.

Kenneth Muir has suggested that Sonnet 85 of Sidney's *Astrophel and Stella* may be a source for Romeo's final speech:

> I see the house, my heart thy self contain,
> Beware full sails drown not thy tottring barge:
> Lest joy by Nature apt sprites to enlarge
> Thee to thy wrack beyond thy limits strain . . .

5. The connection between these two speeches was first noted by Walter Whiter in *A Specimen of a Commentary on Shakespeare 1794*, ed. A. Over and M. Bell (London, 1967), p. 112.

But give apt servants their due place, let eyes
　　See beauty's total sum summed in her face:
　　Let ears hear speech, which wit to wonder ties.
Let breath suck up those sweets, let arms embrace
　　The globe of weal, lips Love's indentures make
　　Thou but of all the Kingly Tribute take.

This is very convincing, with its parallel references to eyes, arms and lips, and the notion of 'indentures' (though the bargain here is with Love, not Death), but again the wreck is only threatened (by an excess of joy) and the outcome is happy. It seems to me possible that Shakespeare added to his use of Brooke and Sidney here a darker and more suicidal aspect of the voyage-motif from Chaucer, who uses it quite frequently and may indeed have influenced Brooke too.[6]

At an early point in the poem Troilus uses the image of a storm-tossed ship to describe the state of love itself (as opposed to any particular crisis):

> Al sterelesse within a bote am I
> A midde the sea, a twixen windes two
> That in contrarie stonden ever mo.
> 　　　　　　　　(i. 416–18)

And Chaucer begins his second book with a complete and rather self-conscious stanza on the theme:

> Out of these blacke wawes for to saile
> O winde, the weder ginneth clere
> For in the see, the bote hath such travaile
> Of my conning, that unneth I it stere
> This see clepe I the tempestous matere
> Of dispaire, that Troilus was in
> But now of hope the Kalendes begin.
> 　　　　　　　　(ii. 1–7)

Most significantly, it appears at the climax of the poem, in Troilus's desperate song to his absent lady, given us by Chaucer immediately before he relates the actual betrayal. Troilus sings:

6. In his discussion of this image in *Shakespeare's Sources*, vol. i (London, 1957), pp. 27–30, Kenneth Muir suggests first-hand experience of the sea as Brooke's source.

> O sterre, of which I lost have all the light
> With hart sore, wel ought I to bewaile
> That ever derke in turment, night by night
> Towards my deth, in winde I stere and saile
> For which the tenth night, if that I faile
> The gliding of thy bemes bright an houre
> My ship and me Caribdes woll devoure.
>
> (v. 638–44)

The linking of the image with real disaster and specifically with the hero's death does not occur in Brooke, though he does describe Romeo as 'stearles' quite early on (800). As Kenneth Muir remarks, Brooke was a very feeble poet and 'could give Shakespeare little beyond the story and a few phrases and images'. In working this material up to the level of poetic intensity he achieved Shakespeare might well have turned to the writer of the greatest love-tragedy he knew as well as to the best of the sonneteers.

Whether it can be proved that he did or not is a question which need not take absolute precedence over the matter of whether it is valid and interesting to read these two great works alongside each other. It is possible that to travel along this road is more important than to arrive. It throws certain things about both works into greater prominence, in particular a series of contrasts between love and death, comedy and tragedy, passion and judgement. By setting the love against a background of hostility (the Greek/Trojan war, the Montague/Capulet feud) both works emphasize its fragility as well as its power. By allowing a greater but more generalized good to emerge at the end both achieve an effect of ultimate comfort after great grief and pathos.

At the same time the comparison highlights by implication the differences between the works and provokes us to consider these. *Troilus and Criseyde* is of course a much darker work, containing the painful truth of the betrayal, and this may be one reason why many people find it more deeply moving. Criseyde is less admirable than Juliet but she is also more satisfactorily complex, and the whole of Chaucer's Book v explores an aspect of suffering which, as C. S. Lewis remarked, is usually avoided in tragedy.[7] By comparison the

7. *The Allegory of Love* (Oxford, 1936), pp. 195–6.

ending of *Romeo and Juliet* might be seen as escapism. We are almost too deeply involved in the pain of Troilus and the guilt of Criseyde whereas Romeo and Juliet retreat into a kind of rhetorical simplicity. For many people the death of Mercutio is the most tragic part of the play (H. A. Mason comments, 'The moment remains so powerful that the deaths at the end of the play seem by contrast merely parts of a story').[8] There is no equivalent for this in *Troilus and Criseyde*; nor is there any need for this kind of bolstering of the seriousness of the whole.

8. *Shakespeare's Tragedies of Love*, p. 30.

4

Troilus and Cressida

Shakespeare's *Troilus and Cressida*, as the only work of his which has the same title as a poem by Chaucer, would seem an obvious place to look for the influence of the earlier poet. But, as I have said, critics are by no means agreed that the play shows first-hand evidence of the poem, and while most are prepared to admit a high degree of probability, since Chaucer's *Troilus and Criseyde* was not only the best-known English version of the story but also the Chaucerian poem most highly esteemed by the Elizabethans, attempts to prove a definite relationship have not been sufficiently convincing to gain general acceptance. It is true that there has been no detailed full-length comparison of the two works from this point of view, but the very absence of this implies a general assumption that the relationship between them is not close enough to merit this kind of approach. It is also true, on the other hand, that there is no single serious rival to Chaucer as the major source for the love-story, and those who deny his influence have to attribute Shakespeare's knowledge of it to literary and popular traditions or to lost plays.

What exactly has been said on this subject? It is necessary to give a brief survey of all significant scholarship before putting one's own arguments. The Variorum edition of *Troilus and Cressida*, published in 1953, provides a summary of the work done on the play's sources up to that year, and the conflicting opinions recorded are typical in this field. The editor quotes and summarizes the argument of R. A. Small, who found considerable evidence for the use of Chaucer in the play and who cited several points of comparison in characters, incidents, and specific speeches, although it was of subsidiary importance in his book, *The Stage-Quarrel between Ben Jonson and the so-called Poetasters.*[1] On the other hand, J. J. Jusserand is quoted as saying 'Shakespeare seems never to have read Chaucer's admirable version of the story',[2] while K. Deighton, editor of the 1906 Arden edition, took a moderate position, believing Chaucer's influence to be likely but not proved. Critics like W. W. Lawrence[3] and H. E. Rollins[4] had accepted Chaucer's influence and explained the change in tone in terms of social conditions (love outside marriage being no longer acceptable) and popular tradition, but J. S. P. Tatlock[5] and W. B. D. Henderson[6] had minimized the Chaucerian element in favour of 'tradition' and Lydgate respectively. The editor of the Variorum himself is a good representative of the middle view, and his comments at the end of the section on Chaucer are worth quoting in full as a summary of the position at this stage. He says

The relation of the play to the poem deserves more careful study than it has yet had. This much can be safely said: that if Shakespeare used Chaucer he did so rather casually, borrowing remarkably little, and giving nowhere evidence of that careful attention which he was wont to employ on Plutarch and Holinshed. So far as action and characters are concerned, a general recollection of the poem would serve his needs. The passage which Small compares (IV. iv. 75 ff.) and one or two others argue a closer knowledge of the text, but in no respect is an intimate knowledge required, and such resemblances as Small has collected are all possible under the hypothesis that Shakespeare was revising an older play. It is altogether probable, however, that Shakespeare had read Chaucer, just as it is altogether probable that he had a general acquaintance with the *Iliad*. Therefore the burden of proof is on those who question his connection with a poem which everyone knew to be the authoritative treatment of the Cressida story.[7]

1. Breslau, 1899.

2. *A Literary History of the English People* (London, 1909), iii. 253–4.

3. 'The love-story in *Troilus and Cressida*', *Shakespearean Studies*, ed. B. Matthews and A. H. Thorndike (New York, 1916), pp. 187–211.

4. 'The Troilus-Cressida story from Chaucer to Shakespeare', *PMLA*, xxxii (1917), 383–429.

5. 'The siege of Troy in Shakespeare and Heywood', *PMLA*, xxx (1915), 673–770.

6. 'Shakespeare's Troilus and its tradition', *The Parrot Presentation Volume*, ed. H. Craig (Princeton, 1935), pp. 127–56.

7. Appendix, p. 449.

Before the next summary of work on the sources of *Troilus*, provided by Geoffrey Bullough in 1966,[8] much discussion had taken place, and the general tendency had been to accept Chaucer's influence, though no 'proof' had been produced either way, and the editor of the New Cambridge text was an important exception. Bullough himself considered that Shakespeare used Chaucer. He quoted Small (still the most detailed study) and commented: 'Some of these parallels might be imaginative coincidences; but enough remains to make it certain that Shakespeare was indebted to Chaucer for many important features of the Troilus–Cressida relationship.'

He added a few parallels of his own and discussed the changes in characterization and attitude in terms of tradition. His opinion was shared by Kenneth Muir, who saw Chaucer's poem as the main source for the love-story and made a brief comparison of the structural outlines of the play and the poem as well as commenting on the changes in the characters.[9] A similar approach was followed by M. C. Bradbrook in an article written in 1958 on the specific subject of 'What Shakespeare did to Chaucer's *Troilus and Criseyde*',[1] where she also considered the effects of the dramatic concentration of the action in the light of Shakespeare's intention to deflate romantic idealism through irony. This is the nearest thing to the 'more careful study' that the Variorum editor had thought necessary, but there is not much room for a detailed comparison in an eight-page article, and Small's list of Chaucerian references remains the most extensive.

Two other periodical articles have a bearing on the subject, in that they deal with non-Chaucerian sources for some aspects of the love-story. In 1955 Kenneth Muir suggested the influence of Greene's *Euphues his Censure to Philautus* on the characterization of Shakespeare's Troilus and Cressida and on some atmospheric details in the play.[2] This is seen as a subsidiary source rather than as a rival to Chaucer, as is the

8. *Narrative and Dramatic Sources of Shakespeare*, vi (London, 1966), 83–111.
9. *Shakespeare's Sources*, i (London, 1957), 78–96.
1. *Shakespeare Quarterly*, ix (1958), 311–19.
2. 'Greene and *Troilus and Cressida*', N & Q, cc (1955), 141–2.

Troilus play put on by the Admiral's Men in 1599 (mentioned in Chapter 2) a lost play surviving only in a short fragment from which Geoffrey Bullough attempted to reconstruct its main outlines in 1964.[3] These are the only specific works to be given even this level of importance by critics.

Finally, there are a few books and articles from the last twenty years which have a more general relevance to the subject. R. K. Presson's book, *Shakespeare's 'Troilus and Cressida' and the Legends of Troy*,[4] did analyse the play's sources, but his attention was focused on the war-story rather than on the love-story. In his discussion of Shakespeare's use of Lydgate's *The Hystorye Sege and Dystruccyon of Troye* and Caxton's *The Recuyell of the Hystoryes of Troye* he cited several incidents from the play which are not found in these writers but which could have been found in Chaucer; he was, however, prepared to admit the possibility of a lost play containing them. Robert Kimbrough's full-length study of the play, *'Troilus and Cressida' and its Setting*[5] was more confident about accepting Chaucer's influence, but the 'setting' it concentrated on was the contemporary one—what Shakespeare did with the story rather than where he found it. I have already had cause to refer to Nevill Coghill's article on 'Shakespeare's reading in Chaucer' which did not deal directly with *Troilus and Cressida* at all but argued for Shakespeare's general familiarity with Chaucer from at least 1593, so could be used as a kind of supplementary support.

Thus, although there has been a considerable amount of comment on *Troilus and Cressida* and its sources, no-one has really attempted a critical comparison between Shakespeare's play and Chaucer's poem in a detailed way. A connection between the two has been assumed more by default than by any positive evidence, and it is still possible to deny that there is any connection at all. The fullest comparison remains the one made by R. A. Small in 1899 in a book in which it was virtually a digression, and most critics have based their assumptions on his rather perfunctory proof.

3. 'The lost *Troilus and Cressida*', *Essays and Studies*, xvii (1964), 24–40.
4. Wisconsin, 1953.
5. Oxford, 1964.

As I said in Chapter 1, it is common for Renaissance-centred critics to misunderstand Chaucer's poem and misread it in the light of Shakespeare's play, which is particularly hazardous when the play is seen as a 'problem' and the sources are studied in order to solve it.

The result of all the work so far seems to be a somewhat haphazard collection of insights and distortions which centre around such obvious points as 'the character of Cressida' and neglect what might be more interesting if less tangible correspondences of themes, ideas, and attitudes. Even on the basic level of plot and character the approach has been piecemeal rather than thorough, with many significant omissions; Troilus, for example, has suffered a strange neglect, and the scene in which Calchas appears (III. iii) has been tacitly assigned to the war-story and is never related to Chaucer. As for thematic influence, the notion that Shakespeare could have been interested in anything other than external matters of plot and characterization in this poem, which enjoyed a very high reputation among the Elizabethans as a piece of philosophical verse, does not seem to have been considered at all, despite a general agreement that *Troilus and Cressida* contains more abstract thought than most of Shakespeare's plays.

Apart from the general probability that Shakespeare, like every other educated man of his time, would have read Chaucer's *Troilus and Criseyde*, I hope I have already given sufficient evidence from his other plays, particularly *Romeo and Juliet*, to prove that he was familiar with it from early in his career. His other medieval sources for *Troilus*, Lydgate and Caxton, refer frequently to Chaucer, especially in connection with the love-story, of which they give abbreviated accounts, relying on their readers' knowledge of his authoritative version. Even if Shakespeare had not read the poem before beginning work on the play, it seems unlikely that he would ignore all these references and not glance at the version generally acknowledged to be definitive.

But to say that it is reasonable to suppose that Shakespeare had read Chaucer's *Troilus and Criseyde* at least once by this time is not, of course, to say that Chaucer is a major source for the play, nor does it imply that Shakespeare's knowledge

of the poem can necessarily be deduced from the text—
evidently not, or someone familiar with the text as an editor
would not deny it. This lack of obvious verbal evidence
might lead one to believe that Shakespeare did not read
Chaucer's poem for the first time at this date, since it would
have left more apparent traces. It seems possible that his
memory of the poem was good enough for him to fill out the
love-story, recalling the general structure and some specific
instances, and perhaps looking up a few important passages,
but not following the older poet in close detail. This, however, is speculative, and there is a need for a thorough study
of the play to establish the basic evidence for the connection.
The best way to do this is to go through the play following
Shakespeare's own structure and bringing in the Chaucerian
material where it is relevant. This is likely to be more comprehensive, and perhaps closer to Shakespeare's own method
of working, than to start with an abstraction from the
drama such as 'the character of Cressida'. It would be
tedious to relate each point to the critics who have noted it
before (usually quite independently of each other), so I shall
refer only to the earliest and most important comparisons in
each case. Most of the material is original, as it has never
been attempted on this scale before. The comparison which
follows treats matters of fact. Afterwards I shall attempt a
critical evaluation of the significance of my findings in relation to the content and structure of the play as a whole.

Analysis of the play

Act I, scene i

Call here my varlet; I'll unarm again . . .

The first words of Troilus seem a deliberate anti-climax to
the play's Prologue, and a warning to the audience that this
play, in contrast, perhaps, to that put on by the Admiral's
Men, is not going to take the ideals of heroism and romance
at their face value, but is more intent on exploiting the ironies
of opposing them to reality. The character of Troilus is a
suitable focus for both areas of aspiration and defeat since he

is both the pattern of the faithful romantic lover and the 'second Hector' of the medieval versions of the Troy story. It has been said that Shakespeare took the romantic figure from Chaucer and the martial one from Caxton and Lydgate and combined them in his hero, but Chaucer's hero at least is not as simple as that, and there may be other influences.

The Troilus of Caxton's *Recuyell* is very much a soldier: 'In force and gladnesse he resemblid moche to Hector and was the seconde after him of prowesse, and ther was not in all the royame a more strong ne more hardy yong man.'[6] His love affair is passed over briefly with the advice to 'rede the book of Troyllus that Chawcer made'. Lydgate presents him in a similar light:

> The seconde Ector for his worthynesse
> He called was, and for his hye prowesse,[7]

again referring us to 'my mayster Chaucer' for the full account. Such information as these writers give on the love-story is concerned with the parting of the lovers and the subsequent career and death of Troilus, and will be considered later. Neither has anything to say about the early stages of the affair, and neither depicts the love-sorrows of Troilus at any length. This leaves Chaucer master of the field apart from the complications of popular traditions and lost plays, neither of which can be analysed.

In some ways, Chaucer's Troilus is a contrast to this love-sick youth of I. i since, in accordance with the traditions of courtly love, he is ennobled by his passion and

> eek did such travayle
> In armes, that to thinke it was mervayle.
> (i. 475–6)

Although Chaucer tells us a great deal about the enervating power of love, with its accompanying pathos and self-pity, his first book ends triumphantly with a eulogy on how love has improved Troilus in every way. By contrast, Shakespeare's first scene, which corresponds in subject-matter to this book, although ending with Troilus's return to the battlefield, seems

6. *The Recuyell of the Hystoryes of Troye*, G. Bullough, *Sources*, vi. 194.
7. *The Hystorye Sege and Dystruccyon of Troye*, in G. Bullough, *Sources*, vi. 160.

to illustrate his inconsistency in this rather than his renewed
valour. The Troilus who describes himself as being

> weaker than a woman's tear,
> Tamer than sleep, fonder than ignorance,
> Less valiant than the virgin in the night,
> And skilless as unpractis'd infancy. (9–12)

takes on the worst aspects of Chaucer's character, his helplessness and his tendency to dramatize his pathos (Chaucer's
Book v is a source here, as well as Book i). One particular
detail, the image of love as a sickness and a wound is common
to both. It is possible that the references of Shakespeare's
Troilus to 'the open ulcer of my heart' and 'every gash that
love hath given me' were suggested by similar images in
Chaucer in the same context, as when Pandarus encourages
Troilus to reveal his love by saying

> who-so list have helping of his leche,
> To him bihoveth first unwrye his wounde,
>   (i. 857–8)

though it is a fairly common analogy.

Both heroes think of Cressida exclusively in terms of physical beauty at this stage (Chaucer i. 276 ff., Shakespeare i. i.
50 ff.), although Chaucer's Pandar can also emphasize her
superior moral qualities (i. 880 ff.). In the changed circumstances, Shakespeare's Pandarus is unable to do the same,
but after comparing Cressida's beauty with that of Helen
(cf. Chaucer i. 455) he resorts, appropriately enough in the
light of the next scene, to praising her witty talk. When
Troilus develops the metaphor of the lover as a sailor:

> Tell me, Apollo, for thy Daphne's love,
> What Cressid is, what Pandar, and what we?
> Her bed is India; there she lies, a pearl;
> Between our Ilium and where she resides
> Let it be call'd the wild and wandering flood;
> Ourself the merchant, and this sailing Pandar
> Our doubtful hope, our convoy, and our bark.
>   (97–103)

Shakespeare may be recalling the powerful versions of this in
Chaucer which I have already mentioned in connection with

Romeo and Juliet: if he was relying on Chaucer for the earlier play it is probable that he would do so again here.

The dependence of Troilus on Pandarus has become a much more degrading thing by Shakespeare's time than it is in Chaucer. Chaucer's Pandarus is a kind and well-meaning friend with love-problems of his own (i. 667 ff.), and he can take pleasure in helping his friend without the disgust that comes in Shakespeare from his declined reputation and the linking of Troilus's love with the vicarious lust of an old man. There are frequent references in Chaucer to Pandarus's good intentions (e.g. i. 589 ff., 990 ff.), and a long justification of his actions (iii. 239 ff.) in which a careful distinction is made between those who 'maken wommen unto men to comen' for money and those who do it out of friendship. There is nevertheless a hint of lewdness in his character, as is shown in his cynical reply to Troilus's innocent avowal of his good intentions:

> But herke Pandare o word, for I nold
> That thou in me wendest so great foly
> That to my lady I desiren should
> That toucheth harme, or any vilany
> For dredelesse me were lever die
> Than she of me aught els understood
> But that, that might sownen in to good
>
> Tho lough this Pandarus, and anon answerd
> And I thy borow, fie no wight doth but so.
>   (i. 1030–8)

In the helplessness of Chaucer's Troilus to 'ease his own smart', we have the reason behind the words of Shakespeare's character, 'I cannot come to Cressid but by Pandar', and Chaucer's hero also gives his simplicity and 'innocence' as his excuse (especially at ii. 1046 ff.). Of course Chaucer's Pandarus is not at all 'tetchy to be wooed to woo', but very eager to help, in a friendly way, and Shakespeare's Pandarus is further degraded by his cheap use of salesmen's tricks in this context (cf. Paris's words to Diomede at IV. i. 77:

> Fair Diomed you do as chapmen do,
> Dispraise the thing that you desire to buy . . .)

pretending indifference to sharpen Troilus's desire. Chaucer's Pandarus compares himself with a whetstone at i. 631 (a word used of Shakespeare's Cressida by Thersites at v. ii. 76), but his usual attitude is that of a comrade. In general, Shakespeare's Pandarus is much more remote from his Chaucerian prototype than is his Troilus, but the hero is proportionately the more lowered by his dependence on this despicable figure.

The attitude of Shakespeare's Troilus towards the war contains some interesting variations on ideas from Chaucer. His awareness of the stupidity of it all ('Fools on both sides!' etc.) is more worthy of the perception of Shakespeare's Hector or Diomed and is inconsistent with his later actions and words, when he becomes incapable of applying the sense of proportion and recognition of objective value he advocates here to either the war or his love for Cressida. Chaucer's Troilus also has a moment when he realizes in sober truth the cause of 'the quarrel', but he is able to relate the public situation to his private problems and to make it a reason for moderation. This happens in Book iv, when he knows the plan to exchange Criseyde and Pandarus advises him to 'ravisshe her', but Troilus refuses because

> this toun hath al this werre
> For ravisshing of wommen so by might.
> (iv. 547–8)

His perception of the general situation and his own place in it is much more an integral part of his story than these chance remarks are in Shakespeare. Nevertheless he is presented as a convinced fatalist, especially in the long Boethian soliloquy in iv. 960–1082, and even at an early stage in the story is blaming the gods and seeing his fate as a punishment for mocking at love (i. 206–7, 519 ff.). It is possible that the words of Shakespeare's Troilus here, 'O gods, how do you plague me!' and a few similar remarks later in the play ('How my achievements mock me' at iv. ii. 69, and 'the blest gods, as angry with my fancy . . .' at iv. iv. 24, for example) echo this tendency to abdicate a personal responsibility for his deeds, which is compatible with his over-dependence on Pandarus, and that both were suggested by Chaucer.

A final parallel with Chaucer in this fairly short scene is to be found in the notion that Troilus's absence from the field may be thought to be due to cowardice ('womanish it is to be from thence'). This is an accusation made in jest by Pandarus in Chaucer at i. 553, 'Han now thus sone Grekes made you lene?' and it occurs again at v. 411 ff. where Pandarus again tries to rouse his friend by telling him people will think he stays at home because he is afraid.[8]

Act I, scene ii

This scene introduces Shakespeare's Cressida, so it is necessary to look again at the non-Chaucerian sources both for her and for further aspects of the character of Pandarus that are revealed here, the more appropriately since the two follow a close course through literature and tradition.

Caxton, who calls Cressida Breseyda, does not mention her at all until Calchas asks for her return, and he says nothing about the early part of the story and her love for Troilus in Troy. What he says about the later events will be relevant below; here it is significant that he refers to Chaucer, but that his tone is one of strong moral disapproval and generalized anti-feminism. Lydgate is less censorious and refers Cressida's fault to the general tragedy of 'Kyndes transmutacyon'. He too begins his story with the parting of the lovers, and neither of these writers mentions Pandarus at all.

I have already described the contemporary reputations of Cressida and Pandarus, and the influence of Henryson's sequel on them. Shakespeare's previous references to the story as described in Chapter 3 display his cognizance of the tradition, and there are a couple of specific points of comparison with Henryson later in the play. It is also possible that the disease imagery of the play and the references to divine retribution were partially suggested by the *Testament*. Another source for Shakespeare's Cressida, or perhaps just an analogue, is Greene's *Euphues his Censure to Philautus* (1587),

8. There is in fact a truce going on at the time, as the previous stanza tells us. Shakespeare is equally careless about such things, as when Ulysses says 'tomorrow We must with all our main of power stand fast' (II. iii. 255) when we know that this particular day of the 'dull and long-continued truce' has been set aside for Hector's challenge (I. iii. 260).

which, as Kenneth Muir has pointed out, presents the heroine as 'tickled a little with a selfe conceipt of hir owne wit',[9] which suits her character in this scene.

The self-possessed girl we meet here is of course a complete contrast to the modest and fearful heroine of Chaucer's poem who first appears 'Wel nigh out of hir wit for sorwe and fere' (i. 108) and who is dressed 'in widowes habit blak' during the early part of the poem. As in Shakespeare, we first see her through the eyes of Troilus and Pandarus, but in Book ii (as in Shakespeare's scene ii) she comes into her own, when Pandarus tells her about Troilus's love and she reacts with considerable distress:

> With this he stint, and cast done the heed
> And she began to brest and wepe anone
> And said, alas for wo, why nere I deed
> For of this world, the faith is al agone
> Alas, what shoulden straunge unto me done
> When he that for my best frend I wend
> Rate me to love, and should it me defend
> (ii. 407–13)

and can only be brought to a favourable position by appeals to her 'pitee' and moving descriptions of Troilus's pain and danger. She is presented very much as the innocent victim in Chaucer, and one could cite many passages to illustrate the careful sympathy and subtlety of the poet's portrayal of her character. In Shakespeare, however, it is she who seems to have the upper hand throughout this scene; she is manipulating Pandarus rather than vice versa. Nevertheless there are several points of comparison in the way the dialogue and incidents are handled, as R. A. Small was the first to note, and the detail of this is the more impressive in the midst of the over-all contrast.

The device of letting the general talk move towards Troilus by way of Hector is in both versions, and in both it is the woman who first mentions Hector. It is natural in the poem that Criseyde 'gan asken him how Hector ferde' (ii. 153) since Hector is not only the greatest Trojan warrior, but is

---

9. See A. B. Grosart (ed.), *Complete Works of Robert Greene* (London, 1881–6), vi. 166.

presented at the very beginning of the poem as Criseyde's personal protector after her father is declared a traitor (i. 110 ff.). Pandarus, however, sees his cue, and begins to talk about 'his fresche brother Troilus' after a few words about Hector (i. 155 ff.). Criseyde, innocent of any personal implication, is quite happy to talk about both brothers, and the two extol the virtues of their heroes at some length, with Pandarus biding his time and quite willing to give Hector his full due.

Shakespeare uses the same situation, but it is completely changed by the fact that Cressida is fully aware of her uncle's meaning from the beginning, and is praising Hector only in order to tease her uncle with the possibility that she admires him more than Troilus. As in Chaucer, Pandarus is quick to take up the hint—'there's Troilus will not come far behind him'—but Cressida is not innocent or honest enough to admit the comparison, so instead of Chaucer's dignified and sincere praise of both heroes, each is denigrated by one of Shake-speare's characters in favour of the other, and as Cressida flaunts Hector as a rival to Troilus, Pandarus introduces Helen as one who 'loves Troilus better than Paris'. As in Chaucer, the talk of the men leads on to a reference to the real matter in hand, but Cressida's ominously jocular 'I'll spring up in his tears an 'twere a nettle against May' is the very opposite of Criseyde's fearful realization of the serious responsibility of her position.

For the subsequent sight of Troilus, Shakespeare has com-bined two scenes in Chaucer. Immediately after Pandarus has told her about his love, Criseyde sees Troilus out of her win-dow (where she is sitting alone), and Chaucer gives us a care-ful analysis of her feelings to show how this is the point at which 'pitee' begins to turn into love:

> For I saie nat that she so sodainly
> Yafe him her love, but that she gan encline
> To liken him tho, and I have told you why
> And after that, his manhode and his pine
> Made that love within her gan to mine
> For which by processe, and by good service
> He wanne her love, and in no sodain wise.
>
> (ii. 673–9)

A later scene in the same book is arranged by Pandarus, who has told Troilus to ride past while he is visiting his niece

> And if thee list, than maiest thou us saluwe,
> And upon me make thou thy contenance.
>
>   (ii. 1016–17)

When Criseyde sees him she wants to withdraw but is prevented so we have the scene where Troilus 'bekked on Pandare' as Chaucer puts it (ii. 1260) in Criseyde's presence. Shakespeare's Pandarus does not arrange the incident, but he certainly encourages Cressida to look ('here's an excellent place') and betrays his intention—'mark Troilus above the rest'. Cressida, like Criseyde, is ashamed when she realizes the obviousness of the device ('speak not so loud'), and the references to Troilus 'giving Pandarus the nod' echo the salutation in the poem. Pandarus's hopeful 'do you not hear the people cry "Troilus"?' is perhaps a reminiscence of the earlier of the two scenes in Chaucer in which this does happen:

> But as she sat alone, and thought thus
> Thascrie arose at skarmoch all without
> And men cried in the strete, se Troilus
> Hath right now put to flight the Grekes rout.
>
>   (ii. 610–13)

> And aie the people cried, here cometh our ioie
> And next his brother, holder up of Troie.
>
>   (ii. 643–4)

and the hacks on Troilus's helm are mentioned by both writers:

> his helm more hack'd than Hector's
>   (Shakespeare, l. 223)

> His helme to hewen was in twentie places
>   (Chaucer, ii. 638)

Pandarus's words to Cressida 'Had I a sister were a grace, or a daughter a goddess, he should take his choice', recall hints in two different parts of Chaucer's poem. In Book i, before Pandarus knows whom Troilus loves, he promises him

> Were it for my suster, al thy sorwe,
> By my wil, she sholde al be thyn tomorwe.
> (i. 860–1)

and in Book iii Troilus reciprocates by offering Pandarus any
of his own sisters (407–10). The somewhat surprising mention
of Achilles as a possible candidate for Cressida's love which
follows soon after (an unlikely notion, before there is any
idea of her leaving Troy) may also come from Chaucer,
whose heroine speaks of him in the same context (ii. 414–18).

Cressida's final calculating soliloquy:

> Yet hold I off. Women are angels, wooing:
> Things won are done; joy's soul lies in the doing.
> That she belov'd knows nought that knows not this:
> Men prize the thing ungain'd more than it is.
> That she was never yet that never knew
> Love got so sweet as when desire did sue;
> Therefore this maxim out of love I teach:
> Achievement is command; ungain'd, beseech.
> Then though my heart's content firm love doth bear,
> Nothing of that shall from mine eyes appear.
> (278–87)

seems a deliberate travesty of Chaucer's heroine's concern
that

> But nathelesse, with goddes governance
> I shal so doon, mine honour shal I kepe
> And eke his life.   (ii. 468–9)

but in Chaucer as well as in Shakespeare 'honour' is an ambiguous concept and is often (as Chapman noticed) a matter
of mere appearances. Stripped of her author's sympathy,
Criseyde is little better than Cressida in this respect, and one
feels that Shakespeare deliberately cut through the defences
and destroyed his heroine's delicate moral position by making her the initiator of situations rather than the unconscious
victim; the events are the same.

The way Pandarus praises Troilus may have been suggested by many similar passages in Chaucer. Perhaps the most
relevant in this context are the speeches at ii. 155–61, 204 ff.,
and 673 ff., though none is very close verbally. The 'token
from Troilus' which Shakespeare's Pandarus promises to

bring may be the letter mentioned in this book in Chaucer
(especially ii. 1005 ff.), and the suggestion that he is a bawd
is one that is hovering uncomfortably in the poem. When
Pandarus first reveals Troilus's love, he reassures Criseyde

> For me were lever, thou and I and he
> Were hanged, than I should ben his baud,
> (ii. 352–3)

and I have already mentioned the long justification of his
actions, on the grounds that they are not mercenary, which
comes in Book iii (393 ff.). Again, the defence is thin, and very
vulnerable to a cynical attack.

The knowingness of Cressida's speech is, as I said above,
closer to some lines in *The Wife of Bath's Prologue* than to
anything in *Troilus and Criseyde*, through Criseyde does
soliloquize on how she should conduct this affair in a surprisingly practical way:

> That thought was this: alas sith I am free
> Should I now love, and put in ieopardie
> My sikernesse, and thrallen libertie . . .

> For love is yet the most stormie life
> Right of himselfe, that ever was begonne . . .

> And after that her thought gan for to clere
> And said, he which that nothing undertaketh
> Nothing acheveth . . .
> (ii. 771–3, 778–9, 806–8)

She is not as calculating as Shakespeare's heroine, but her
wish to please Troilus without becoming too deeply involved
herself is a modest version of Cressida's conscious 'holding
off'. She does not see this as a means of increasing his desire,
but again she is acting in the same way out of well-meaning
innocence. The notion of manipulating people which is so
repellent in Cressida here, and which is to recur in the parallel
war-story with the machinations of Ulysses beginning in the
next scene, is very remote from the spirit in which Chaucer
shows us the delight Pandarus takes in arranging things, as
he thinks, for the best. Many of the ideas in this scene are
present in Chaucer but are given such a different twist by
Shakespeare that his version becomes a very subjective inter-

pretation, showing the same facts in a totally opposed light, and seeming to throw out Troilus's own challenge 'What's aught but as t'is valued?'

Act III, scene ii

This is the next major scene of the love-story, in which Shakespeare compresses the first meeting of the lovers and the consumation of their love into a single occasion. Chaucer is still the only one of his sources to offer any material on this part of the story. As I. i corresponded roughly to Chaucer's Book i, and I. ii to his Book ii, this scene gives a version of his Book iii, with some use of the end of Book ii.

The first meeting of Chaucer's lovers is the result of a complicated plot by Pandarus involving a dinner given by Deiphobus at which Troilus pretends to be sick. Shakespeare may have used the notion of the dinner ('supper'), the excuses, the use of Troilus's brothers as unconscious conspirators, and the presence and behaviour of Helen on this occasion for some of the comedy of his III. i. In his version it is Cressida who is falsely represented as ill ('. . . your disposer is sick'), but the idea probably came from Chaucer nevertheless. His second meeting is also arranged by Pandarus and is more directly relevant to Shakespeare.

In both versions, the hero is completely dependent on Pandarus, and is presented as almost helpless with fear. The anxiety of Shakespeare's Troilus about his ability to appreciate the height of his ecstasy is paralleled by the incapacitating love-sickness of Chaucer's character who actually does swoon and 'lose distinction in his joys' at the bedside. He also indulges in some high-flown rhetoric just before the crucial moment (iii. 712–35, cf. Shakespeare 8 ff., 17 ff.), and both writers emphasize this by juxtaposing it with Pandarus's down-to-earth replies. Both heroes are struck dumb with shyness: on the first occasion, Chaucer says of Troilus

> his lesson, that he wende conne,
> To preyen hir, is through his wit yronne,
> (iii. 83–84)

and on the second occasion he is equally fearful and has to be encouraged by Pandarus (iii. 736–7); Criseyde is also silent, 'She could not a word a right out bring' (iii. 958). In Shakespeare, we find Pandarus chattering desperately and urging Troilus 'Why do you not speak to her?' Like Chaucer's Pandarus he is more intent on deeds than words, though he does not go quite so far as actually to put Troilus into bed and undress him:

> For this or that, he into bedde him cast
> And saied, O thefe, is this a mannes hert
> And of he rent all to his bare shert.
> (iii. 1097–9)

Both Pandars realize at one point that they are unnecessary ('I'll go get a fire'—cf. 'This light nor I ne serven here of naught', iii. 1136) but Shakespeare's character quickly returns to the scene.

Chaucer makes much of the role of Pandarus here, and presents it affectionately as verging on broad comedy, because his lovers are to be seen as an innocent pair incapable of reaching this point of their own: Criseyde is virtually a victim of her uncle's plot[1] and Troilus, though conscious of it, is presented sympathetically as one driven to it by the agony of his love. By comparison, Shakespeare's lovers are a fallen pair, and they talk about the 'execution' and 'performance' of love in a manner quite alien to Chaucer's characters. Cressida has already revealed that she is not only conscious of what is happening but willing to manipulate it, and she displays more of her calculated charms and encouragements here. If anyone is the victim it is Troilus, whose ideals and language about love are misunderstood and mocked by his lady and his friend. The fear that Pandarus attributes to Cressida ('she fetches her breath as short as a new-ta'en sparrow') seems no more than an affected parody of Criseyde's genuine and characteristic apprehension ('Right as an aspes leef she gan to quake', iii. 1200).

Both the heroines make a confession of love at this point. Criseyde's is all the more sincere for its touch of humour; when Troilus says 'Now yeldeth yow, for other boot is noon' (iii. 1208), she replies

---

1. She does suspect something: see iii. 569 and 575–6.

> Ne hadde I er now, my swete herte dere,
> Ben yolde, y-wis, I were now not here!
> (iii. 1210–11)

We can take a pleasure in witnessing this consummation of a relationship founded on mutual understanding and trust which is impossible in the play, where Cressida's confession is not as artless as she makes it seem, with its clever 'pretty abruptions' and self-accusations. We feel she does indeed 'show more craft than love'.

Shakespeare follows this with the exchange of vows which he makes into a self-conscious tableau of stereotyped characters. Both writers have two scenes in which the lovers promise to be true, one here at the consummation and one at the parting, but Shakespeare telescopes the two events into a single night. Chaucer's Troilus is simple and direct:

> This dar I seye, that trouthe and diligence,
> That shal ye finden in me al my lyf.
> (iii. 1297–8)

This is comparable with Shakespeare's 'Few words to fair faith . . . what truth can speak truest, not truer than Troilus', but the simplicity is elaborated into a rhetorical speech in the play, and given the exaggeration of the self-conscious prototype. We know that Shakespeare's Troilus is not at all direct and simple in his speech, and we are perturbed by the complacent tone here which seems to be saying 'I am famous for my truth' rather than 'I will be true'. For once Shakespeare's heroine seems to be closer to her predecessor. Chaucer's Criseyde is given some uncharacteristically extravagant protestations:

> first shal Phebus fallen fro the sphere,
> And everich Egle been the Doves fere,
> And every roche out of his place sterte,
> Er Troilus go out of Creseides herte!
> (iiii. 1495–68)

We know the comparative weakness of her character, but Chaucer does not detract from these words by pointing it out, and we cannot question her sincerity. Shakespeare's Cressida is also unusually moving at this point, partly because her words are less 'tired with iteration' than those of Troilus:

> If I be false, or swerve a hair from truth,
> When time is old and hath forgot itself,
> When water drops have worn the stones of Troy,
> And blind oblivion swallow'd cities up . . .
>   . . . when they have said 'as false
> As air, or water, wind, or sandy earth
> As fox to lamb, as wolf to heifer's calf,
> Pard to the hind, or stepdame to her son;'
> Yea, let them say, to stick the heart of falsehood,
> 'As false as Cressid'.   (180–92)

There is a general resemblance between the two visions of an unrecognizable world described by the heroines but no specific parallels. The height to which Cressida rises here has been seen by some critics as an example of how she adjusts to the level of her companions, but the influence of Chaucer's Criseyde seems to me more likely than that she or anyone would be inspired by the trite similes of Troilus.

Chaucer does not remind us of the end of the story here, but finishes his Book with a joyful eulogy of love as if nothing were going to go wrong, while in the play we cannot help being aware of the end from Shakespeare's use of the clichés 'as true as Troilus' and 'as false as Cressid', even if he did not use Pandarus to seal it. Chaucer keeps Pandarus out of the poem here and takes over himself to express his confidence in the nobility of love and the happiness of his lovers (iii. 1772 ff.). Pandarus's comment to the audience at the end of Shakespeare's scene—

> And Cupid grant all tongue-tied maidens here
> Bed, chamber, pandar, to provide this gear!—

seems a deliberate parody of this author-to-reader comment at one of the highest points in the poem, and it happens again at the very end of both works, as M. C. Bradbrook pointed out. To the extent that the Pandarus of the poem has many of the qualities Chaucer gave to the image of himself which he projected into other poems, it seems very bitter that Shakespeare should use such a debased version of the character to comment on the play at these moments. If it is deliberate, 'merry Chaucer' was never presented quite so harshly and cynically as a lewd old man.

Act III, scene iii

The first part of this scene, in which Calchas asks the Greek princes for the return of his daughter in exchange for Antenor, treats material which is to be found in Caxton and Lydgate as well as in Chaucer. Caxton's account is short and not very clear. He tells us that Thoas was exchanged for Antenor and goes on to say that 'Calcas . . . prayd to Kynge Agamenon and to the other prynces that they wolde requyre Kynge Pryant to sende Breseyda to hym'. He does not give any of the arguments Calchas used.[2] Lydgate is more prolix and detailed. He agrees that Thoas was exchanged for Antenor, but goes on to introduce Calchas and his request that Cressida should be included in the deal. He is seen as a very humble figure, depending on the pathos of his grief to gain the Greeks' pity. He is said to be despised by the Trojans as a traitor, so their consent to the embassy, led by Diomede, is reluctant.[3] In both these versions Calchas is a minor figure brought on at this point in the story and not mentioned elsewhere. He is far more important in Chaucer's poem which begins with an account of his defection and its consequences (i. 64 ff.). The scene in which he requests the return of his daughter comes at the beginning of Book iv, and he is presented as quite a strong character. He reminds the Greeks of how he gave up his home in Troy in order to join them and share with them his foreknowledge of the end of the war (iv. 73–91), and he asks for the return of his daughter as recompense for the comfort he has given them. He speaks of the remorse he felt when he left her behind and the grief he still feels, but combines his pathos with a reminder of an obligation:

> Rewe on this olde caitif is distresse,
> Sin I through yow have al this hevinesse!
>
> (iv. 104–5)

Chaucer's Calchas does not specify who should be exchanged, but he is given Antenor, and the embassy, headed by Diomede, is sent 'to bringen hoom King Thoas and Criseyde'.

2. *The Recuyell* (as cited), p. 201.
3. *The Hystory* (as cited), pp. 163–4.

Shakespeare's Calchas is nearer in spirit to Chaucer's character than to either of the other medieval sources. He speaks of 'recompense' for 'the service I have done' and emphasizes what he has left for the Greek cause (ll. 5–10), repeating that he did all this 'to do you service'. He is more specific about the benefits 'registered in promise' than Chaucer's Calchas, and he actually asks that his daughter be requested in exchange for Antenor.[4] His reference to the fact that the exchange has been requested before and refused by the Trojans is not in any of the sources, but all three speak of the difficulty of obtaining Criseyde after this particular request. Caxton and Lydgate attibute this to the hatred of the Trojans for Calchas, but Chaucer makes Hector voice the objection 'in parlement' that Criseyde is not a prisoner to be exchanged in this way. Shakespeare, like Chaucer and unlike the other medieval sources, dwells on the importance to the Trojans of Antenor at this point (Chaucer iv. 192 ff.), though he does not exploit Chaucer's comment on the irony of this preference for one who was 'after traytour to the toun'.

Act iv, scenes ii and iv

As is apparent from the last scene, the story has now arrived at the point where Caxton and Lydgate take it up and become alternative sources to Chaucer. All three describe the effect that the news of the exchange has on the lovers and the actual parting, though both Caxton and Lydgate refer to Chaucer for the full authentic version, and his account is by far the longest and most detailed. Shakespeare treats this material in these two scenes, with iv. iii as a brief interruption.

iv. ii actually uses an incident which is described by Chaucer alone: the parting of the lovers after their first night together. The events are so foreshortened in the play that it is also their last, but they are not conscious of that, though the audience is. In both writers we find the conventional 'aubade' tradition, and it is impossible to claim specific

---

4. Shakespeare wisely omits Thoas, about whom Lydgate himself is confused, telling us later that Criseyde was exchanged 'For Anthenor and for the Kynge Thoas' (172).

borrowings when the situation and allusions are so common, though there are some interesting parallels and differences. Cressida is the first to cry out against the night in both (Chaucer iii. 1435–7), but Chaucer's heroine is given three lyrical stanzas which are reduced in the play to the comment 'Night hath been too brief'. Shakespeare gives all the lyricism in this scene to Troilus, in keeping with the greater discrepancy between the two characters that he has already established. Some of the images are the same, but the tone is different.

Chaucer does not allow Pandarus to interrupt this scene, but he shows him teasing his niece the next morning after Troilus has gone. He pretends the rain must have kept her awake (iii. 1555–8), and asks her jestingly how she is. Criseyde gives him a straight answer, 'never the bet for yow', but she is ashamed and hides her face (iii. 1569–70). Pandarus knows she is not really angry and offers to be punished— 'Have here a swerde, and smyteth of myn hedde' (1573)—but Criseyde is too honest to rail against him and pretend she is not really pleased with her situation, so Chaucer tells us she 'foryaf' him 'and with hir uncle gan to pleye' (1578).

Shakespeare's version of the scene is coarsened by the lack of innocence or honesty on the part of Cressida. She is still treating love as a power-game, and betrays her knowledge (or experience) in such words as 'You men will never tarry'. Like Criseyde, she accuses her uncle of responsibility for what has happened; having less justification she is more insistent. It is possible that her words to him 'Go hang yourself' are a reminiscence of Chaucer's 'Have here a swerde' speech, significantly transferred to her. All the references are of course much more explicit in the play, and the fact that Troilus is present while Pandarus and Cressida talk makes their teasing more indelicate. Again it is basically a similar situation altered by a different appraisal of the characters, especially the heroines. Both are complex, but Criseyde's complexity lies more in her creator's subtle portrayal of what is really a straightforward and simple character, while Cressida has a personal complexity which is simultaneously sophisticated and crude. Shakespeare again does violence to Chaucer's description of motive and feeling by concentrating on the brute facts and by presenting his heroine as one who 'meant naughtily' all along. He does violence to the love itself by having Aeneas knocking on the door before the lovers are up, so that disaster follows immediately upon consummation. Although Chaucer's poem is heavy with a painful consciousness of its own ending, there are also moments when we are tempted to share the happy ignorance of the characters, and this is one of them; Book iii ends on a strong upwards note, though Book iv is to begin with ominous intimations.

While the 'morning after' scene could have come from Chaucer alone, the second parting of the lovers, the final parting made in full knowledge of the exchange of Cressida for Antenor, is related by Lydgate and Caxton too. Caxton does it quite briefly, referring the reader to Chaucer as usual. He does not say precisely how the news of the exchange came to either of the lovers (p. 202). Lydgate's version is longer and is, as he says, based on Chaucer. He gives many of the details we find in the earlier poem, such as Criseyde's swoon and Troilus's readiness to kill himself, and he has many reflections on mutability and the transience of worldly pleasures (p. 168). It is such a full retelling that critics have doubted whether Chaucer is necessary as an additional source for this scene, but apart from the fact that Shakespeare would be unlikely to dispense with Chaucer at this point if he had been using him so far, there are some things in the scene that could have been suggested only by Chaucer's account.

By having Troilus return to the stage alone to see Aeneas and receive his message and then leave with him, so that Pandarus has to break the news to Cressida, Shakespeare achieves the same kind of structural effect as Chaucer, who gives us a separate 'revelation and reaction' scene for each of his lovers before they come together to express their grief. The reaction of Shakespeare's Troilus at this point has had considerable influence on critical interpretations of his whole character, since it is possible to be favourably impressed by his 'stoic' acceptance of the blow, or to see it as another example of evasion of responsibility.[5] Either way, I think it is

---

5. See M. C. Bradbrook (as cited), p. 317, and Bullough, *Sources*, vi. 104 for the first, and R. Kimbrough, '*Troilus and Cressida' and Its Setting* (Oxford, 1964), p. 85 for the second.

traceable to the attitude of Chaucer's Troilus, who is present at the council scene when Criseyde is requested and who does not say anything, mainly because he is unwilling to damage her reputation or to do anything at all before consulting her (iv. 150 ff.), and I have already referred to his awareness of the cause of the war itself and how this prevents him from expressing his feelings in violent action. He does, of course, give them vent at great length when he is alone, but his moments of self-control in public are the only precedent in the medieval sources for the behaviour of Shakespeare's Troilus here: elsewhere the emphasis is on the expression of grief rather than its restraint.

The grief of Pandarus, which intervenes here, has also some points of agreement with Chaucer, though Chaucer's Pandarus, in accordance with his position, had been present at the council scene and heard the decision himself. He is most concerned about the emotional effect on Troilus, which may explain why Shakespeare's Pandarus first says 'The young prince will go mad' rather than worrying about his niece with whom he seems, in this version, to have a closer affinity. Although the scene in Chaucer ostensibly builds up to a hope that the lovers can find some solution if they meet and talk it over sensibly, the more powerful impression is of a cruel but inevitable turn of Fortune's wheel, and the underlying acceptance of this by both characters is paralleled in Shakespeare's scene.

In the poem, the news comes to Criseyde by rumour at first, and then Pandarus arrives to confirm it. She is grieved for Troilus more than for herself, but she accepts the fact that she will have to go. She curses her father, and Chaucer stresses her indifference to him:

> she which that of hir father roughte,
> As in this cas, right nought. (iv. 667–8)

She swears she will starve herself to death if she is forced to go, but Pandarus encourages her to be moderate and optimistic. Shakespeare's Cressida is comparable in her explicit rejection of her father and in her impassioned expression of loyalty to Troilus, though she responds differently to her uncle's plea for moderation: while Criseyde agrees 'I shal don

al my might, me to restrayne ...' (iv. 940), Cressida cries
dramatically 'Why tell you me of moderation?' She does not
have Criseyde's unselfish consideration for Troilus either.
The way in which she expresses her grief is traditional:

> I'll go in and weep ...
> Tear my bright hair, and scratch my praised cheeks,
> Crack my clear voice with sobs and break my heart,
> With sounding 'Troilus'.   (104–8)

but both Chaucer and Lydgate refer to her bright hair, and
her 'clear' voice is mentioned twice in Henryson's *The Testament of Cresseid* where its 'cracking' is one of her punish-
ments for cursing the gods (ll. 338, 443–5).

Before Chaucer's lovers come together again, Troilus has
fortified himself with Boethian philosophy and become convinced 'Thus to be lorn, it is my destinee'. Nevertheless he is
ready to attempt suicide when Criseyde swoons and he thinks
she is dead. After some emotional exchanges they try to discuss the matter objectively and Criseyde puts forward some
weak but superficially convincing arguments that she will be
able to return soon. Troilus would rather they eloped together, but such a course seems very desperate to the fearful
Criseyde and she says he doesn't trust her, which leads to
mutual vows of faith and the closing of the subject. Chaucer
brings out the darker side of things by over-emphasizing the
good, as he goes out of his way to tell us that all Criseyde's
arguments were 'seyde of good entente' (iv. 1416), and that
she 'was in purpos ever to be trewe' (1420). Such reassurance
is anything but a comfort here. When Shakespeare's lovers
meet, Troilus's speech about 'Injurious Time' enforcing a
'rude brevity' seems an appropriate description of what
Shakespeare is doing to Chaucer as well as being another
example of our hero's tendency to blame supernatural forces
like his fatalistic prototype. The additional presence of
Pandarus in this scene has its usual coarsening and trivializing
effect, and the extreme haste does not allow the lovers to
make any plans. Both seem to accept the necessity of the
parting, but Troilus is more like Chaucer's Criseyde in his
comparative self-possession, while Cressida seems unable to
take it in at first. The harping on the woman's loyalty seems

very Chaucerian, but Criseyde is given a long and eloquent vow of loyalty while Cressida seems to have exhausted her ability in this vein in iii. iii.

Chaucer's Troilus is afraid of rivals and that Calchas will make his daughter marry a Greek. He is worried about their accomplishments:

> Ye shul eek seen so many a lusty knight
> Among the Grekes, ful of worthinesse,
> And eche of hem with hert, wit and might
> To plesen yow don al his businesse,
> That ye shal dullen of the rudenesse
> Of sely Troians, but-if routhe
> Remorce yow, or vertue of your trouthe.
>
>   (iv. 1484–90)

It has been pointed out by Small and subsequent critics that this is a possible source for the speech made by Shakespeare's Troilus beginning 'The Grecian youths are full of quality', in which he too is concerned about 'how novelties may move and parts with person'. This does not accord much with our previous knowledge of his character: he seems very much one who could sing, 'heel the high lavolt', 'sweeten talk', etc., and Shakespeare has even stressed the fact that the Trojans are 'ceremonious courtiers' (i. iii. 234), and likely to be at least as 'prompt and pregnant' in these things as the Greeks. This discrepancy seems to make the likelihood of a somewhat careless borrowing from Chaucer more convincing, since it is not a speech which would have occurred naturally in Shakespeare's independent version of the story.

For the references to 'truth', Shakespeare combines the premonitions Chaucer's Troilus had of Criseyde's disloyalty earlier on (iv. 1422 ff.) with the insistence of the heroine on her own sincerity at this point (iv. 1606 ff.), and achieves a heightened effect by playing them off in dramatic counterpoint instead of treating them separately. Troilus's statement 'the moral of my wit Is "plain and true"' seems a reminiscence of Chaucer's hero, who says 'At shorte worde wel ye may me leve' (iv. 1658), and to whom the words seem more appropriate. He realizes the vulnerability of his simplicity later (v. 1266–7), while Shakespeare's Troilus says now that 'it is my vice'. There is no trace of this discussion or any vows of faith in the other sources.

The exchange of tokens uses material gathered from different parts of Chaucer's poem. After their first night together his lovers exchange rings and Criseyde gives Troilus a brooch (iii. 1366), and later we have a reference to a brooch given by Troilus to Criseyde (v. 1040–1) which she gives to Diomede. She also gives Diomede 'a pencel of her sleve' (v. 1043), and he has previously acquired a glove as a love-token (v. 1013). The glove is mentioned by Caxton in the same context, but neither he nor Lydgate, nor indeed Chaucer, has any reference to tokens exchanged at the parting of the lovers.

The idea that the gods may be envious is in the poem (iv. 274 ff.), but Chaucer's hero is puzzled because he is now obeying the god of love whom he had formerly mocked. Chaucer makes it clear that there is a higher system of values of which Troilus is ignorant, and Shakespeare's hero is perhaps aware of this when he sees his love as an alternative to religious devotion:

> . . . the bless'd gods, as angry with my fancy,
> More bright in zeal than the devotion which
> Cold lips blow to their deities, take thee from me.
>   (IV. iv. 24–26)

His somewhat smug speech about his virtues seems a less sympathetic version of the praise of Troilus by Criseyde at the end of Chaucer's Book iv, which gives us good reasons for believing in the seriousness of her love.

The introduction of Diomede is very different in the two versions. Chaucer's Diomede is at least courteous on the surface, though his motto seems to be 'he is a fool that wol foryete himselve', but he suffered a decline in literary and popular tradition and appears in Lydgate and Caxton in a very unfavourable light, both of them being influenced by his treatment in Henryson.[6] Shakespeare's Diomede has already established himself as a realist in iv. i and verbally at least he seems more genuinely 'plain and true' than Troilus. In all three medieval sources he begins to talk of love to Criseyde on the way back to the Greek camp, but there is no hint of

6. See Bullough, *Sources*, vi. 158–9 and 193.

the open confrontation with Troilus that we have in the play. In the poem Troilus does not suspect Diomede as a rival until Cassandra interprets his dream at v. 1513 ff., but in the play each event is always rushing on to the next. Lydgate and Caxton are vague about whether Troilus accompanied his lady out of the city, and it may be Chaucer's reference to him waiting at 'the yate ther she sholde oute ryde' (v. 32) that suggested Shakespeare's 'At the port . . . I'll give her to your hand'. Chaucer's Troilus is of course far more discreet than Shakespeare's hero at this point, and is glad to get in a few quiet words to Criseyde (v. 78–84) rather than claiming the need openly. Still, the idea of the lovers talking to each other as Criseyde is taken away is common to both versions.

Act IV, scene v

This scene describes the arrival of Cressida in the Greek camp and seems mainly derived from Caxton (p. 203), though Shakespeare has considerably altered it from a friendly fatherly occasion to the sight of Cressida being kissed 'in general'. Chaucer's Criseyde is not received by anyone except her father, and she is too preoccupied with the grief of being separated from Troilus to be more than polite to him (v. 193–4). It is some time yet before she even comprehends Diomede's intentions in Chaucer, but Lydgate and Caxton compress the events almost as much as Shakespeare. Her witty and crude replies to the Greeks are in total contrast to her stunned silence in Chaucer and again show Shakespeare taking the worst possible view of the medieval character, foreshortening events to make her seem even more fickle and heartless.

Shakespeare chooses Ulysses to comment on this, and the speech can be seen in relation to the one he makes about Troilus later in the scene, though the first is a direct observation and the second a repetition of what Aeneas told him seven years ago. It is interesting that Chaucer interrupts his narrative at exactly this point to give us some formal and almost entirely external portraits of Diomede, Criseyde, and Troilus in that order. If we include the sketch of Diomede given by Ulysses at the beginning of this scene

'Tis [Diomed], I ken the manner of his gait:
He rises on the toe. That spirit of his
In aspiration lifts him from the earth,

(14–16)

Shakespeare is like Chaucer in following this slightly ambiguous description with a fuller, detached, and (relatively
speaking in Chaucer's case) condemnatory view of the
heroine, and then finishing with a favourable passage about
Troilus (Chaucer v. 799 ff., 806 ff., 827 ff.). Chaucer's portraits have the effect of distancing the characters and preparing for the withdrawal of sympathy which is necessary to
make the impending tragedy less painful. We have never felt
very close to Shakespeare's characters, so this is superfluous
in the play, though the devastating change in Cressida from
her attitude in the scene immediately preceding this one is an
effective and brutal way of destroying any faith that we could
have had in her love for Troilus. Both descriptions of Troilus
concentrate on his martial prowess. We have more reason to
think well of him in Chaucer, since we find it difficult to
believe that Shakespeare's Troilus is 'deedless with his
tongue', etc., though we are soon to discover that he is indeed
'more vindicative than jealous love'. In both cases he is
established more clearly as the tragic hero, but the audience
is not allowed full confidence in this: Chaucer is beginning to
undermine it with the pathos of his position and Shakespeare
has not given us much evidence for Ulysses's opinion. The
fact that Ulysses, the most practical of the Greeks, voices
opinions which are authorial in the source may justify our
seeing him as Shakespeare's spokesman, but I do not feel this
can be felt consistently throughout the play, and even here the
position is dubious.

The silence of Troilus during this scene and his reticence
in conversation with Ulysses at the very end help to support
the favourable view of him and give him rather more dignity
than he has had before. His attempt to conceal his love may
be related to the many efforts made by Chaucer's hero in the
same cause throughout Book v of the poem, and Chaucer is
also aware that 'a mock is due' to any display of self-pity in
this context, as he shows by a stanza like v. 617 ff.:

And of him selfe imagined he oft
To ben defaited, pale and waxen lesse
Than he was wont, and that men saiden soft
What may it be? who can the soth gesse
Why Troilus hath all this hevinesse
And all this nas but his melancoly
That he had of himselfe such fantasie.

Troilus's reference to Fortune in the last line of the scene again links him with the helpless and fatalistic hero of the poem.

Act v, scene ii

None of the medieval sources describes Troilus witnessing his betrayal by Cressida. Both Lydgate and Caxton refer to Chaucer and refrain from specifying how Troilus came to know that Diomede was his rival, though they deal with the enmity of the two men. Chaucer's Troilus experiences an agony of waiting, dragged out with letters and significant dreams, but he does not see Criseyde again. He comes closer to it than any other source both in his unfulfilled plans to go to the Greek camp and see his lady (v. 1576–82), and in the dream in which he sees a boar (said by Cassandra to symbolize Diomede) in whose arms 'Lay kissing ay his lady bright Criseyde' (v. 1241). The reversals from belief to disbelief, hope to despair, experienced by Troilus in this book are compressed by Shakespeare into a single unambiguous moment of great dramatic effect. If any other source is needed apart from his own instinct for a successful stage scene, Shakespeare may have recalled the scene in *The Two Gentlemen of Verona* (IV. ii) in which Julia witnesses the treachery of Proteus: the structure is very similar and it seems quite possible that he decided to make even more effective and complicated use of Montemayor's device. The only version in which Troilus and Cressida do meet again is Henryson's *Testament*, but the circumstances are so different that this can scarcely be described as a 'source'.[7]

7. John Bayley, however, argues for a closer relationship between the two works in 'Shakespeare's only play', *Stratford Papers on Shakespeare*, ed. B. W. Jackson (Toronto, 1963), pp. 58–83.

Lydgate and Caxton describe the love of Diomede and Cressida in tones quite different from that of Chaucer. They both attribute any delay in its progress to her calculation rather than to any lingering love for Troilus, and they have not portrayed her in such a way that we can understand and pity her at this point, as we can in Chaucer. Even so, Chaucer seems to be so hurt by this part of the story that he rushes through it as fast as he can, telling us very little about Criseyde's real feelings and putting all the blame on his sources:

> The morrow came, and ghostly for to speke
> This Diomede is come unto Creseide
> And shortly, lest that ye my tale breke
> So wel he for him selfe spake and seide
> That all her sighes sore, doun he leide
> And finally, the soth for to saine
> He reft her the great of all her paine.

> And after this, the story telleth us . . .

> I find eke in stories elswhere . . .

> But truely the story telleth us . . .
>   (v. 1030–7, 1044, 1051)

Shakespeare is of course hostile in his interpretation of his heroine and to that extent he is un-Chaucerian in this scene.

The tokens, however, may come from Chaucer. Lydgate and Caxton both mention the horse which comes into the play at v. v, but say nothing of any letters or gifts. Chaucer, as I have said, has used tokens earlier, as Shakespeare has, and he mentions both a glove and a sleeve again here, as the characters do in the play. Both of them are given to Diomede in the poem, the glove at v. 1013, and the sleeve at v. 1043, together with a brooch given to Criseyde by Troilus. Chaucer cannot refrain from commenting on this 'and that was litel need' (1040), and it may have been his recognition of this as one of the worst and most unnecessary things about the betrayal that made Shakespeare elaborate it into the painful play with the sleeve in this scene. Chaucer's Troilus is also particularly struck with the cruelty of this treatment of his token (v. 1688 ff.) and sees it as a spiteful action deliberately intended to show how little Criseyde cares for him now. Chaucer, however attributes considerable regret and sorrow to his heroine, together with pathetic attempts to justify herself by generalization—'al be I not the first that dide amis' (v. 1067)—rather as Cressida speaks of 'poor our sex'. It has been suggested that Criseyde's words here 'Throughout the world my bel shal be rong' (v. 1062) gave Henryson the idea for his vision of her wandering and begging 'with cop and clapper, lyk ane lazarous'. If so, Shakespeare seems to throw out a similar hint of the well-known ending to the story when he makes Cressida say 'I shall be plagued'.

In the poem, there are two separate occasions when Chaucer's Troilus believes he has lost Criseyde. The first is when he has the dream I have already mentioned and is on the point of despair, but Pandarus persuades him to write to her. This elicits an elaborate reply 'of which he fond but botmelees bihestes' (v. 1431), and Chaucer comments that it is all over (1432. ff). Troilus himself is not convinced until he sees the brooch he gave Criseyde on a cote-armoure taken from Diomede by Deiphobus (1646 ff.), whereupon he cries out bitterly against Criseyde and human faith in general: 'who shal now trowe on any othes mo?' (1681). Despite this he cannot change his fundamental feelings towards her; earlier he had rejected Pandarus's suggestion of another lady with the words 'It lyeth not in my power, my leve brother' (ii. 458), and we find the same notion in the pathos of his speech here:

> I see that clene out of your mind
> Ye have me cast, and I ne can nor may,
> For all this world, within mine hart find
> To unloven yow a quarter of a day.
>
> (v. 1695–8)

At the same time he turns violently against Diomede:

> Now god, quod he, me send yet the grace
> That I may meten with this Diomede
> And truely, if I have might and space,
> Yet shal I make I hope his sydes blede,
>
> (v. 1702–5)

and his last words are of suicidal despair:

> Myn owne death in armes wol I sech;
> I retch nat how soone be the day!   (v. 1718–19)

I have quoted quite extensively here as I think that, despite
the different circumstances, Chaucer's version could have
been a strong influence on Shakespeare's treatment of
Troilus's reaction. He is particularly moved by Cressida's
giving Diomede his token and he is at first reluctant to
believe what he sees. He cannot go on hoping as desperately
or as long of course. He is also inclined to generalize from
this instance of betrayal, and see it as a threat to universal
harmony. Various sources have been suggested for this vision
of chaos, but it is possible to trace the ideas to Chaucer,
whose hero addresses love as 'Benigne Love, thou holy bond
of thinges' (iii. 1261), and whose eulogy on the subject sees it
as the principle of all order in the universe:

> Love, that of erth and sea hath governaunce
> Love, that his heestes hath in heven hie
> Love, that with an holsome aliaunce
> Halt people ioyned, as him list hem gie
> Love, that knitteth law and company ...
>
> That, that the world with faith, which that is stable
> Diverseth so his stounds according
> That elements that ben discordable
> Holden a bond, perpetually during
> That Phebus mote his rosy day forth bring
> And that the mone hath lordship over the nights
> All this doeth love, aie heried by his mights.
>
> (iii. 1744–8, 1751–7)

There is an ambiguity in the poem here, in that Chaucer is
really celebrating Christian love, which remains when worldly love is shattered, but his hero shares the short-sightedness
and the despair of Shakespeare's character. The portrayal of
Cressida makes it impossible for us to be as impressed by
Troilus's feelings as we are in Chaucer, where we have seen
the love itself as a noble thing. Shakespeare's Troilus turns
quickly to disgust, though he does not deny the sincerity of
his love in the past ('Never did young man fancy With so
eternal and so fixed a soul'). Finally, like Chaucer's hero, he
turns his love into jealousy and revenge:

> as much as I do Cressid love,
> So much by weight hate I her Diomed.

The feeling is the same, though Shakespeare adds the idea of an exact equivalent between love and hate, the 'by weight' reminding us of Diomede's comment on the contenders for another 'light' woman: 'He as he, the heavier for a whore' (IV. i. 68).

Act v, scene iii

The violence of Troilus's revenge runs through the rest of the act as he seeks 'honour' in war after losing it in love. All the medieval sources tell of this, and Lydgate and Caxton describe how he is killed by Achilles in the way Shakespeare's Achilles kills Hector. In all three versions he outlives Hector and has his heroic moments as supreme champion of Troy. Chaucer in particular emphasizes the alteration in Troilus's method of fighting by his repeated use of the word 'cruel' to describe it:

> In many cruell battaile out of drede
> Of Troilus, this ilke noble knight
> (As men may in these old bokes rede)
> Was seen his knighthood, and his great might
> And dredelesse his ire day and night
> Ful cruelly the Grekes aie about
> (And alway most this Diomede) he sought ...

> And God it wote, with many a cruel heat
> Gan Troilus upon his helme to beet ...
>   (v. 1751–7, 1761–2)

and Shakespeare puts an even greater stress on it in the argument with Hector, where Troilus chides his elder brother for his 'vice of mercy' and advocates 'venomed vengeance'. Both ignore Cassandra, as they did in II. ii, though Hector called her words 'high strains of divination' there while Troilus termed them 'brain-sick raptures'. Here again Hector seems to respect the accumulated weight of prophecies and omens, but he goes to the field because he 'holds honour far more precious-dear than life', while Troilus dismisses them out of hand:

This foolish, dreaming superstitious girl
Makes all these bodements.

In Lydgate and Caxton Troilus is not present during this
scene, in which Andromache is more important than Cassandra, and in which her requests succeed in moving Priam to
prevent Hector from fighting. Chaucer does not mention
Cassandra here, though he has a couple of stanzas foretelling
the death of Hector and the fall of Troy (v. 1541–54) slightly
earlier in the story, and immediately following a confrontation between Troilus and Cassandra in which her prophecies
are rejected in much the same spirit as they are in Shakespeare. The subject at issue is his dream, which she rightly
interprets as meaning 'This Diomede is in and thou art oute'
(v. 1519), but he is angry and contemptuous:

> Thou seyst nat sothe, quod he, thou sorceresse,
> With al thy false ghost of Prophecie!
> Thou weenest been a greet devineresse;
> Now seest thou not this foole of fantasie
> Painen hir on ladyes for to lie?   (v. 1520–4)

Since there is no encounter between the two in Shakespeare's
other sources, it seems likely that Troilus's attitude here and
in II. ii was influenced by a reminiscence of Chaucer.

The incident that closes the scene, the appearance of
Pandarus with the letter, is also found only in Chaucer, who
tells us about two letters from Criseyde, at v. 1423 ff. and
v. 1587 ff., the first of which I have already mentioned as that
in which Troilus found 'botmelees bihestes'. The second is
even less reassuring, and causes him to feel that he cannot
believe in her at all (v. 1632–8). Both seem very like the one
said in the play to contain 'no matter from the heart' and the
recipient's reaction is similar. Chaucer's Pandarus is shocked
and completely at a loss for words (v. 1723–9), rather like
Chaucer himself, and I think this may be why Shakespeare's
Pandarus is allowed a moment of pathos here which he does
not merit anywhere else in the play, though this is perhaps an
over-sympathetic interpretation, since the pathos consists in
his references to his illness and impending death and the
specific illness mentioned is the 'bone-ache'.

Act v, scenes v–x

In the battle-scenes that follow, we have further examples of the recklessness and despair of Troilus. Shakespeare seems to be relying on Lydgate and Caxton for the events, and he follows them in making more of the incident of Troilus's horse than he could have found in Chaucer who mentions it briefly earlier on (v. 1038–9). It is possible that Ulysses's attribution of Troilus's success to 'luck' (v. v. 41) is derived from the emphasis given by Chaucer to 'fortune' at this stage of the story (e.g. v. 1745, 1763), which is not in the other sources. The cry of Troilus in v. vi,

> Fate, hear me what I say!
> I reck not though thou end my life today,

is in accordance with this fatalism, and closely comparable to the suicidal words of Chaucer's hero:

> Myn own death in armes wol I sech
> I retch not how sone be the day!
> (v. 1718–19)

In fact this is the nearest thing to an exact verbal parallel I have found. It is not very close, but there is nothing like it in the other sources and it is a very memorable moment in Chaucer.

As I have said, Shakespeare uses the account of the death of Troilus given by both Lydgate and Caxton for the death of Hector, presumably not wishing to give Troilus the dignity of death in battle or the chance of contrasting favourably with Achilles. The choice of Troilus to announce his brother's death in v. x and the emphasis on his reaction may well be signs of Chaucerian influence, since neither Lydgate nor Caxton dwells on this but Chaucer makes a special point of the grief of Troilus on this occasion and the effect it had:

> And in this wo gan Troilus to dwell,
> That, what for sorow, love and for unrest,
> Ful oft a day he bad his hert brest.
> (v. 1566–8)

So Troilus's martial valour is motivated by a mixture of love for Criseyde and revenge for Hector in Chaucer as it is in

Shakespeare, factors left vague though no doubt assumed in
the other sources. The line in this scene which looks as if it
might come directly from a medieval source, 'Hector is dead;
there is no more to say', does not in fact occur in either
Chaucer or Lydgate. They both use the tag 'there is no more
to say' quite frequently, Lydgate rather more than Chaucer,
but the nearest parallel I have found to this is in Lydgate's
description of the woe of Troilus on hearing Criseyde must
leave him:

> He was but dede, there is no more to sayne.
>
> (p. 168)

Chaucer's Troilus is of course finally allowed to share his
author's wider view of life as he looks back at the earth
from his place in heaven

> And dampned all our werks that foloweth so
> The blind lust, which that may nat last,
> And sholden al our hert on heaven cast.
>
> (v. 1823-5)

Shakespeare's hero has no such moment of recognition, being
denied any insight into the meaning of what has happened to
him as he is denied a tragic death. Instead we have the final
entry of Pandarus, who speaks directly to the audience as he
did at the end of III. ii. When discussing that passage, I suggested it was a deliberately debased substitute for Chaucer's
address to the reader in the poem, and the same thing may be
happening here, with a very harsh contrast between the piety
of Chaucer's ending and this passage about 'traders and
bawds'. If the play has been following the structure of the
poem as closely as I have maintained, it should not end with
the grief and rage of Troilus, but with some kind of detached
comment, and it is appropriate that Pandarus should do this
(however out of place he may be on the battlefield) if he has
been used in this role before. As Chaucer is more explicitly
Christian and serious at this point in his poem than ever
before, Shakespeare's Pandarus is more overtly base and
crude. Far from being an extraneous afterthought as some
critics have argued, the 'epilogue' is quite devastating in its
artistic rightness.

Chaucer's influence and its significance

I think this examination of the play has shown that there is a considerable amount of reference to Chaucer in it, perhaps more than has been recognized, but that it is not very close reference and that there are very few places where a direct verbal parallel can be claimed. There is, however, a similarity of structure and the same basic sequence of incidents, including even such details as the way in which the news of the exchange is revealed to the lovers separately, and perhaps the use of direct comment at two important points. The way in which Shakespeare compresses his material, often drawing on two or more parts of the poem to produce a concentrated effect, seems to show his familiarity with it as a whole, and the number of times he 'coincides' with Chaucer in his depiction of something which is not in any of the other sources gives strong support to the assumption from general probability that he knew it well. It is the complete contrast in tone which makes the two works so different in their final effect and which has obscured the relation between them; I have pointed out more than once that the facts are the same but the interpretations are at variance. Chaucer's sympathy for the characters is the more difficult and remarkable achievement, but it depends very much upon the narrative presentation and the opportunities this gives the author to extenuate and persuade. The drama must concentrate on the deeds, and inevitably throws the story into a different light.

Even if Chaucer is accepted as one source for the play, it would be dangerous to consider his influence in isolation from other factors such as the fashions of the contemporary theatre, as well as Shakespeare's wider intentions in this particular play which I shall try to bear in mind as I discuss the significance of my findings. I have been concentrating on Chaucer and the love-story, but *Troilus and Cressida* is a large and complex play and is typically Shakespearian in its use of multiple sources. I have had cause to mention Caxton, Lydgate, Greene, a lost play, and some elusive ballads, but have not needed to comment on the use of Chapman's Homer (and earlier translations into Latin and English), Golding's Ovid, and Sir John Harington's *Metamorphosis of Ajax*, all of which have been proved to be likely sources. Alice Walker notes that Ulysses's speech on 'degree' has been traced to Plato, Elyot, Hooker, one of the Homilies, and *The Faerie Queene*,[8] which perhaps proves only that it is a very orthodox view, but it does not seem wise to discount sources, or to ridicule them on account of their ever-increasing numbers, when we seem to be accumulating more and more evidence that Shakespeare read very widely and had an excellent memory for what he read.

It remains to be established in exactly what sense he used his sources, and whether his use of Chaucer in *Troilus and Cressida* is part of a general pattern. J. Oates Smith makes an interesting comment on this play in an essay in which she points out the difference between 'merely clever art based upon cultural knowledge of earlier art, and art that is deadly serious and wants absolutely to recreate and reinterpret the world'.[9] She gives T. S. Eliot's poetry as an example of the former variety, and Shakespeare's *Troilus and Cressida* for the latter. I would agree that Shakespeare is not a self-consciously literary man making careful allusions to an earlier poet for the benefit of an intellectual minority alone. Chaucer's poem was very well known, and the use he makes of it is not prohibitively esoteric, but this does not mean that it is not possible or part of the intention that one who knows the poem will see a further level of meaning in the play. I would also agree that the play is a 'deadly serious' reinterpretation of life, but I think there is another, less lofty reason for the use of older authors than the two Smith gives, and one that must not be omitted in a discussion of this particular work, namely the purely practical 'use' of an author as a quarry for plots and source of commercial exploitation by a hard-headed playwright with his eye on the box-office. Although Shakespeare's first reading of Chaucer did not, I think, have this motive, the popularity of Troy plays in the late 1590s[1] can hardly have escaped the notice of the man

8. See her New Cambridge edition of the play (Cambridge, 1957), p. xxx.
9. 'Essence and existence in Shakespeare's *Troilus and Cressida*', *Philological Quarterly*, xlvi (1967), 167–85.
1. The fullest list is given by J. S. P. Tatlock in 'The siege of Troy in Shakespeare and Heywood', *PMLA*, xxx (1915), 673–770.

Alfred Harbage has called 'the most attentive and assimila-tive of the Elizabethans',[2] and must have encouraged him to think of the older poet in a more practical way than before.

Shakespeare's *Troilus*, then, is at least three things in respect to its use of Chaucer. It is, more than has been recog-nized, 'clever art' based on knowledge of another piece of literature shared by author and audience, it is 'deadly serious' art which carries out its reinterpretation of life by means of a story which has been used before, and it is commercial art, a play by a man who needs a good story and who is (and has to be) responsive to the trends in the theatre and the demands of the audience.

The theatrical context of *Troilus and Cressida* is, unfor-tunately, comparable to the source-problem in complication and in lacking the convincing evidence that would ensure general agreement. It has been questioned whether it was performed at all, or, if it was, whether the performance was public or private. More important perhaps is the discussion of whether it is a deliberate contribution to the 'war of the theatres', complete with topical references, since this would have a more direct bearing on the details of the play's content, but the Prologue (ll. 23–25) seems to deny this quite explicitly, and it is impossible to pretend that *Troilus* contains the kind of personal and contemporary satire we find in plays like *Poetaster* and *Satiromastix*. Nevertheless, Shakespeare was aware of what was happening in the theatre, and he may well have been influenced in his attitude towards his subject by the cynical tone which was becoming more popular on the stage (especially in the 'private' theatres) about the turn of the century. There may have been a commercial advantage too, in offering to the audience at the Globe their own version of the fare which was fashionable at the more exclusive theatres: perhaps Shakespeare was aiming at an audience who agreed that the sentimental version of the Troilus story put on by the Admiral's Men was naive, but who did not want their afternoon taken up with the abuse and in-jokes of professional rivalry. It seems more than coincidence that Shakespeare's most overtly satirical play was produced at this time, but we need not necessarily assume that he felt

2. *Shakespeare and the Rival Traditions* (New York, 1952), p. 118.

obliged to adopt this particular tone without any option. He was not, at this date, in the position of one who had to write what the management wanted exactly to order, having acquired a 10 per cent share in the company in 1599, and being the only shareholder with any experience of the actual writing of plays. He was more likely to be guided by his own tastes and his feeling for what would succeed with the audience.

A satirical tone was by no means new to Shakespeare. His plays had often, indeed regularly, contained a satirical or critical element and this was increasingly important in the plays immediately preceding *Troilus*, as can be seen in such different examples as *As You Like It* and *Hamlet*. The use of satire with a love story (to protect it from external attack) occurs from the very beginning, with plays like *The Two Gentlemen of Verona* and *Love's Labour's Lost*, and Shakespeare had been practising such things as a satiric detachment from character, the use of explicit comment and implicit dramatic irony, and the mockery of idealism and subjective values all through his romantic comedies. The difference in *Troilus* comes from an overbalancing in the direction of the critical element and the use of a plot which excludes a compensatory happy ending rather than from any real innovation in technique or philosophy.

In the circumstances, the material to which Shakespeare went for his work on 'the matter of Troy' would have positively encouraged satirical treatment. The pretensions of Chapman's Homer invited ridicule, and the accounts of Lydgate and Caxton were full of ludicrous (and apparently innocent) discrepancies and ambiguities, such as their descriptions of the heroes:

> Of Ulixes what shall I also sayne
> That was so noble and worthy in his dayes,
> Full of wyles and sleyghty at assayes.
> In menyuge double and deceyvable
> To forge a lesynge also wonder able.
>   (Lydgate 4598–602; Bullough, p. 158)

Dyomdes was grete and had a brode breste and mervayllous stronge, of a fiers regard and sight, false in his promesses, worthy in armes, desirous of victorye, dredde and redoubted. For he was gretly injuryous to his servantes, luxuryous, wherfore he suffryd many paynes.   (Caxton, Book, iii; Bullough, p. 193)

Chaucer's poem, while a great deal less crude than this, must have seemed very vulnerable in its sympathetic treatment of a heroine like Cressida. The consistent use of irony in the poem foreshadows in a restrained form the biting satire of the play. Shakespeare gives his play a unity of tone by treating both the romantic and heroic materials with the same deflating cynicism, exposing self-interest, and sordid intrigue on all sides. His use of Thersites as commentator on both plots furthers this intention and allows him to point out some general parallels:

> Still wars and lechery! Nothing else holds fashion.
> (v. ii. 194)

> Hold thy whore, Grecian; now for thy whore, Troyan.
> (v. iv. 23–24)

> The cuckold and the cuckold-maker are at it.
> (v. vii. 9)

Troilus and Diomede fighting over Cressida are just another version of Paris and Menelaus fighting over Helen and the origin of one of the most seminal narratives of the European tradition is simply 'a war for a placket'. Shakespeare indicates many parallels between the love-story and the war-story which are often of a complex and indirect nature. The problem of how to evaluate the worth of a human being, for example, is illustrated not only by Cressida and Helen but also by Achilles and Ajax, indicating that romantic love is not the sole area in which the judgement may be at fault though it is probably the most notorious. It is on this thematic level that I have found the influence of Chaucer to be most interesting and profound. *Troilus and Criseyde* contains many of the ideas that Shakespeare used, not only in his retelling of the love-story but as thematic links between that and the rest of his material. It gave him many hints as to how to weld the two parts of the play together on this level, more than he could have found in his other sources.

One of the most remarkable things about *Troilus and Cressida* is the intense and self-conscious nature of its questioning of intellectual and philosophical attitudes. It has been considered by many to be overburdened by the amount of abstract discussion it contains. The theory that it was performed privately at the Inns of Court relies partly on the view that the play is too 'difficult' and intellectual for the public theatre. A large number of themes have been discovered in the play and given varying degrees of prominence. Topics such as order and disorder, appearance and reality, the consciousness of time and human mutability, fame, honour, the problem of subjective and objective evaluation, idealism, and the traditional opposition between the will and the reason have all been seen to be important aspects of the play, and it is valuable to see how far these are present in Chaucer's poem. *Troilus and Criseyde* was famous as a philosophical poem and *Troilus and Cressida* has been seen as the work in which Shakespeare comes nearest to discussing abstract philosophy, and most deeply questions the meaning of life, so a comparison of the ideas in the two works is appropriate. Sometimes it is possible to claim the direct influence of Chaucer's poem on the themes of Shakespeare's play while at others one can simply note coincidences of interest. I think most of the important themes of the play centre around the broad concepts of order, time, and value, so I shall consider the Chaucerian elements in each of these. I shall also look at Shakespeare's manner of presentation and his attitude towards his material, since this is another important area of Chaucer's influence.

Some critics have taken 'order', as it is set out in Ulysses's great speech, to be the controlling idea of the play, and have satisfactorily demonstrated that the action fails to maintain these high standards. Shakespeare, however, had already discussed the evils of civil disorder in the *Henry IV* plays and *Julius Caesar*, and the distinctive feature of *Troilus and Cressida* is that this kind of order and disorder is set against another kind of order, that created by love, and it is the latter which is given more serious treatment, and whose breakdown is more deeply felt. Moreover, it is Chaucer who speaks of love as the 'holy bond of things' (iii. 1744 ff.), although with

a certain ambiguity, as the author and the reader are aware
of the Christian implications of love, while the hero puts his
faith in the earthly variety. All Shakespeare had to do to
Chaucer's poem to produce the vision of chaos we find in his
play was to omit the higher level of values that would provide
an alternative to the cynical materialism of Ulysses and the
misplaced idealism of Troilus. H. Swanston, who sees the
play as an experiment in 'baroque' dialectical structure, sees
the omission of 'truly divine values' as a truncation of the
baroque system denying a final synthesis,[3] but does not
relate this to the sources, whereas I think it could be part of
what I have been describing as Shakespeare's deliberate distortion of Chaucer.

As modern critics have sometimes shown, it is very easy to
simplify and reduce Chaucer's poem by ignoring his more
serious and explicitly religious frame of reference, and it was
the obvious course of action for a playwright producing a
satirical version. Shakespeare must have perceived the
ambiguity of his source and made a deliberate decision to
change the final effect by providing no corrective to the
shortsighted vision of his characters on either the romantic or
the heroic level. Both writers see their characters seeking constancy and lasting happiness in things unstable by their
mortal nature, and being governed by apparently irrational
forces and accidents beyond their control, but Chaucer moves
beyond this lower level of the Boethian vision of life and
finally takes his hero with him, while Shakespeare leaves his
characters in the disorder of mortality.

Another aspect of the discussion of order in the play is the
debate between the will and the reason which was a common-
place in the Middle Ages as well as in the Renaissance. It is
frequently found in Shakespeare and has been seen as the
major theme of *Troilus*, and the factor which links the two
plots. R. K. Presson is an advocate of this view, which he
relates to the source, but only in terms of contrast.[4] He says
Shakespeare has turned Chaucer's courtly love story into a

3. 'The Baroque element in *Troilus and Cressida*', *Durham University Journal*, xix (1957–8), 14–23.
4. 'The structural use of a traditional theme in *Troilus and Cressida*', *Philological Quarterly*, xxxi (1952), 180–8.

moral exemplum, but it does not seem to me that a great deal of transformation was necessary. Chaucer explicitly describes his hero as being 'with desyr and resoun twight' (iv. 572) and his whole poem is concerned with the disastrous effects of allowing the will, specifically sexual desire, to overrule the higher elements in man. In the last stanza he condemns 'the blinde lust, the which that may not laste' and makes explicit the contrast between the two levels of apprehension that Boethius discusses as the higher and lower reason. This is such a common theme in Shakespeare's time that one would hardly claim a 'source', but it is another parallel which has been obscured by misconceptions about Chaucer.

Shakespeare's concern with time in *Troilus and Cressida* is a problem for those who try to see the play as a comedy, since this kind of awareness has essentially tragic implications. The most explicit statement in connection with the love-story is Troilus's speech on 'Injurious Time' in IV. iv where the concentrated language itself 'jostles roughly by' in imitation of the experience. We are always conscious of the precariousness of love in time, especially here when Troilus says he loves 'with so eternal and so fixed a soul' while Cressida thinks that 'things won are done'. The whole theme is echoed in the war-story, with the additional stress on fame and opinion. Agamemnon hopefully sees time combining with bad fortune to bring out 'persistive constancy in men', but the more impressive view is that of Ulysses when he tries to persuade Achilles that not only his reputation but his virtue itself depends on constant motion and applause (III. iii). In both contexts human activity is deprived of dignity and meaning and reduced to the insane kind of 'progress' pictured by Shelley in *The Triumph of Life*. This view of time is of course relevant to the notions of order and value, since both are challenged by the threat of oblivion.

Again this is not a new theme for Shakespeare and his contemporaries, and its association with Troy was predictable. E. M. W. Tillyard has pointed out the connection between Shakespeare's *Rape of Lucrece* and his *Troilus* in their common use of 'the great inherited conception of Troy as the rich and wonderful city whose fall was one of the most striking and exemplary achievements of Time'.[5] Here and in the Sonnets there is the influence of the last book of the *Metamorphoses*: Ovid's 'tempus edax rerum', in contrast to the optimistic view of time as the unraveller of problems that is implicit in the plots of the comedies, and occasionally explicit too, as in Viola's 'O time! thou must untangle this, not I' (II. ii. 38).

The tragic consciousness of time broods on mutability, which J. W. Lever, thinking mainly of the lyric and narrative poetry, has called 'the deepest concern of the age'.[6] It is certainly central to literary works as different as *The Faerie Queene* and *Troilus* itself. In the plays of the turn of the century, this awareness of time combines with the fashion for satire to produce a cynicism about values similar to that of Shakespeare's play; Marston's work of this period (*Jack Drum's Entertainment* and *What you Will*) is perhaps the best example: lines like 'all that exists Takes valuation from Opinion', and 'Doth not Opinion stamp the current passe Of each man's valew, vertue, quality?'[7] could almost be quotations from *Troilus*. Shakespeare had shown his interest in such notions in the *Henry IV* plays, *Julius Caesar*, and *Hamlet*, but neither he nor anyone else had written a play quite so obsessed with time and mutability before *Troilus*.

Chaucer's poem is also pervaded with the consciousness of mutability, and it is something an Elizabethan reader would not have missed. There are constant references to Fortune and her variation (e.g. i. 843, 946; iv. proem) and to Time itself (ii. 393 ff.). The consummation of the love itself is framed by remarks on its transience (iii. 820, 828, 1636) and the whole structure of the poem is directed towards the contrast between eternal values and values that are subject to time. Chaucer speaks of the political and social aspects of mutability too: it is no accident that Criseyde is reading the story of Thebes when Pandarus comes to tell her of Troilus's love, since this was another exemplum of mutability, and is used again when Cassandra reveals the power of Fortune to

5. *Shakespeare's Problem Plays* (London, 1950), p. 40.
6. *The Elizabethan Love Sonnet* (London, 1956), p. 167.
7. From *What You Will* in H. H. Wood (ed.), *The Plays of John Marston*, iii. 237, 269.

Troilus in Book v. There is an even greater stress on Fortune as the story nears its end, when the fortunes of Troilus and of Troy are verging on destruction:

> Fortune, which that permutation
> Of all things hath, as it is her committed
> Through purveyance and disposicion
> Of high Jove, as reignes shall been flitted
> Fro folk in folk, or whan they shall ben smitted
> Gan pul away the fethers bright of Troy
> Fro day to day, till they been bare of ioy.
>
> (v. 1541–7)

Chaucer's attitude to this complex of ideas is of course influenced by Boethius, and it sometimes seems possible that Shakespeare is using ideas directly from Boethius without the medium of *Troilus*. For example, Boethius speaks twice about the idea that 'contrarious Fortune profiteth more to men than Fortune debonaire' (Chaucer's translation, Book ii, Prose viii and Book iv, Prose vii), and follows it the second time with Agamemnon and Ulysses as examples of men who have suffered ill fortune and turned it to good (Metre vii of Book iv). This is very suggestive of the opening of Shakespeare's I. iii.[8]

Chaucer related the Boethian philosophy of mutability both to his story of courtly love and to his explicitly Christian viewpoint. Because of the latter he is able to provide a more comforting solution to the problem, but it has to remain external to the story until the end, and it is a comfort that Shakespeare excludes altogether. As in his other plays with a pre-Christian setting he seems to use references to 'the gods' in rather vague conjunction with stoicism, but I think the medieval-Renaissance tradition of Boethius was as important as strictly classical influences in forming his attitudes. Lydgate is also interested in the problem of mutability (especially in Books iii and iv), but his work has so much less poetic

8. Other critics have claimed direct influence of Boethius in Shakespeare, namely R. Soellner who claims an influence on *Romeo and Juliet* in 'Shakespeare and the *Consolatio*', N & Q, cxcix (1954), 108–9, R. K. Presson, 'Boethius, King Lear and "Maystresse Philosophie" ', *JEGP*, lxiv (1965), 406–24, and F. Markland, 'The order of *The Knight's Tale* and *The Tempest*', *Research Studies*, xxxiii (Washington, 1965), 1–10.

power than Chaucer's that the latter is more likely to have influenced Shakespeare, especially as it seems that he knew the whole of *Troilus and Criseyde* and must have understood its over-all concerns, while he may have only dipped into Lydgate for pieces of plot and not read as extensively as would be necessary to achieve this.

The human values which are vulnerable to both the effects of disorder and to mutability are themselves questioned in so far as they dwell in appearances or in the subjective will. Critics have oversimplified the play by romanticizing Troilus and the Trojans as the representatives of noble, if outdated, virtues, while the Greeks appear as cynical political realists bringing about the triumph of the modern rational world. But Shakespeare is by no means uncritical in his attitude towards the Trojans: one of the main 'problems' about the play is that there is no character with whom we can straight-forwardly identify and no 'right' viewpoint in this welter of arguments and comparative values. Although Hector knows in II. ii that 'Tis mad idolatry To make the service greater than the god', a statement which could be a comment on the whole tradition of 'courtly love', his heart is not in his own sober, rational arguments from the beginning and he has already committed himself to further action in the cause of 'honour'. The play does not do anything so obvious as to uphold rationalism against idealism, but faces the fact that there *are* values which cannot be debated and analysed in terms of cold reason, and the difficulty is to find some other standard by which to judge them and the 'attributive' element in them. The touchstone of value for Ulysses, the rational man, is as subjective as that of the emotional and idealistic Troilus, consisting as it does in the 'reflection' of popular acclaim and the assumption that value is not absolute but can only be assessed at second-hand as it were, in terms of the emotional reactions of other people. It is significant that the Greeks are as much deceived by their own rhetoric in I. iii as the Trojans are in II. ii.

This question of finding a reliable standard of evaluation for non-material things is very important in Shakespeare. His constant use of language, metaphors, and literal devices which illustrate the discrepancy between appearance and reality shows this, and the concern is particularly strong in plays like *Hamlet*, *All's Well*, and *Measure for Measure*, written close in time to *Troilus*. Other contemporary satirical plays are concerned with the problem of true and false values, the exposure of folly and self-deception and so on, but other writers (and one thinks particularly of Jonson) are much more sure of their own viewpoint than Shakespeare seems to be here, and we are not left with such an apparently unresolved confusion.

But for all its complexity, the play is in many ways rather crude in comparison to *Troilus and Criseyde*, and the discussion of values in the context of the love-story is one example of this. Chaucer is careful to give the maximum value and attractiveness to his presentation of romantic love while simultaneously reminding us through his constant irony that it is not the highest good. The subtlety of this consistent double vision is quite a different thing from Shakespeare's satire. Chaucer, like Jonson, is sure of his ultimate standards, but he does not ridicule or condemn his characters for not measuring up to them. He uses irony as an evaluative technique but does not, like Shakespeare in this play as well as Jonson, find this incompatible with a genuine sympathy for the characters (Shakespeare achieves this in *Antony and Cleopatra*). It is made easier for Chaucer by the form in which he presents his work, the narrative making it possible for him to give a great deal of explanatory material, whereas it is very difficult to combine irony with sympathy in drama. Both Chaucer and Shakespeare are close to Boethius in their choice of appearance/reality metaphors. Ulysses's reference to 'dust that is a little gilt' is a common image in *The Consolation*, and there are other general resemblances. The tradition was so widespread for many of these ideas that there need not be a direct link, but Shakespeare is still concerned with the same problems as the medieval writers.

This is indeed the somewhat surprising fact that has kept emerging from this study of ideas in Shakespeare's play and Chaucer's poem: the play in which Shaw saw Shakespeare as 'ready to start the twentieth century' and which Jan Kott describes as 'amazing and modern' turns out to be full not only of Chaucerian ideas but of the traditional medieval commonplaces that go back to the sixth century.[9] To put it in such terms is misleading since it places the emphasis on the contents rather than on 'what Shakespeare made of his material', but it certainly implies a greater continuity between medieval and Elizabethan preoccupations in literature and philosophy than is apparent at first sight. Despite the greater scepticism of his treatment, Shakespeare is concerned with many of the same problems as Chaucer and Boethius before him and even comes to some of the same conclusions. He agrees with them about the problems of life in time and the difficulty of establishing true meanings and values in the face of human inadequacy and the shifting and arbitrary misrule of Fortune, but he rejects their solutions with some bitterness. This is what is 'modern' about the play: Shakespeare does not provide the answers to the questions he raises and he does not point out an escape-route.

If there is any escape from the play's dilemmas it is in the comparative detachment with which Shakespeare treats the characters. We are never allowed to come close enough to them to feel that the incoherence of their lives is directly relevant to our own or to the author's basic convictions. This is obvious when we consider our reaction to Troilus's realization of Cressida's falsehood. Although we see him facing chaos we have no reason to identify with him, and the very structure of the scene (and Ulysses's comments) prevent this, as does our knowledge of Cressida herself: we had expected no better. We do not feel (as we might in the case of Desdemona) that this particular betrayal signifies the breakdown of truth itself, and we can only feel an external pity for Troilus rather than an identifying sympathy. We are engaged with the ideas in this play more than we are with the characters. The action itself is not presented in such a way as to justify the momentous philosophical implications discovered by some critics and it is possible to falsify it by paying insufficient attention to some of the play's rather peculiar technical aspects.

Shakespeare's 'technique' in *Troilus and Cressida* is unusual in the light of the rest of the canon. There is more

9. See *Shaw on Shakespeare*, ed. E. Wilson (Harmondsworth, 1969), p. 266, and Jan Kott, *Shakespeare Our Contemporary* (London, 1965).

detachment than we ever find elsewhere. This has been generally recognized by critics, perhaps most explicitly by T. McAlindon who says:

In *Troilus and Cressida* one occasionally has the strong impression that Shakespeare is simultaneously scrutinizing characters in action and his own play in the making; that in exposing to censure the contemptuous treatment of the Greek and Trojan heroes by Patroclus, Thersites and 'envious and calumniating Time' he is ruefully contemplating the discourteous truthfulness of his own art, and wondering if it is he, not they, who is guilty of a failure to treat the subject with a proper decorum.[1]

His article is mainly concerned with 'indecorum' in relation to the style and language of the play, but the question of the sources does not seem irrelevant. Whatever one believes about Shakespeare's direct use of Homer and Chaucer one can hardly deny him an awareness that their versions existed, and this awareness helps to explain his unusual attitude.

The satirical plays of the period encouraged a detached tone, and some critics have seen this aspect of *Troilus and Cressida* as distinctively 'Jonsonian' and as evidence for the influence of the 'poetomachia' plays. In terms of technique, however, these plays are usually so crude that it is impossible to see *Troilus* as an attempt to imitate them. Jonson's method of providing detached comment in plays like *Every Man Out of his Humour* and *Cynthia's Revels* is decidedly undramatic, and the 'author's spokesmen' set up by Marston in *Histriomastix* and *Jack Drum's Entertainment* are little better, although they are involved in the action. The comment tends to be external, obtrusive, and verging on the didactic, while Shakespeare's criticism is more likely to be implicit in his presentation of plot and theme than explicit in choric form. It is true that he allows his characters to discuss each other here,[2] but this evaluation is incorporated into the play's theme of subjective and objective judgement and is not provided as authorial comment.

1. 'Language, style and meaning in *Troilus and Cressida*', PMLA, lxxxiv (1969), 29–43.
2. Robert Kimbrough has pointed out the parallel between Alexander's description of Ajax in I. ii and Mercury's description of Crites in *Cynthia's Revels* (II. iii) in *The Origins of 'Troilus and Cressida'*, p. 196.

As I have said, the Troy material provided plenty of encouragement for a satirical treatment, most of all in the highly studied irony of Chaucer. He too is self-conscious about the use of this familiar material and is constantly alluding to his authorities, impressing on us (whether they are real sources or not) that the story is an old one and the ending predetermined. Like Shakespeare, but again in a more subtle way, he fully exploits the irony of this situation. Neither writer is concerned with 'suspense' over the outcome of the love-story: Chaucer tells us the end at the beginning and Shakespeare does not need to, but both see the effectiveness of contrasting the knowledge of the audience with the ignorance of the characters. Both allow the latter painfully ironic moments of fragile happiness and equally ironic premonitions of disaster. Chaucer employs several different devices to distance himself from his material. Despite his 'medievalization' of some things he is very conscious of historical distance, and the importance of time and mutability is part of this. By constantly referring to his sources he forces the reader to see not just the story but the way in which he, the narrator and interpreter, is manipulating it. He points out the problem of being tied by his climax, especially as this approaches and passes, and of course he is standing at a philosophical and religious distance from his characters and expects his readers to share in this.

It is difficult, then, to avoid seeing Chaucer's poem as a very self-conscious aesthetic object, as we share the author's problems and his sense of detachment. He is certainly not troubled by any naive theory of art as a consistent illusion which must not be broken by authorial intervention. Neither, I think, was Shakespeare, allowing for the much narrower scope afforded him by his dramatic form. He frequently seems to challenge the conventions of his plays by referring to acting and illusions, and he is not nearly as concerned with consistent naturalism as some of his critics have expected. Most obviously, he will allow his persons to speak 'out of character' to achieve a particular effect, he is careless about details of plot and motivation, and the Comedies and Romances especially call attention to themselves as art. In the case of *Troilus* it would seem that all the factors combined to make him consider the subject with more detachment than usual. The result is a play in which the involvement of the audience is rather different from the usual situation in Shakespeare, or in drama in general. Our feelings are deliberately distanced from the characters, but our minds are engaged by the ideas that are at issue, and we are emotionally involved with these abstractions. This is not the same as saying that the characters seem mere puppets invented to illustrate a thesis—an accusation one might sometimes make against Jonson. Shakespeare's characters are 'real' enough, but Shakespeare, like Chaucer, has reasons for standing back from their reality and viewing their problems from the outside. We are hardly aware of any difficulty in the other sources; Lydgate and Caxton present a flat narrative from an easy didactic viewpoint.

How far Shakespeare was following Chaucer in adopting this distance can hardly be determined. The effect is very different in that we have the distance without the compensation of another kind of realism and another level of values, and the method is different in that Shakespeare allows his critical attitude to emerge from the speeches and the action without authorial comment of a Chaucerian or a Jonsonian variety. He could hardly have failed to notice Chaucer's self-consciousness about the subject and this must have added to his own. Similarly he must have noticed the devices Chaucer used to exploit his materials and to withdraw from them when necessary. Chaucer withdrew to avoid the pain of the tragedy, and this risk was so much greater for Shakespeare, having no higher level to which to retreat, that his detachment may have had a similar motive. In *Troilus and Cressida* he was testing ideas and values which were important for him as severely as he could, showing their weaknesses and embodying them in unattractive characters. We know from his later work that he continued to believe very strongly in the importance of trust, love, and loyalty between people, since he regularly presents these things as positive and even redeeming factors (as in *King Lear* and the Romances), while their absence or destruction heralds disaster. Although *Troilus* leaves its characters in a very bleak position, it did not shake its author's faith in the better aspects of human nature. Perhaps Shakespeare saw how, despite his precautions, Chaucer did become unhappily involved in his subject-matter, and took this as a warning to present it in such a way that this could not happen to him. The bitterness of the play sometimes seems to be directed against Chaucer himself, but the reason for it seems to lie in Shakespeare's awareness that the retreat into a total unquestioning acceptance of Christianity is not as easily available for him.

Thus I would argue that Chaucer's poem was not only an important influence on the detailed presentation of the love-story in Shakespeare's play but that the ideas it contained offered many suggestions of structural and thematic importance to the play as a whole. Moreover Chaucer's continuous and explicit discussion of the problems of dealing with a well-known story which is at once both tragic and sordid inspired the peculiar tone and attitude which Shakespeare adopted in this particular play.

5

The Two Noble Kinsmen

This play, written in collaboration with John Fletcher about 1612–13, is the only other play in which Shakespeare's use of Chaucer is as direct and extensive as it is in *Troilus and Cressida*. Moreover, this debt is acknowledged in the Prologue:

> [our play] has a noble breeder and a pure,
> A learned, and a poet never went
> More famous yet 'twixt Po and silver Trent.
> Chaucer, of all admir'd, the story gives,
> There constant to eternity it lives. (10–14)[1]

Although critics have unanimously accepted the truth of this statement, Shakespeare's actual use of *The Knight's Tale* is very like his use of *Troilus and Criseyde* over which there has been so much argument. In both plays he shows his familiarity with his source-poem by a free adaptation, using situations, ideas, and verbal details scattered through the whole work rather than adhering strictly to its own narrative sequence. The most striking difference between the two plays is in the attitude towards the material and the extent to which this differs from Chaucer's attitude. In *Troilus* Shakespeare's overtly satirical approach transformed the material, whereas in telling the story of Palamon and Arcite it is Chaucer who takes the more comic approach, mocking and deflating his subject-matter, and forcing the reader to see it with detached irony, while Shakespeare treats it seriously.

In so doing he is occasionally at odds with his collaborator, who, without copying Chaucer's irony, nevertheless adopts a much lighter tone, thus setting up many tensions and inconsistencies within the play as I shall describe below. I should

1. Quotations from *The Two Noble Kinsmen* are from the Regent's Renaissance edition by G. R. Proudfoot (London and Nebraska, 1970).

say at this point that I accept what is by now the orthodox position on the division of scenes, which is as follows:

Shakespeare: I. i–v; III. i, ii; V. i, iii–v, probably II. i and IV. iii.
Fletcher: II. ii–vi; III. iii–vi; IV, i, ii; V. ii.

Roughly speaking, this gives the first and last acts to Shakespeare and the middle three acts to Fletcher, excluding the beginning of Act III and the play's only two prose scenes, II. i and IV. iii. Naturally I did not begin my work on this play determined to accept the orthodox position, but I have come to this view mainly because my detailed study of the use of the source in different parts of the play confirmed it so strongly.[2] The contrast between the two dramatists does in fact become the most important focus of this chapter, since the basic question of whether Chaucer was the source or not does not need to be argued. Shakespeare and Fletcher clearly saw completely different things in *The Knight's Tale* and dramatized it in quite independent ways. From the point of view of the play's over-all success it is unfortunate that some final revision did not iron out all the discrepancies, but from the point of view of the scholar this gives us a unique opportunity to study the genesis of a late Shakespearian Romance (very probably his last work for the stage) and to observe the many differences between that and the new genre of Fletcherian tragicomedy.

Chaucer's *Knight's Tale* is similar to his *Troilus and Criseyde* in being more obviously suited to a narrative medium than to a dramatic one. Many readers have had little confidence in the basic story at all; Harold Littledale, editor of the major nineteenth-century edition of *The Two Noble Kinsmen* commented

Not even Shakespeare could have created a great play, full of high and passionate thoughts, and possessing firm dramatic unity, from the tale of Palamon and Arcite.[3]

2. This is not the view of Paul Bertram, who argues from the use of the source, amongst other things, that the whole play is by Shakespeare in his book *Shakespeare and 'The Two Noble Kinsmen'* (New Brunswick, 1965). I shall be discussing some of his arguments below.

3. *The Two Noble Kinsmen*, New Shakespeare Society edition (London, 1876, 1885), Introduction, p. 24.

and Theodore Spencer's article on the play agreed with him:

> The story of Palamon and Arcite, whether told by Boccaccio, Chaucer or Shakespeare and Fletcher, is intrinsically feeble, superficial and undramatic.[4]

Presumably a playgoer living in the Elizabethan/Jacobean era would have disputed this point, since *The Knight's Tale* was not only the most popular and admired of Chaucer's poems after *Troilus*[5] but had already been dramatized twice (in the lost *Palamon and Arcite* plays of 1566 and 1594 referred to in Chapter 2) and used extensively by Shakespeare in *A Midsummer Night's Dream*. It all depends on what one expects a play to be like. *The Knight's Tale* is not promising material if one's criteria for judging drama incorporate the high standard of naturalism customary in the nineteenth-century novel. It might look better if one allowed stylization, ritual, and symmetry the dramatic power on stage that they can achieve in religious contexts. It is a curiously impersonal story which takes an absurd yet tragic plot as the basis for a meditation on the wider implications of love, friendship, and human destiny.

W. Spalding has in fact argued in *A Letter on Shakespeare's Authorship of 'The Two Noble Kinsmen'* that *The Knight's Tale* is a typically Shakespearian choice of subject, reflecting his liking for old and familiar stories rather than Fletcher's taste for new or strange ones.[6] The plots of the late plays show a reversion on Shakespeare's part to the old-fashioned rambling romances that Sidney had regretted and ridiculed thirty years earlier, and *The Two Noble Kinsmen* fits into this group. Indeed E. C. Pettet differentiates it from the other romances only on the grounds that 'its substance and spirit derive more completely than any of them from the oldest layer of the romantic tradition',[7] and he shows how Shakespeare has deliberately emphasized and sometimes heightened the 'unrealistic' conventions of medieval chivalry and

---

4. 'The Two Noble Kinsmen', *Modern Philology*, xxxvi (1939), 255–76.

5. The evidence is to be found in Caroline Spurgeon's collection of Chaucer allusions (as cited).

6. London, 1833, p. 64.

7. *Shakespeare and the Romance Tradition* (London and New York, 1949), p. 172.

romance. Shakespeare was not concerned with the same kind of 'drama' at this stage in his career as he had been earlier, and it is hard to believe that he either chose *The Knight's Tale* for its potential as a naturalistic love-story or abandoned it on realizing that he had assessed that potential wrongly.

It is not necessary to resort to the attitude of Frank Kermode, who believes that 'although he probably wrote a great deal of the play Shakespeare had nothing to do with the plot'. Of the first scene he says 'it is difficult to believe he planned it', on the grounds that it is 'slow, falsely posed and ceremonial'. Hence he concludes that 'it is best thought of as a play by Fletcher to which Shakespeare contributed'.[8] Philip Edwards, on the other hand, has argued that Shakespeare *did* plot the whole play, and that there is a unity of design and subtlety of theme perceptible in it which can hardly be attributed to Fletcher.[9] He points out that much of Shakespeare's work from *Pericles* onwards is 'undramatic' in precisely the same way as *The Two Noble Kinsmen*, so that this aspect of the play is an argument for rather than against Shakespeare's controlling hand. These views are supported by a recent editor of the play, Clifford Leech, who adds some specific parallels with Shakespeare's romances, especially *Pericles*.[1]

But, having granted that the story was not, for Shakespeare in 1612, a complete non-starter, one has to admit that some basic changes are needed to make it stageable. At whatever distance of time or place Shakespeare and Fletcher collaborated (a crucial matter on which we are totally ignorant) they agreed on such alterations as a drastic compression of the time-scheme, a general tightening of the structure and a greater emphasis on characterization. They introduced two subsidiary actions, that of the Jailer's daughter and that of the schoolmaster Gerrold and his rustic pupils. The latter is more of an inserted episode than a sub-plot, involving only two scenes, II. iii and III. v (almost always attributed to

8. *William Shakespeare: The Final Plays* (Writers and Their Work Series, London, 1963), pp. 51–52.

9. 'On the design of *The Two Noble Kinsmen*', *A Review of English Literature* [REL], v (1964), 89–105.

1. See the introduction to his Signet edition (New York, 1966).

Fletcher). It consists entirely in the preparation and performance of an entertainment before the Duke and his court, in
which respect it is similar to the offerings of the rustics in
Love's Labour's Lost and *A Midsummer Night's Dream*
though the entertainment is a dance rather than a play,
suggesting parallels with the rustic dances in *The Winter's
Tale* and *The Tempest*.[2]

The Jailer's daughter, who releases Palamon from prison
and runs mad for love of him, is more important to the play
both structurally and thematically. She was probably invented by Shakespeare, since she first appears in one of the
two prose scenes attributed to him (II. i), and the other prose
scene presents her distraction with what many critics have
felt to be a Shakespearian delicacy and pathos (IV. iii).
Elsewhere, however, her role is awkward and isolated from
the rest of the play: four scenes (II. iv and vi, III. ii and iv,
mostly attributed to Fletcher) are given over entirely to her
soliloquies, while III. v yokes her to the other subsidiary
action by the somewhat desperate expedient of having her
join in the rustics' dance. Thematically her role is to provide
another example of amorous passion, pathetic and self-
destructive as the love of the kinsmen though on a different
plane. Like Emilia, she is the victim of extreme desire (though
in Emilia's case the desire is not her own), and like Emilia
she is involved with two men, reaches a point where she
seems to have decided in favour of one of them but finally has
to accept a substitute. This however is more an hypothesis
than a direct reading of her blurred role in the play as it stands.
One explanation might be that Fletcher was unwilling or unable to follow up Shakespeare's intentions in creating the part.

As in the case of *Troilus and Cressida*, there has been no
detailed comparison of the play with its source. This is perhaps less surprising for *The Two Noble Kinsmen* since
critical interest has tended to centre on the authorship problem.[3] Two nineteenth-century editors, Littledale and Skeat,

2. More specifically, the schoolmaster here may derive from Rhombus in
Sidney's entertainment *The Lady of May* and the list of dancers given at III. v.
121–9 closely parallels those in the second anti-masque in Beaumont's *Masque
of the Inner Temple*.

3. There is a useful survey of contributions to this debate in D. V. Erdman
and E. G. Fogel (eds), *Evidence for Authorship* (New York, 1966), pp. 486–94.

gave lists of parallels without commenting on how exactly the source was used,[4] while some critics have referred to the source in a general way when discussing the play as a whole. As with *Troilus* I shall follow the structure of the play itself in my comparison.

The prologue

The major part of this prologue (probably written by Fletcher) consists of a tribute to Chaucer, which is remarkable since there is no explicit acknowledgement of the source in any of the other extant Chaucerian plays of the period, and the only comparable instance I know is the tribute to Sidney in John Day's *The Isle of Gulls* (1606). Evidently the dramatist expected the audience to be impressed by the mention of Chaucer and to share his enthusiastic admiration for him: the prologue advertises the play and the implication is that Chaucer's name had considerable selling power.

The image of Chaucer conveyed here is in many ways typical of the age. He is 'noble' 'famous', 'of all admir'd', and above all 'learned'. Perhaps the praise is exaggerated to emphasize the modesty of the present offering, since the audience is told 'it were an endless thing And too ambitious to aspire to him', and that the subsequent scenes will be 'below his art', but this overestimation of Chaucer is also typical of the writers of the time who spoke of Chaucer as the 'father of English poetry' and referred to him rather more than his actual influence seems to justify. The vision of Chaucer's dismay at the irreverence of 'such a writer That blasts my bays and my fam'd works makes lighter Than Robin Hood' reflects the opposite end of the scale of possible attitudes towards him when publications like *The Cobbler of Canterburie* and *The Wanton Wife of Bath* were exploiting the more dubious side of his reputation. Chaucer the philosophical poet and Chaucer the teller of bawdy stories were confused in the often ambiguous references to him in the literature of the time, and I think something of this ambiguity is present

4. Littledale's edition is cited above. W. W. Skeat's edition was published in Cambridge in 1875.

in *The Two Noble Kinsmen*. Shakespeare, who based his other Chaucerian work on the sententious *Troilus*, seems to see something very serious, not to say gloomy, in *The Knight's Tale*, while Fletcher, who used *The Wife of Bath's Tale* elsewhere, exploits the more comic and superficial elements of the story such as absurdity and suspense.

Speght, who makes much of the philosophical content of Chaucer's *Troilus*, takes up a fairly neutral position in the 'Argument' prefixed to *The Knight's Tale* in his 1602 edition, which runs:

Palamon and Arcite, a paire of friends and fellow prisoners, fight a combat before Duke Theseus, for the ladie Emelie, sister to the queene Ipolita wife of Theseus. A tale fitting the person of a knight, for that it discourseth of the deeds of Armes, and love of Ladies.

The 'sentences' he marks for special attention are generally well-known proverbial sayings. He ignores the Boethian material Chaucer adds to his source (e.g. at 1663 and 1251 ff.), but heavily marks the rather comic speech of Egeus at 2843 ff. where Chaucer is self-consciously using platitudes. It seems likely that part of the attraction of *The Knight's Tale* for Elizabethan readers lay in 'the deeds of Armes and love of Ladies', elements which appealed to their own taste in literature and which rather surprisingly proclaimed the affinity of this ancient English poem with such things as the Italian romances, *The Arcadia*, *The Faerie Queene*, and their own dramatic comedies. The prologue to *The Two Noble Kinsmen* does not however reveal what aspect of *The Knight's Tale* attracted the dramatists' attention apart from the fact that it was written by a famous poet.

Act 1, scene i

Since the play proper begins with Shakespeare's work, the relationship to the source is one of free adaptation rather than the faithful retelling we find in some of Fletcher's scenes (and of course in Shakespeare's own use of some other writers). This allegedly 'undramatic' scene is loosely based on lines 859–1032 of *The Knight's Tale*. It shows us Theseus on

the very brink of marriage with Hippolyta when he is interrupted by the plea of the bereaved queens that he will avenge
their husbands' deaths and redeem their bodies for burial.
The scene differs from Chaucer most notably in the addition
and fuller treatment of some of the characters and in the
introduction of thematic conflicts that are not explicit in the
source. Some of the changes are directed towards greater
stage effectiveness: Shakespeare's three queens, for example,
are more impressive than Chaucer's 'compaignye of ladies',[5]
and while Chaucer's women all pray to Theseus and the only
dialogue is between him and 'the eldest of hem alle', Shakespeare creates a powerful effect of ritual and symmetry by
having his three queens kneel to and address the three
principal characters in turn. He may have been influenced by
Chaucer in employing this regularity of design, since his
queens are introduced very symmetrically ('tweye and tweye,
Ech after oother'), and there is a great stress on order (and
especially on threes) in his poem.[6] This change increases the
sense of formality and can be extremely good theatre.

Meanwhile, the same device serves the needs of the drama
on the more naturalistic level of characterization. The queens
are hardly individualized, but Theseus comes over strongly
and Shakespeare uses Hippolyta and Emilia, who play no
part in this scene in the poem. He introduces Emilia's role in
the play with the lines

> for the love of him whom Jove hath mark'd
> The honour of your bed, and for the sake
> Of clear virginity,

in the third queen's prayer to her. This speech and Emilia's
reply are slightly longer than the others and are further
stressed by being last in the sequence. Shakespeare follows
Chaucer in selecting the widow of King Capaneus to state
the women's griefs. The substance of her speech is similar,
though Shakespeare omits the references to Fortune and to
the wait in the temple of the goddess 'Clemence' and con-

5. A notable contrast with Lydgate who also used this episode in *The Knight's
Tale* but altered it in the opposite direction to produce 'a thousand wymen
outher tweyne' at line 4455 of *The Siege of Thebes*.

6. This is detailed by Charles Muscatine in 'Form, texture and meaning in
Chaucer's *Knight's Tale*', *PMLA*, lxv (1950), 911–29.

centrates on the image of the corpses. She introduces herself in Chaucer, but Shakespeare makes Theseus recognize her, giving occasion for a moving, if unchivalrous, reflection on the decay of her beauty: 'O grief and time, Fearful consumers, you will all devour.' The suggestion may be in Chaucer, who says of Theseus at the same point

> Him thought that his hert would all to break,
> Whan he saugh hem so pitous and so maat,
> That whilom were of so greet estaat. (954-6)

He is so moved that he promises to help at once, and Chaucer brings this episode to a close with a vision of immediate action (ll. 965 ff.). Shakespeare's Theseus however, despite the first queen's confidence that his 'first thought is more Than others' labored meditance', seems more reflective, less the man of action. He has already digressed to recall the wedding of King Capaneus and to muse about the effect of love on his hero Hercules,[7] and now he turns aside to ponder —'Troubled I am'—after asking the queen to pray to Bellona for him.[8] The fact that he does not commit himself at once allows for the speeches of the other queens and the replies of Hippolyta and Emilia, a sequence in which Shakespeare may be using material from later in the source, the scene in which the women pray successfully to Theseus to change his mind when he condemns Arcite and Palamon to death on finding them fighting in the wood (cf. Chaucer, ll. 1748 ff.). This scene is necessary to the play later, and Fletcher's 'strange conjurings' in III. vi repeat the situation Shakespeare draws on here.

The use of more speaking characters in this scene allows Shakespeare to break up and dramatize some of the material Chaucer gives as sheer informative statement. The Amazonian war mentioned in Chaucer's opening lines is brought in and given thematic significance as an instance of war overcoming love as the male overcomes the female by the second queen at 77 ff., and of course it helps to characterize Hippo-

---

7. The admiration of Theseus for Hercules, here and at III. vi. 175-6 and v. iii. 119-20, is not in Chaucer and probably comes from the Life of Theseus in North's Plutarch.

8. As I said above, this reference may come from Chaucer's *Anelida and Arcite*.

lyta who is being addressed. Similarly, the praise of Theseus
is put into the mouths of the queens (e.g. at 131 ff.). The fact
that Theseus and Hippolyta are not yet married is an alteration to the source which may be a reminiscence of *A Midsummer Night's Dream* and which allows Shakespeare to
develop the will/reason theme, stated by Theseus himself
later in the scene:

> As we are men,
> Thus should we do; being sensually subdued,
> We lose our human title.   (231–3)

This sentiment is expressed by Chaucer's Theseus in the later
incident Shakespeare may be recalling here, when the discovery of Palamon and Arcite fighting causes him to reflect on
the absurdities performed by men under the influence of the
god of love (1785 ff.). As in Chaucer, the wise, mature love of
Theseus and Hippolyta is to be contrasted in the play with
the hot-headed passion of Palamon and Arcite which is soon
to arise. The suppliant queens stress the difficulty of putting
duty before pleasure:

> O when
> Her twinning cherries shall their sweetness fall
> Upon thy tasteful lips, what wilt thou think
> Of rotten kings or blubber'd queens? (177–80)

and throughout this scene Shakespeare hints at the complexity of the relationship between love and war: Theseus
was right to overcome Hippolyta by both methods; love is
greater than war ultimately, but it is wrong to be 'sensually
subdued'. Paradoxically within this scene it is the passion of
grief (the call of duty) which has disrupted the ordered ritual
of the marriage (representing pleasure), but Theseus shows
himself able to keep both under control: directing one officer
to summon the army against Thebes, he instructs Pirithous
to 'lead on the bride'. In Chaucer too the women are sent on
(971 ff.) although the wedding has already happened (868).

There are a few incidental correspondences between this
scene and *The Knight's Tale*, such as the reference to Mars
'spurning his drum' for love (l. 182) which probably alludes
to his passion for Venus, described by Chaucer's Arcite in his

prayer to Mars (2382 ff.), and the list of suicides given by the third queen:

> Those that with cords, knives, drams, precipitance,
> Weary of this world's light, have to themselves
> Been death's most horrid agents,   (142–4)

which reminds us generally of the description Chaucer gives of the power of Mars over all sorts of violent crimes and deaths, including suicide (1955–2008).

The scene as a whole is ponderous and ritualistic, indicating clearly that Shakespeare was interested both in the stylization of *The Knight's Tale* and in its rather sombre strain of philosophical reflection.

Act I, scene ii

This scene is not in the source, but is added by Shakespeare in order to introduce Palamon and Arcite. It is not strictly necessary to the plot, and much of its interest is thematic. Chaucer's influence in this area is apparent, especially in the references to a mysterious but powerful fortune governing men's affairs (66 ff., 102 ff.) and in Arcite's words of resignation at the end of the scene,

> Let th'event
> That never-erring arbitrator, tell us,
> When we know all ourselves, and let us follow
> The becking of our chance,   (113–16)

which prefigure the recognition of human ignorance and limitation (shown by Theseus at the end of the play) which is a recurrent topic of Chaucer's poem, especially in the Boethian vision of men seeking happiness blindly and missing it by not knowing what they really want (e.g. 1251 ff.). The image of the metaphorically 'dronke' man, the helpless victim both of his own passions and of the arbitrary gods, clearly impressed Shakespeare at this time.

The political theme in general is not particularly Chaucerian: his kinsmen have no qualms about whether they should fight for Creon. Perhaps the passage of time and the decay of feudal conventions made Shakespeare feel

obliged to explain why his heroes are first encountered
fighting on the side of an acknowledged villain. It adds to the
feeling that individual lives are governed by larger, uncon-
trollable forces. Lydgate is much stronger on the political
aspects of the story, and devotes some space to the oath of
allegiance sworn to Creon by the Thebans and the obligation
under which this put them (4391–9). Shakespeare probably
read Lydgate's *Siege of Thebes* since it was published at the
end of the editions of Chaucer from 1561. He used the *Troy-
Book* for *Troilus and Cressida* so it seems reasonable to
suppose that he read this poem which was shorter and more
easily available. Lydgate does not cite Juno's jealousy and
anger as a cause of the ill-luck of Thebes at all, and it may be
that Shakespeare is recalling Ovid in the reference to Juno's
'ancient fit of jealousy' here (l. 22), but he says no more than
he could have learned from Chaucer (1329 ff. and 1543 ff.,
and *Anelida*, 51), and gives the idea no more importance
than it has in *The Knight's Tale*.

In general the scene succeeds in telling us more of the
kinsmen than Chaucer does at this point, mainly by allowing
them to discuss the moral problems of individuals in a cor-
rupt society. They are not strongly differentiated in this
scene, and do not reveal the characteristics that the plot and
Fletcher are later to give them. Palamon shows a certain
amount of pride (e.g. 44 ff.) and refuses to be less than first in
anything (58–60), which fits in with his later indignation at
Arcite's presumption in loving the lady he saw first, and indeed with his consistent air of self-righteousness, but he also
seems more 'the martialist' than his cousin here (15 ff.).
Both are aware of their dilemma and of the uselessness of
'reason' to solve it: it is a more explicit version of Hector's
problem in *Troilus and Cressida*.

Act 1, scene iii

This again is virtually an addition to the source. The 'plot' is
contained, as Littledale noted, in 966–74 of *The Knight's
Tale*, in which we are simply told that Theseus did not enter
Athens but set off for Thebes at once, although he did send
the women into the town. Shakespeare turns this into a 100-

line farewell scene mainly with the effect of giving the women
more importance and preparing for Emilia's later role in such
a manner as to make it dramatically credible. Her speech
about her childhood friendship with Flavina (55 ff.) prepares
us for the conviction that she will never 'love any that's
called man',[9] and, coming after the broken vows of the first
two scenes, shows us how Shakespeare is interested in exploiting the discrepancy between intention and action just as
Chaucer is.

The theme of friendship, already introduced in relation to
Palamon and Arcite in the previous scene is repeated in this
feminine version and in the talk of the love of Theseus and
Pirithous that occasions Emilia's outburst. Shakespeare
seems to be preparing a contrast between these relationships
and the broken one of the Theban kinsmen but this never
becomes very explicit after Fletcher takes over. Shakespeare
makes more of the notion of the women as Amazonian warriors than Chaucer does, but here as in scene i such references
centre around Hippolyta: neither writer encourages us to see
Emilia in a military capacity.

Act I, scene iv

Chaucer moves straight from the opening scene outside
Athens to a brief description of the war against Creon (975–
93) in which Theseus kills him

> And to the ladies he restored againe
> The bodies of her husbandes that were slain
> (991–2)

The latter action is dramatized by Shakespeare in the stage
direction and opening lines of this scene. Theseus's reference
to 'Th'impartial gods' (4) is consistent with the emphasis on
superhuman powers in the poem, and the herald here was
probably suggested by the 'heraudes' at l. 1017 of *The
Knight's Tale*. Shakespeare's Theseus remains present for the
discovery of Palamon and Arcite, who are brought in on

---

9. Friendships between people of the same sex are often presented in this
nostalgic way by Shakespeare, especially when they are threatened with
destruction e.g. *As You Like It*, I. iii. 69–72, *A Midsummer Night's Dream*, III.
ii. 203–14, *The Winter's Tale*, I. ii. 67–74.

hearses, as in Chaucer they are 'carried softe unto the tente of Theseus' (1021–2), but Shakespeare omits his grimly realistic picture of the 'pilours' ransacking the corpses for their armour.

Theseus's praise of the kinsmen's valour (17–21) is an addition to the source, and, like I. ii, gives the heroes greater prominence at this stage than they have in the poem. They are recognized in the same way, 'by hir coat-armours, and by hir gere' in the poem and 'By their appointment' in the play. The closest parallel comes in the exchange 'They are not dead?—Nor in a state of life' (24–25) which echoes Chaucer's 'Nat fully quicke, ne fully dede they were' (1015). Theseus's concern for them is added,[1] but his reflections on the irrational motives by which men can be ruled (40–45) again seem Chaucerian in origin, though it is much later in the poem (1785 ff.) that Chaucer's duke discourses on this. Here as in I. i Shakespeare can be seen to be developing the meditative tendency of Theseus earlier than his source.

Both writers end the sequence with a move back to Athens (Chaucer 1026, Shakespeare 48–49), but Shakespeare, though making Theseus seem highly considerate of his prisoners (33–37) omits Chaucer's bleak and repeated statement that this is to be 'Perpetuelly, he nold hem not ransoun', and the explicit contrast between the duke living in happiness and luxury and the kinsmen in misery and discomfort with which Chaucer finishes. Even so, Theseus's words

> Rather than have 'em
> Freed of this plight and in their morning state,
> Sound and at liberty, I would 'em dead;
> But forty thousand fold we had rather have 'em
> Prisoners to us, than death.   (33–37)

have a similarly grim effect, and reveal a less attractive side of his character.

Act I, scene v

Shakespeare reverses the order of the source here to give a brief impression of the kings' funeral which Chaucer called 'al to long for to devise' (994). The effectiveness of the short

1. Possibly from Boccaccio, *Teseida*, ii, stanza 89.

scene is increased by the way in which the procession is a visual echo of I. i's marriage procession. Shakespeare links death and marriage in this Act as the story forces one to do, and as Chaucer does later when he follows the description of Arcite's funeral rites (2853 ff.) with the speech of Theseus which advocates acceptance of death and the continuation of life in marriage (2987 ff.). Shakespeare uses some of this material later on (see v. iv), but does not treat either of these long passages in anything like Chaucer's detail, probably because he had already created the effects and used many of the ideas in scene i. The closing lines of the scene

> This world's a city full of straying streets,
> And death's the marketplace, where each one meets.
> (15–16)

are close to some words spoken by Chaucer's Egeus immediately before the funeral of Arcite

> This world is but a thoroughfare full of wo
> And we been pilgrimes, passing to and fro
> Death is an ende of every worldes sore.
> (2847–9)

but, as Littledale points out, the sayings are proverbial. I. v is like the rest of Act I in drawing its material from different parts of Chaucer's poem and in setting out the themes and ideas that are to be important in the play or would have been if Shakespeare had written the whole.

Act II, scene i

This scene seems to be Shakespearian in its use of prose and its general style as well as in the fact that it has some points of inconsistency with the next which is undoubtedly Fletcher's. For example the Jailer's daughter tells us in II. i that Palamon and Arcite 'have no more sense of their captivity than I of ruling Athens' and that they 'discourse of many things, but nothing of their own restraint and disasters' (34–37), but when they appear some twenty lines later they talk exclusively of their own sad condition. There is no Jailer's daughter in *The Knight's Tale*, though this sub-plot may have been suggested by a hint in Chaucer who tells us vaguely that Palamon 'by helping of a freend, brake his prisoun' (1468). The Jailer's daughter (and her wooer) become the play's first victims of the destructive effects of amorous passion if we read her final comment 'Lord, the difference of men!' (50) as the first indication of the transfer of her affections to Palamon.

Act II, scene ii

At this point, it is generally agreed, Fletcher takes over. The action speeds up at the same time as it narrows in scope and declines in seriousness. Fletcher follows *The Knight's Tale* more closely than Shakespeare, though (as in *Women Pleased*) he makes some alterations which are difficult to justify in terms of dramatic effect, as well as some that are easily explicable.

One example of the latter is the change in the time-scheme. Chaucer allows a vague interval, perhaps of several years, at this point:

> And in a toure, in anguish and in wo
> Dwelleth Palamon, and his felowe Arcite
> For evermore, there may no gold hem quite.
>
> Thus passeth yere by yere, and day by day
> Till it fell ones in a morowe of May ...
>
> (1030–4)

while Fletcher allows the kinsmen to see Emilia almost immediately after their imprisonment, judging from the way they speak of it as a new misfortune to which they must adjust. After what the Jailer's daughter had said they are surprisingly self-pitying at first:

> ... here the graces of our youths must wither,
> Like a too-timely spring. Here age must find us
> And, which is heaviest, Palamon, unmarried;
>
> (27–29)
>
> We shall know nothing here but one another;
> Hear nothing but the clock that tells our woes;
> The vine shall grow but we shall never see it;

> Summer shall come and with her all delights
> But dead-cold winter must inhabit here still.
>
> (41–45)

Having displayed his considerable talent for this sort of
pathos, Fletcher returns to the source for Arcite's sermon on
patience and the virtues of prison:

> Let's think this prison holy sanctuary,
> To keep us from corruption of worse men:
>   —here with a little patience
> We shall live long and loving.   (71–86)

which must have been inspired by the speech of Chaucer's
Arcite

> For goddes love, take all in pacience
> Our prison, for it maie none other be
> Fortune hath yeven us this adversite.
>
> (1084–6)

though this comes more effectively in the poem as a response
to the cry Palamon lets out at the sight of Emily, thought by
his cousin to be a cry of despair at his imprisonment. Both
speeches contain commonplaces on the theme of enduring
one's destiny, but Fletcher adds the positive side of the speech
in Arcite's description of the 'mere blessings' of prison. He
also adds the heavily ironic stress on the men's friendship
just before the entrance of Emilia:

> PALAMON: I do not think it possible our friendship
> Should ever leave us.
> ARCITE: Till our deaths it cannot,
>
> (114–15)

Chaucer had opened this sequence with a description of
Emilia (1034–55), while Fletcher begins with the men. In
both, of course, her appearance interrupts the kinsmen's
conversation (and their lives). Fletcher gives her a companion
to talk to, as Shakespeare had provided Hippolyta as confidante in I. iii, but the conversation here contrasts abruptly
with our earlier view of the heroine who cannot 'love any
that's call'd man'. Fletcher's Emilia criticizes Narcissus for
not loving women and praises her companion for saying she
would not be 'hard-hearted' to men. She has a short speech

describing a rose as 'the very emblem of a maid' but the conversation ends on a note of light-hearted sexual innuendo.

The quarrel over her that follows is based on Chaucer but trivializes the main issue by omitting Palamon's reminder that they both swore

> That never for to dyen in the payne
> Till that the deth departe us twayne
> Neither of us in love to hindre other.
> (1135-7)

so that his 'I saw her first' claim becomes ridiculous. Arcite's reply is likewise simplified. Fletcher uses the woman/goddess quibble (used by Shakespeare in Love's Labour's Lost) but ignores the argument from necessity (1163 ff.) and the wry comment on the absurdity of their quarrel:

> We striven, as did the houndes for the bone
> That fought al day, and yet her part was non
> Ther cam a cur, whil that they wer so wroth
> And bare away the bone from hem both.
> (1177-80)

His Arcite would clearly agree with the 'each man for himself' axiom delivered by Chaucer's character, and in both works we have a contrast set up between the more rational, realistic Arcite and the passionate Palamon. The self-congratulatory note sounded earlier in the scene comes up again in the discussion of who is more worthy of the lady.

After the quarrel, Chaucer leaves another vague time-gap (beginning the next episode 'It happed on a day', as if several days at least have intervened) and then introduces 'Perithous'[2] for the first time, emphasizing the friendship between him and Theseus (1191-3) with ironic effect just after the kinsmen's quarrel. Chaucer tells us that Perithous had known and loved Arcite in Thebes which is why he requests and obtains his release (1202-6), whereas his motive is left uncertain in the play. The condition of the release (banishment) is the same in both (poem 1209 ff., play 247-9), but Chaucer describes Arcite's reaction at once (1219 ff.) while Fletcher, who has removed him from the scene, allows Palamon to vent

2. Spelt thus in Speght's 1602 Chaucer. 'Pirithous' in North's Plutarch.

his feelings first. His thought that Arcite will now raise an army and win Emily is the same (*The Knight's Tale*, 1285 ff.), but Fletcher ignores the powerful Boethian outcry against the 'cruel goddes' and the apparent injustice of life that follows (1303 ff.). This speech in the poem contains several themes, such as the irrationality of fate, the cruelty of the gods, the problem of the will and man's bestiality (ironically he is less fortunate than the animals), which are used by Shakespeare in his parts of the play but neglected by his collaborator, as here.

There are a couple of incidental echoes of Chaucer: Emilia's reference to Narcissus (119), used again by Fletcher at IV. ii. 32, may be a reminiscence of Chaucer's use of him in the description of the temple of Venus (1941), and the roses she gathers may be the 'floures, partly white and rede' that Chaucer's heroine picks. (Chaucer refers to roses in connection with Emily's skin at 1038.) Also the Jailer replies to Palamon with the same proverb, 'There is no remedy' that Arcite uses at this point in the poem (1274).

The most striking instance of an alteration which weakens the sequence is at the end: Chaucer brings his episode to a climax with the following 'demande d'amour':

> You lovers aske I now this question
> Who hath the worse, Arcite or Palamon?
> That one may se his lady day by day
> But in prison mote he dwel alway
> That other where him list may ride or go
> But sene his lady shall he never mo.
>
> (1347–52)

We cannot weigh up the situations of the two lovers in the play since Fletcher's Palamon is to be moved to a different part of the prison where he will not be able to see his lady, so Arcite is at this point in a much more favourable position. In contrast to the humorous detachment of Chaucer's ending, Fletcher closes his scene on a pathetic note with Palamon's words,

> Farewell kind window,
> May rude wind never hurt thee, O my lady,
> If ever thou hast felt what sorrow was,
> Dream how I suffer.—Come, now bury me.
>
> (276–80)

Act II, scene iii

Arcite's opening soliloquy here derives from his speech in the poem at 1223 ff. Both characters note the irony that freedom on these terms is worse than prison and both express envy for Palamon. Chaucer's Arcite, like his Palamon, generalizes from his affection and muses on Fortune and the blindness of men. The Boethian theme that 'We witen nat what thing we preyen here' (1260) is one developed by Shakespeare in his parts of the play, but Fletcher's heroes have a narrower, more personal outlook.

Both works imply the passage of time here; Chaucer lets Arcite suffer from love for 'a year or two' before returning to Athens and Fletcher interposes this scene with the country-men and the next with the Jailer's daughter before continuing with the main plot. Both Arcites form a resolve to return in disguise, though the method of Chaucer's hero is more gradual as he begins by offering to 'drugge and drawe' in Athens (1416), becomes employed by Emily's chamberlain for another 'year or two' and is finally promoted for his merits to the position of squire of Theseus. Fletcher's device of the games offers a faster route to the top if we recall the rapid advancement of heroes like Orlando in *As You Like It* and the disguised Pericles by this method.[3] The part of the scene with the country people rehearsing their entertainment is based on dramatic precedent (notably *A Midsummer Night's Dream*) rather than the poem.

Clifford Leech notes that Arcas, a name given to one of the country people here and at III. v. 45, is the son of Callisto, mentioned in *The Knight's Tale* at l. 2056.[4] It is also one of the names of Mercury who appears to Arcite at this point in the poem.

Act II, scene iv

This is the first of the Jailer's daughter's soliloquies. It picks up the theme of I. i that it is degrading to be 'sensually subdued':

3. Fletcher was to use this device again in *Women Pleased*, as described above.
4. Signet edition (New York, 1966), p. 190.

What pushes are we wenches driven to
When fifteen once has found us! (6–7)

By declaring her passion for Palamon, the Jailer's daughter
keeps him (the 'real' hero of the play if we judge by the ending) firmly in mind while Arcite is the focus of the main
action; she describes his grief-stricken but courteous deport-
ment in prison and reveals her plan to set him free in order to
win his love.

Act II, scene v

This scene records Arcite's triumph in the games which is
rewarded by a position at court. It is ironic that Theseus asks
Pirithous (the man who obtained his release from prison) to
dispose of him and that he is instantly put into the service of
Emilia. There is also irony (for those who know the story)
in the line that comes as a climax to his modest description
of his merits, 'I would be thought a soldier' (15): Fletcher is
careful in these central Acts to stress the contrast between
Arcite the soldier and Palamon the lover. (Already Arcite has
triumphed in running and wrestling while Palamon has
unwittingly triumphed over the Jailer's daughter.) Emilia
promises to be 'a loving mistress' (57).

Fletcher's additions include the mention of Emilia's
birthday (another echo of *Pericles* perhaps), the explicit
discussion of Arcite's virtue 'breaking through' his 'baser
garments' (a common theme appearing in most of Shakespeare's Romances and in many of Fletcher's plays), and the
speeches at the end which carry the action on by referring to
the May-Day celebrations as taking place 'tomorrow'. Paul
Bertram, who analyses a sequence of scenes (II. v, III. i, iii,
and vi) in detail in his attempt to prove Shakespeare's sole
authorship of the play, makes much of the consistency of the
additions and alterations to the source throughout the
sequence, citing especially such things as the gift of horses to
Arcite mentioned here (53–54) and again in III. i (19–20) and
v. iv (49–50) and other invented details. However, only one
of his sequence of scenes, III. i, and not a very large part of
that, has been generally assigned to Shakespeare, and most of
his argument is devoted to proving the internal consistency

of scenes that have always been attributed to one writer (Fletcher) anyway. Even if one did prove total consistency between the two parts, this could be due to a time-lag in the writing, whereby one writer was enabled to read what the other had written, but Bertram does not consider this notion, which seems as reasonable as to deduce single authorship. He rejects the idea that Shakespeare could have written Acts I and V and the opening soliloquy of Act III without writing the rest of the play, apparently on the assumption that he must always have begun writing at I. i and worked straight through to the end—a notion that would be opposed by anyone who has ever written anything, and which E. A. J. Honigmann has attacked in so far as Shakespeare is concerned, arguing convincingly that it was usual for him to write the most important passages of a play or those which most interested him first.[5]

As for the use of Chaucer, it is not possible to believe that the treatment of *The Knight's Tale* is consistent throughout the play after a careful examination of both texts. Already we have seen how the loose adaptation of the source in Act I is different from the close adherence to it in Act II, but Bertram uses this closeness as evidence for Shakespeare's authorship of Act II since

The close verbal relationships between many passages in Shakespeare's text and his sources, Holinshed and North for example, are too familar to need illustration.[6]

This is true, but it is also true that Shakespeare felt free to adapt loosely on occasion, particularly when he knew his source well, and that this is exactly what he did in his other Chaucerian play, *Troilus and Cressida*. What is curious about *The Two Noble Kinsmen* is that it does have a high degree of internal coherence in details of the kind Bertram cites alongside the much more glaring and frequently noted discrepancies of style, theme, and characterization.

5. *The Stability of Shakespeare's Text* (London, 1965), chap. xi.
6. Op. cit., p. 246.

Act II, scene vi

Here we return to the Jailer's daughter in soliloquy describing how she has in fact released Palamon from prison. Fletcher does not use Chaucer's suggestion that the jailer was drugged (1470 ff.). Palamon's reluctance to be freed—'He made such scruples of the wrong he did To me and to my father'(25–26) is added by Fletcher: Chaucer's hero has no such scruples and later declares 'I out of prison am astert by grace' (1592), not acknowledging any harm in the deed.[7] Fletcher is careful to point out that the passion is not mutual:

> And yet he has not thank'd me
> For what I have done; no, not so much as kiss'd me;
>
> (21–22)

Act III, scene i

The beginning of this scene was clearly written by Shakespeare but Fletcher may have taken it over (or revised it heavily) after about the first seventy lines. The ritual of doing observance to May has been anticipated by Theseus in II. v (48–51), and this scene begins with Arcite explaining in soliloquy how the members of the royal party have become separated from each other. In *The Knight's Tale* at this point Arcite has gone out into the woods alone (though for the same reason) and his brief song in praise of May

> Maie, with all thy floures and thy grene
> Welcome be thou faire freshe Maie
> I hope that I some grene get maie
>
> (1510–12)

is followed by a comic description of his recollection of Emily:

> Into a studie he fell sodenly
> As doen these lovers in their queint gires
> Now in the crop and now doun in the brires
> Now up now doune, as boket in a well
> Right as the fridaie, sothly for to tell.
>
> (1530–4)

---

7. Davenant's adaptation of *The Two Noble Kinsmen*, called *The Rivals* (1668) actually presents the scene described here with the Jailer's daughter having to persuade Palamon to escape.

Shakespeare turns the 'roundel' into a moving paean of praise for Emilia:

> O queen Emilia,
> Fresher than May, sweeter
> Than her gold buttons on the boughs, or all
> Th'enamell'd knacks o'th'mead or garden, yea
> We challenge too the bank of any nymph
> That makes the stream seem flowers; thou O jewel
> O' th' wood, o' th' world, hast likewise blest a place
> With thy sole presence.   (4–11)

He presents the love more seriously than Chaucer, though he omits the long speech on the wrath of Juno and the ill-fortune of Thebes (1542 ff.) and picks up the source again with his pitying reference to Palamon—'Alas, alas, Poor cousin Palamon, poor prisoner', which echoes Chaucer's 'wreched Palamon That Theseus martyreth in prison' (1562). In the poem we already know that Palamon is overhearing this speech (1516 ff.), so his eruption from hiding when Arcite goes on to talk of his love for Emily is less surprising than it is in the play.

Palamon's accusation in the play is close to that in the poem. The desire for a weapon (30 ff., cf. Chaucer 1591) and the notion that Arcite is false to him in continuing to love Emily (35 ff., cf. 1580 ff.) are common to both. Chaucer's Palamon also accuses his cousin of treachery to Theseus, a point omitted by Shakespeare, perhaps because it was to be used later (and in III. vi) or simply because it is true and detracts from the honour of Arcite who is presented sympathetically here. His calm response (45 ff.) contrasts with the anger of Chaucer's hero (1596 ff.), and this distinction between the cousins continues throughout the scene, with Arcite refusing to be angry again at 69 ff. and 105 ff. If Shakespeare set the pattern in the first of these speeches, and if he wrote his part of the play first, Fletcher extended it when finishing the scene and when writing II. ii.

Chaucer's Arcite, although he is angry and returns Palamon's threats (1596 ff.) offers to bring weapons and food, while in the play Palamon asks for them in a speech which seems very Fletcherian in its pathos, self-conscious nobility, and evocation of death:

Quit me of these cold gyves, give me a sword
Though it be rusty, and the charity
Of one meal lend me. Come before me then,
A good sword in thy hand, and do but say
That Emily is thine—I will forgive
The trespass thou hast done me, yea, my life,
If then thou carry't; and brave souls in shades
That have died manly, which will seek of me
Some news from earth, they shall get none but this—
That thou art brave and noble.   (72–81)

The offer to give up Emily if the duel is lost also comes from
Arcite in the poem (1617 ff.) and from Palamon in the play.
Chaucer follows the dialogue with some ironic reflections on
the fact that 'love ne lordship Wol nat, his thankes, have any
fellowship' (1623 ff.), while Fletcher gives his heroes some
lines of mutual admiration. Towards the end of the scene
he brings in the deception of Theseus (110 ff., cf. Chaucer
1585) which Shakespeare had omitted from Palamon's part
earlier.

The additions to the source here are again used by Bertram
in his argument, but his conclusions do not necessarily
follow. It seems likely that the perfumes Arcite promises here
(86), for example, were put in by Fletcher anyway, so it is not
surprising that they appear again in III. iii. He does not mention one detail of internal consistency, namely the mention of
Theseus and Hippolyta hunting at the beginning of the
scene and the way this is taken up and made the reason for
the ending. (In Chaucer this conversation is not interrupted.)
After the Shakespearian opening of the scene, which seems
about to diverge from the source, we have a fairly close
version, altered in obvious ways such as the extension and
multiplication of speeches (Palamon and Arcite have only one
speech apiece in Chaucer, not counting Palamon's brief reply
'I graunte it thee') and the addition of some conventional
sentiments and metaphors.

Act III, scene ii

This scene, the third of the Jailer's daughter's lonely soliloquies, has occasionally been claimed for Shakespeare, most

recently by Cyrus Hoy,[8] partly on the grounds that the sensitive treatment of impending madness here contrasts with Fletcher's semi-comic treatment of it elsewhere in the play. The confident tone of II. vi has changed to one of bewilderment and pathos:

> What if I hallow'd for him?
> I cannot hallow. If I whoop'd, what then?
> If he not answer'd, I should call a wolf
> And do him but that service, ...
>   Alas,
> Dissolve my life; let not my sense unsettle,
> Lest I should drown, or stab, or hang myself.
> O state of nature, fail together in me,
> Since thy best props are warp'd!
>   (8–11, 28–32)

While not directly Chaucerian, this scene continues to illustrate the tragically destructive effects love can have on its helpless victims.

Act III, scene iii

In a sense this is an addition to the source, since Fletcher provides an extra scene for Arcite to bring the 'food and files' while Chaucer goes straight on to the fight, delayed in the play until III. vi. He does suggest an intervening encounter by making Arcite promise to bring 'mete and drinke' and blankets 'this night' (1615), while he next presents him arriving with the armour and weapons 'on the morwe' (1629). Perhaps Fletcher is exploiting the ironic potential in Chaucer's words on friendship at this point (1625 ff.), but the flippancy of the discussion of women reflects little credit on the heroes, is absent from the source, and, especially in the case of Palamon, notoriously inconsistent with Shakespeare's conception of their characters. Again Arcite is more sympathetically treated, seeming calmer, more generous and less suspicious.

Act III, scenes iv and v

These are both sub-plot scenes, the first of which depicts the

---

8. 'The shares of Fletcher and his collaborators in the Beaumont and Fletcher Canon', Part 7, *Studies in Bibliography* [SB], xv (1962), 71–90.

further disintegration of the Jailer's daughter, alone as usual. (These scenes can, incidentally, be far more effective in performance than one might think from reading them.[9]) The second is the one I have already described in which the country people perform their entertainment before the Duke and his followers. There is very little Chaucer here, except possibly in the reference to the story of 'Meleager and the boar' (17) which comes into *The Knight's Tale* at l. 2071, in the description of Diana's temple.

Act III, scene vi

III. vi returns to Chaucer and presents the first climax of the story, the fight between Palamon and Arcite which is interrupted by the arrival of Theseus. The meeting of the kinsmen is very laconic in the poem:

> Ther nas no 'Good day', ne no saluing,
> But streight, without word or rehersing,
> Everiche of hem helped for to arme oother,
> As freendly as he were his own brother.
>
> (1649–52)

The effect created by these brief ironic lines is quite dissipated when Fletcher spins out the brotherliness in sentimental dialogue. One could hardly expect him to present the encounter 'without word' but he goes to the opposite extreme. Chaucer creates tension by his opening simile which compares the kinsmen with Thracian huntsmen waiting for the lion or bear to rush out of hiding, the atmosphere tense with physical alertness and the grim thought 'here cometh my mortal enemy, Without faille, he must be dead or I' (1643–4). Later Palamon is described as a 'cruel tigre' (1657), and both of them as 'wilde bores' (1658), in comparison with which Fletcher's simile 'Like meeting of two tides' (30) seems almost passive. Indeed Fletcher emphasizes the brotherliness to an almost erotic degree, with the talk of embraces and Arcite's description of Palamon as 'more than a mistress to me' (26).

Chaucer does not dwell on the choosing of weapons and

9. Given the peculiar nature of the play, I have been fortunate to have seen three productions: Bristol University in 1964, a British Council production in 1970, and the New Shakespeare Company at York in 1973.

armour at this point, having already made Arcite tell Palamon to 'chees the beste and leve the worste for me' when he
first offered to bring them (1613). In the play too it is Arcite
who appears in the better light, underlined by Palamon's
'Wilt thou exceed in all?' (46). The idea that Arcite stole the
armour from Theseus is added by Fletcher, and treated more
as a comic note than a reminder of Arcite's treachery, and the
discussion of whether Palamon is 'fall'n away' is new, though
it may have been suggested by Chaucer's description of Arcite
earlier as much disfigured by love: 'lene he wexeth and drye
as is a shaft', etc. (1362).

In *The Knight's Tale* there is a digression here on Boethian
predestination so that Theseus's arrival is seen as inevitable
(1663 ff.). There is no question of the kinsmen hiding, so
Fletcher's lines 107–31 are original and keep up the distinction between the reckless Palamon and the more rational
Arcite. Palamon's 'I know your cunning' (120) undermines
some of his praise of Arcite earlier in the scene. Arcite's 'come
what can come' (128) echoes the proverb he uses at II. iii. 17
and is consistent with the thoughtful fatalism of the ending of
I. ii and with Chaucer's determinism here. Theseus's opening
lines

> What ignorant and mad malicious traitors
> Are you, that 'gainst the tenor of my laws
> Are making battle, thus like knights appointed,
> Without my leave and officers of arms?
> By Castor, both shall die.   (132–6)

are close to his speech in the poem:

> No more, on paine of lesing your hedde
> By mightie Mars, he shall anone be dedde
> That smiteth any stroke, that I maie seen
> But telleth me, what mister men ye been
> That been so hardie for to fighten here
> Without iudge or other officere
> As though it were in listes riall? (1707–13)

and Palamon's reply, impetuously exposing Arcite and con-
fessing his own crime, is also very comparable (136 ff., cf.
poem 1715 ff.). The request that Arcite should die first is in
both, though Fletcher gives it a romantic motive—'That I

may tell my soul he shall not have her'—rather than the practical one that Arcite has offended more by his deception. This is, however, picked up by Fletcher's Theseus:

> I grant your wish; for, to say true, your cousin
> Has ten times more offended, for I gave him
> More mercy than you found, sir, your offences
> Being no more than his.   (180–3)

In both works Theseus's first reaction is to impose the death penalty on both men (180 ff., cf. poem 1743 ff.).

At this point the women intervene to ask for mercy in both versions (185 ff., cf. *The Knight's Tale*, 1748 ff.), although their feelings and requests are generalized in the poem and set out individually in the play in a ritualistic manner that may have been suggested by I. i if that was written first. Pirithous, again an additional character, joins in, and the pleas are successful. Fletcher omits the long explanation given by Chaucer for Theseus's change of mind. Several things in this passage are marked for special notice by Speght, such as Theseus's awareness of the helplessness of love's victims (1767 ff.) and the false pride of a lord who refuses to show compassion (1774) and will not alter an arbitrary decision. Chaucer's duke also discourses on the power of the god of love and the irony of the whole situation (1785 ff.). He confesses to having felt 'loves peine' himself, and so commutes the sentence.

Fletcher may be picking up the discussion of the arbitrary decisions of rulers (*The Knight's Tale*, 1774 ff.) in the references to Theseus's oath and its importance at 224 and 227, etc. Emilia's role is much extended and Fletcher introduces the idea of giving her the choice. Chaucer implies the impossibility of deciding between the lovers (1835), but Fletcher makes this explicit by having Theseus ask her to choose. He adds some speeches on the nobility of the two men (Chaucer's Theseus comments affectionately on their foolhardiness at 1791 ff.), and he adds the explicit lover-soldier distinction:

> PALAMON: If I fall from that mouth, I fall with favour,
>   And lovers yet unborn shall bless my ashes.
>   ARCITE: If she refuse me, yet my grave will wed me,
>   And soldiers sing my epitaph.   (282–5)

The final decision to allow the men to fight for Emily at a
a later date is the same (288 ff., cf. *The Knight's Tale*, 1845
ff.) with simple alterations in the time (a month instead of a
year) and the number of supporters allowed (three instead
of a hundred) for obvious dramatic reasons. Fletcher omits
the references to destiny, Fortune and God in this speech by
Theseus, who says in Chaucer that the question will be
decided if one of the cousins can 'sleen his contrarye, or out
of listes drive'. If either is killed it will be in the fighting, and
there is no mention of the externally imposed death penalty
for the loser added in the play. Clifford Leech notes that the
tournament is to be held in the place where Theseus found
the knights fighting (292), whereas in Chaucer the same
location is to be used again for Arcite's tomb (2858 ff.).[1] The
sequence ends in both versions with the acceptance of
Theseus's ruling and the temporary reconciliation of Palamon
and Arcite.

Act IV, scene i

This is the longest scene in the Jailer's daughter sub-plot,
which includes a description of her attempt to kill herself by
drowning clearly deriving from the death of Ophelia. The
Jailer is told of the events of the preceding scene, and
Palamon is presented in a sympathetic light when we are told
that he has procured the pardon of both the Jailer and his
daughter and has sent a large sum of money for the latter's
marriage. It is never made explicit how far he is aware of her
love for him. When the girl appears her snippets of song
revealing an underlying obsession with the loss of virginity
are again reminiscent of Ophelia.

Act IV, scene ii

The beginning of this scene, presenting Emilia comparing the
pictures of her two lovers, is original to Fletcher; Chaucer's
heroine remains remote from the action to the end. Emilia
seems to be choosing for physical beauty alone, and the truth
of the matter is that she wants both, as she admits:

1. Signet edition (as cited), p. 190.

> I am sotted,
> Utterly lost, my virgin's faith has fled me;
> . . . What a mere child is fancy,
> That having two fair gauds of equal sweetness
> Cannot distinguish, but must cry for both!
>
> (45–54)

This is one of the more notorious examples of the discrepancy in characterization between the two halves of the play, since Shakespeare's Emilia (soon to reappear) remains close to her Chaucerian model in desiring to remain a virgin. It is not of course impossible to imagine the successful portrayal of a heroine who vacillated between wanting both men and wanting neither, but we do not feel here that the contradiction is explicitly recognized by either dramatist. Chaucer's heroine has to do a *volte-face* when Arcite has won her in the battle, and the poet comments on her desertion of virginity in a cynical couplet

> For women, as to speke in comune,
> They follown al the favour of fortune.
>
> (2681–2)

which Speght marked as a 'notable sentence' in his 1602 edition.

The descriptions of the knights who have come to fight in support of Palamon and Arcite contain some very close parallels with Chaucer, though he does not reach this point for over two hundred lines which he spends describing the temples built for Venus, Mars, and Diana at the site of the impending battle. Some of this material is used by Shakespeare in Act v but it is omitted entirely by Fletcher.

Fletcher does not adopt Chaucer's knights without alteration, however. The first knight described by the Messenger in the play has the characteristics of the knight Chaucer describes first, but in the poem he is named as Ligurge and is a supporter of Palamon while in the play he 'stands with Arcite' and is not named. Chaucer describes him thus:

> Blake was his berd, and manly was his face
> The cercles of his eyen in his heed
> They glouden betwixt yelow and reed

And like a Lion loked he aboute . . .[2]
His limmes great, his brawnes strong
His shoulders brode, his armes round and long . . .
His long heare was kempd behind his back
As any ravens fether it shone for blacke.

(2130-3, 2135-6, 2143-4)

Fletcher copies many of these details:

his complexion
Nearer a brown than black, stern and yet noble, . . .
The circles of his eyes show fire within him,
And as a heated lion, so he looks;
His hair hangs long behind him, black and shining,
Like ravens' wings; his shoulders broad and strong;
Arm'd long and round;   (78-85)

He adds a few lines about the man's baldric to distinguish him as a warrior, and finishes

better, o' my conscience,
Was never soldier's friend.   (87-88)

The second knight, described by Pirithous in the play, takes his most notable features from Emetreus, whose description follows that of Ligurge in the poem and includes the lines

His crispe hear like rings was yronne
And that was yelow, and glittering as the sonne . . .
His lippes ruddy, his colour was sanguyne . . .
His voyce was as a trompet sowning.

(2165-6, 2168, 2174)

Of Palamon's supporter in the play we are told

his complexion
Is as a ripe grape ruddy . . .
His head's yellow,
Hard-hair'd and curl'd, thick twin'd, like ivy-tods, . . .
His red lips, after fights, are fit for ladies . . .
When he speaks, his tongue
Sounds like a trumpet;   (95-96, 103-4, 111, 112-13)

Perhaps it was the curly yellow hair that made Fletcher allot this man specifically to the lover's cause, telling us 'He has

2. A notable instance of the value of using the 1602 edition (however bad it often is in some respects) since modern texts read 'And lyk a griffon loked he aboute' for this line.

felt, Without doubt, what he fights for' (96–97), while the stern dark looks of Ligurge betokened martial qualities. Fletcher also gives us a third knight (not in Chaucer), who is described as 'freckle-fac'd' (120), a characteristic omitted from his version of Emetreus who has in Chaucer 'a fewe freckles in his face yspente' (2169). The Messenger says of him

> when he smiles
> He shows a lover, when he frowns, a soldier;
> About his head he wears the winner's oak,
> And in it stuck the favor of his lady. (135–8)

He maintains the suspense by not allotting him to either the lover's or the soldier's party.

Fletcher emphasizes in this scene the cruel tyranny and high cost of love, a Chaucerian theme used more consistently by Shakespeare. Emilia deplores the 'sacrifice' of the princes at 57–64, and her single line later, 'Must these men die too?' (112) is very effective in the midst of the masculine enthusiasm for the warriors. While Theseus seems to have lost his capacity for reflection and is eager for the fight to begin, Emilia goes off saying to herself

> Poor wench, go weep; for whosoever wins
> Loses a noble cousin for thy sins. (155–6)

Act IV, scene iii

Chaucer separates the descriptions of the knights from the sequence of prayers by a passage about how Theseus entertained all the contestants (2190 ff.), while the play inserts another sub-plot scene. This is the second sub-plot scene in the play which is in prose, and may have been written by Shakespeare.[3] It is the scene in which the madness of the Jailer's daughter is considered by a doctor who recommends to her former lover that he pretend to be Palamon in order to cure her (66 ff.). This aspect of the sub-plot anticipates the final substitution of one man for another (Palamon for Arcite) in the main plot, and to that extent it can be seen as an echo of a Chaucerian theme too.

3. See Cyrus Hoy, as cited (p. 191, n. 8).

Act v, scene i

Most of this scene is Shakespearian, but the first thirty-three lines have been attributed to Fletcher.[4] The dialogue between Theseus and Pirithous, and then between the kinsmen themselves, is very like Fletcher's style in Act III. After this we return to Shakespeare and, with the sequence of prayers to the gods, to Chaucer. The order in which they are given (Arcite prays to Mars, then Palamon to Venus, then Emilia to Diana) follows the order of the descriptions of the temples in *The Knight's Tale* rather than that of the prayers, which are arranged according to the astrological system of allocating specific hours to each planet, so that the sequence runs Palamon to Venus, Emily to Diana, Arcite to Mars.[5] Shakespeare combines detail and atmospheric effect from both the sequences in the poem, as in the first speech of Arcite to Mars which recalls the horrors of war depicted on the walls of Chaucer's temple:

> The open warre, with woundes all bebledde . . .
> A thousand slain, and nat of qualme istorve
> The tiraunt, with the praie by force iraft
> The toun destroied, there was nothing ilaft.
>
> (2002, 2014–16)

Shakespeare's Arcite evokes this destructive power:

> Our intercession then
> Must be to him that makes the camp a cistern
> Brimm'd with the blood of men, (45–46)

and he describes Mars as one

> who dost pluck,
> With hand armipotent, from forth blue clouds
> The mason'd turrets, that both mak'st and break'st
> The strong girths of cities; (53–56)

This also reminds us of a speech by Chaucer's Saturn who claims

> Mine is the ruin of the high halls
> The falling of the toures and the walls
>
> (2463–4)

4. See Cyrus Hoy, as cited (p. 191, n. 8).

5. See the Explanatory Note on this in F. N. Robinson's edition of Chaucer (as cited), p. 679.

and Mars is twice described as 'armipotent' in the poem:

> There stode the temple of Mars armipotent   (1982)
> Mars the sterne god armipotent   (2441)

Both Arcites emphasize their youth, as in Chaucer's prayer

> I am young and uncunning, as thou woost
> (2393)

and in the play,

>   ... me thy pupil
> Youngest follower of thy drum, instruct this day,
> (56–57)

Shakespeare's Arcite says little about love but specifically requests to be 'styl'd the lord o' th' day' (60), echoing in thought rather than word Chaucer's Arcite who prays 'Yif me the victorye, I ask thee namore' (2420).[6]

Palamon's prayer to Venus in the play concentrates on the theme that love is painful, irrational, and undignified, which is again the emphasis in Chaucer's description of her temple:

> First in the temple of Venus thou maist se
> Wrought on the wall, full pitously to behold
> The broken slepes and the sighes cold
> The sault teares, and the weimenting
> The fire strokes, and the desiring
> That loves servauntes in this life enduren ...
>
> Thus may you sen, that wisedom ne richesse
> Beauty ne sleight, strength ne hardinesse
> Ne maie with Venus hold champartie
> For as her list the world may she gie.
> (1918–23, 1947–50)

The supremacy of Venus is grimly portrayed in the play in Palamon's descriptions of cripples and old men overcome by passion. He mentions her conquest of Mars which may be transferred from Arcite's speech in Chaucer (2383 ff.). His helpless tone is similar to Palamon in the poem, but his insistence on his own innocence is different from that hero's

---

6. Kenneth Muir notes that this speech is influenced by Elizabethan views on the function of war as a purge of society, in *Shakespeare as Collaborator* (London, 1960), p. 138.

vow to 'hold werre alwey with chastitee' (2236) as well as
being inconsistent with the conversation about women in
III. iii. Both versions contrast the efficient and optimistic
soldier (Arcite) with the tormented lover at this point.

In the poem, Palamon is explicit about his aims:

> I kepe noght of armes still for to yelpe,
> Ne I ne aske tomorwe to have victorye—
> But wolde have fully possessioun
> Of Emelye.   (2238–9, 2242–3)

This prepares us for some kind of trick, but in the play
Palamon says

>   our argument is love,
> Which if the goddess of it grant, she gives
> Victory too.   (70–72)

and

> Give me the victory of this question, which
> Is true love's merit.   (126–7)

These are his closing lines, in contrast to the poem where
Palamon finishes

> This is the effecte, and ende of my prayere
> Yeve me my lady, thou blissfull lady dere.
>   (2259–60)

It is fairly clear in Chaucer that Arcite is asking for victory in
battle while Palamon is asking for Emily but Shakespeare
leaves us less certain. The signs given by the gods are more
ambiguous too: Mars actually murmurs 'Victory' in Chaucer
(2433) rather than responding simply with a 'noise of battle',
and though Palamon's sign in the poem is less obvious (the
statue shakes) he seems confident of its meaning:

> For though the signe shewed a delay
> Yet wist he well, that graunted was his boone.
>   (2268–9)

Both heroes in the play interpret their signs as being favourable, but the question is less straightforward for the audience.

The closing lines of Palamon's speech in the play refer to
Venus as a hunter 'whose chase is in this world, And we in
herds thy game' (131–2), echoing Theseus's description of

men as the 'mortal herd' of the gods in the play at I. iv. 5. This might also be linked with an earlier passage in *The Knight's Tale* when Palamon, reflecting on his fate, asks the gods

> What is mankind more unto yow yhold
> Than is the shepe, that rouketh in the folde?
> For slain is man, right as another beest,
>   (1307–9 ff.)

There are other images of men as animals in *The Knight's Tale*, where, despite all the references to fate, determinism, and the actual intervention of the gods, we are usually given an explanation for what happens in terms of the (animalistic) human will as well. Shakespeare, although he uses the gods less, seems to give them more real power by *not* giving us a human explanation, and by making his characters, especially Theseus, both attempt to rationalize and acknowledge the limitations of reason.

Emilia's prayer is again based on the poem, though it omits the 'vengeance' and 'ire' of Diana feared by Chaucer's heroine (2302). Her basic attitude, 'I am bride-habited, But maiden-hearted' (150–1) echoes the poem, 'well-woste thow that I Desyre to ben a mayde all my life' (2304–5), and compares with the innocence Palamon has just claimed. (It is also equally inconsistent with some earlier moments in the play.) Her request either that she may remain a virgin or that 'He of the two pretenders that best loves me' be victorious (158) is close to Chaucer's lines

> Or if so be my destinie be shapen so
> That I shall nedes have one of hem two
> As sende me him that most desireth me.
>   (2323–5)

The sign given by Diana is more disturbing in Chaucer, where Emily is 'sore agast' at the bleeding branch, but it is also more clearly explained by the appearance of the goddess herself. In the play, the vision of the rose falling from the tree is more conventional. In both versions the heroine goes away in some perplexity (171–3, cf. Chaucer 2361 ff.) although her sign has been the least ambiguous of the three.

Act v, scene ii

Again the sub-plot intervenes. We begin to have more confidence in the ultimate cure of the Jailer's daughter who seems
pleased with her substitute lover. The arrival of the Messenger and the general exodus to see the tournament reflect the
source, since Chaucer describes the enthusiasm of the
citizens at some length here (2483-90, 2513-22).

Act v, scene iii

From this point, the source is considerably altered, and
treated with as much if not more freedom than in Act I.
Chaucer makes Theseus decree that the battle shall not be
mortal (2537 ff.) although this is not really consistent with
the earlier assumption that the elimination of one of the kinsmen is the only possible solution. Shakespeare omits this
merciful gesture (much praised by the citizens in the poem),
increasing the solemnity of the occasion and the pain for
Emilia. She watches the fight in the poem, but the device in
the play whereby she refuses to go on provides a further
chance to describe her feelings and allows Shakespeare to
have the fight reported rather than enacted.

The comparison she makes between the two heroes is
rather like that of IV. ii and quite unlike the remoteness of
Emily in the source. It is quite an abrupt change from her
sentiments in v. i, and shows that Shakespeare too has to
prepare for a switch of allegiance from Diana to Venus.
(Fletcherian interpolations have been suggested in this scene,
but lines like 'his brow Is grav'd and seems to bury what it
frowns on' seem very Shakespearian.) Emilia's fear that her
presence may distract the fighters (60 ff.) may be a recollection of Arcite's death in the poem, where it is at least implied
that he was looking at her instead of at the ground (2679 ff.).
But the situation is more closely paralleled in Sonnet 53 of
Sidney's *Astrophel and Stella* (1582) which may have been the
source:

> In martial sports I had my cunning tried,
>   And yet to break more staves did me address:
>   While, with the people's shouts, I must confess,
>   Youth, luck, and praise, even fill'd my veins with pride;

When Cupid having me his slave descried,
  In Mars's livery, prancing in the press:
  'What now, Sir Fool', said he; I would no less.
  'Look here, I say'. I look'd and Stella spied,
Who hard by made a window send forth light.
  My heart then quak'd, then dazzled were mine eyes;
  One hand forgot to rule, th' other to fight.
Nor trumpet's sound I heard, nor friendly cries;
  My foe came on, and beat the air for me,
  Til that her blush taught me my shame to see.

Chaucer describes the combat in some detail and implies that it lasted a long time:

> And sometime doeth hem Theseus to reste
> Hem to refreshe, and drinke if hem leste.
> Full ofte a day have these Thebans two
> Togither met, and don eche other wo.
>
> (2621–4)

The play keeps up the suspense with the initial triumph of Palamon, but in both versions he is finally beaten. Theseus confidently endorses Arcite's victory and gives him the prize (play 106–8, cf. poem 2656–8). General rejoicing can follow in the poem but Arcite in the play is aware of loss too:

> Emilia,
> To buy you I have lost what's dearest to me,
> Save what is bought;   (111–13)

This is a very prominent theme in the closing scenes of the play, with all the main characters voicing the same thought. Emilia's reaction is to cry 'Is this winning?' (138) and she sees her role to be the comforter of Arcite who 'cuts away A life more worthy from him than all women' (142–3). Hippolyta replies in the same vein:

> Infinite pity
> That four such eyes should be so fix'd on one
> That two must needs be blind for't.   (144–6)

Palamon, when he is in the victor's position later also regrets

> That we should things desire, which cost us
> The loss of our desire! That nought could buy
> Dear love, but loss of dear love. (v. iv. 110–12)

and Theseus comments that 'The victor has the loss' (v. iv.
114) This theme may have been suggested by Chaucer's lines
on Palamon at the end:

> And God, that al this world hath ywrought,
> Sende him his love, that it hath so deer bought.
>
> (3099–100)

But Shakespeare is more insistent on it than Chaucer, and his
mood has changed since writing the other Romances where
loss is usually balanced by restoration and no important
characters are sacrificed. (Though the intensity of Prospero's
loneliness at the end of *The Tempest* is a kind of precedent.)
In his earlier use of similar stories, *The Two Gentlemen of
Verona* for example, Shakespeare had avoided the need for
this sort of painful moment by the use of two heroines, but in
this case he deliberately underlines the fact that sexual love
can destroy friendship.[7] The praise of the kinsmen by
Theseus at 115 ff. is new, and, with its emphasis on the noble
qualities of the doomed Palamon, further stresses the idea of
loss and cost. The resignation to necessity at the end is again
possibly Chaucerian.

Act v, scene iv

Since the losers are not to be put to death in Chaucer's
version, the beginning of this scene is original, though Palamon's speech on the merits of dying at the height of one's
youth, fame, and virtue may have been suggested by a speech
by Theseus later in *The Knight's Tale* when he is trying to
persuade Palamon and Emily to accept Arcite's death with
words like

> And certainly a man hath most honour
> To dien in his excellence and flour.
>
> (3047–8)

and

---

7. *The Merchant of Venice* is a precedent, with its love and friendship theme
and its discussion of love in mercantile terms. Portia says to Bassanio 'Since you
are dear bought, I will love you dear' (III. ii. 315), but the theme is treated lightly
and Bassanio's choice between his friend and his wife over the ring is given a
comic twist.

> Than it is best as for a worthy fame
> To dien when he is best of name.
>
> (3055–6)

Both these passages are marked as 'notable sentences' by Speght. (Lydgate also has a long passage on this theme following the death of Adrastus's son at 3419 in *The Siege of Thebes*.)

The idea of cost and loss appears again in the statement that the other knights who are about to lose their lives for supporting Palamon have 'sold 'em too too cheap' (15), but one of them finds comfort in the thought that their merits equal those of the victors, as Theseus has said in the previous scene, following Chaucer who makes this point at some length (2719–30). Another expresses a Boethian contempt for fortune (19–21). Palamon again inquires after the Jailer's daughter and leads his friends in giving money for her dowry when he hears 'she's well restor'd And to be married shortly' (27–28). Chaucer's Theseus describes Arcite as having escaped 'out of this foule prisoun of this life' in the speech I have already quoted as a source for this scene (3061), and Shakespeare's Palamon uses the same metaphor to the Jailer:

> my friend, my friend,
> Your gentle daughter gave me freedom once;
> You'll see't done now forever.   (23–25)

The entry of Pirithous brings us back to the events of the poem more directly. He says that 'the gods' are responsible for the accident he is about to describe (43–44), but the mechanics of this are not revealed in the play as they are in the poem where the argument of Mars and Venus is settled by the specific intervention of Saturn at this point. The description of Arcite's fatal accident (which one critic called 'decidedly bad, but undeniably the work of Shakespeare'[8]) is close to Chaucer both in its facts (he is thrown awkwardly from his horse) and in the vividness of its details. The fact that the horse is one given to him by Emilia is an addition to the source, but the description of it, 'the hot horse, hot as fire' (65), recalls an earlier moment in the poem when Arcite

---

8. W. Spalding, *A Letter on Shakespeare's Authorship of 'The Two Noble Kinsmen'* (London, 1833), p. 54.

rode out 'to doon his observaunce to May' on a 'courser, startlinge as the fire' (1502). We are given two explanations of the incident in the poem: the fury sent by Pluto at the request of Saturn (who has promised his daughter Venus to give her knight, Palamon, the final victory) and the more mundane notion that Arcite was not looking where he was going but gazing at Emily (2676–91). Shakespeare reduces Saturn to a simile:

> what envious flint,
> Cold as old Saturn and like him possess'd
> With fire malevolent, darted a spark,
>   (61–63)

and we are not told of any fault on the part of the rider, so the event seems more arbitrary.

Arcite does not die instantaneously in either version. The plot moves slowly in the poem where we are given a long, realistic description of Arcite's wounds, sickness, and death (2689–99, 2743–815) relieved by a few humorous remarks from the narrator like

> And certainly ther as nature wol nat wirch
> Farwel physike, go beare the corse to chirch.
>   (2759–60)

while Theseus tries to keep normal life going: 'He would not disconfort hem alle' (2704). Chaucer gives Arcite a thirty-line dying speech in which he reflects on the apparent pointlessness of his own life (2765–97). Speght marks the following lines for special attention:

> What is this world? What asken men to have?
> Now with his love, now in his cold grave
> Alone, withouten any company.   (2779–7)

Then the poem relates the grief of the other characters, the platitudinous counsel of Egeus, the elaborate preparations for the funeral and the event itself, subsequent to which it is only after 'lengthe of certain yeeres' (2967) that Theseus's desire

> To have with certain contrees alliance,
> And have fully of Thebans obeisance
>   (2973–4)

prompts him to encourage the marriage of Emily and
Palamon though Arcite had said to her on his death-bed

> And if that you shall ever been a wife
> Forget not Palamon, the gentle man.
> (2796–7)

In the play he not only passes her on—'Take Emilia, And
with her all the world's joy' (90–91)—but declares 'I was
false' (92) and confesses Palamon's better right (116 ff.). Like
his namesake in Chaucer, Theseus tries to rationalize the
situation. He accepts the unavoidable with a good grace,
declaring 'the deities have show'd due justice' (108–9), but
his final speech expresses bewilderment as well as resignation:

> O you heavenly charmers,
> What things you make of us! For what we lack
> We laugh, for what we have, are sorry; still
> Are children in some kind. Let us be thankful
> For that which is, and with you leave dispute
> That are above our question.   (131–6)

This mood at the close of the play strongly recalls the theme
of *The Knight's Tale* that 'We witen nat what thing we preyen
here' (1260)—men cannot understand their destinies, do not
know how to find happiness and are ruled on the one hand
by their own reckless passions and on the other by arbitrary
and remote deities.[9]

Chaucer, romance, and tragicomedy

Throughout the preceding comparison it has been apparent
that Shakespeare and Fletcher were using their source in
quite different ways. In particular the presentation of characters is inconsistent, most obviously in the cases of Emilia and
Palamon, and Shakespeare's parts of the play (especially
Acts I and v) contain certain themes—for example, the destructive effects of amorous passion on other relationships,
the extent to which men can control their own destinies—

9. The tone of the Epilogue serves to deflate this effect by dismissing the play
rather lightly.

which are not always developed by Fletcher. Some of the discrepancies within the play can be attributed to different interpretations of the source, but, as with *Troilus and Cressida*, it is also necessary to take a wider look at the play and to bring other factors such as the influence of the contemporary theatre and the relation the play bears to the other work of each of its authors into the discussion.

It has often been remarked that there is a general resemblance between the work of the late Shakespeare and that of the early Fletcher, or between Shakespearian romance and Fletcherian tragicomedy. Superficially at least they use similar plots and situations, whether by coincidence, common awareness of new tastes and new theatrical facilities (the use of the indoor Blackfriars theatre from 1609), or by mutual influence.[1] At the same time, several critics have pointed out major differences between the output of Shakespeare and that of Beaumont and Fletcher during this period. John Danby, for example, has related these differences to the two 'traditions' to which the playwrights belonged and to the conditions under which Shakespeare's 'inclusiveness of comprehension' became 'socially unuseable' in the 'snobbish vulgarization and sectional narrowing of the great tradition'. Although Shakespeare used some of the same materials as Beaumont and Fletcher, the resulting plays are not very similar on closer examination, and Danby attributes this to the fact that 'their framework is the large metaphor his work had established for him before Beaumont and Fletcher began to write'.[2] *The Two Noble Kinsmen* becomes a valuable text for further defining these differences since it is very likely that the inconsistencies in the interpretation of *The Knight's Tale* can be related to the wider contrast.

Fletcher conveniently defined the art of tragicomedy in the preface he wrote for the published text of *The Faithful Shepherdess* in 1609:

1. Criticism on this subject has been usefully summarized by Andrew Gurr in his edition of *Philaster* for the Revels series (London, 1969), pp. xlv–l. See also Clifford Leech, *The John Fletcher Plays* (London, 1962), and Richard Proudfoot, 'Shakespeare and the new dramatists of the King's Men, 1606–13', *Later Shakespeare*, ed. J. R. Brown and B. Harris (Stratford-on-Avon Studies 8, London, 1966), pp. 234–61.

2. *Poets on Fortune's Hill* (London, 1952), pp. 152–83.

A tragi-comedy is not so called in respect of mirth and killing, but in respect it wants deaths, which is enough to make it no tragedy, yet brings some near it, which is enough to make it no comedy, which must be a representation of familiar people, with such kind of trouble as no life be questioned; so that a god is as lawful in this as in a tragedy, and mean people as in a comedy.

These words have been much quoted by critics, but it remains uncertain how far the definition was important for Fletcher's actual practice as a playwright. He seems to see tragicomedy as a happy means of combining the materials and effects of both tragedy and comedy but he is not very explicit about the details and the exact method and does not seem to acknowledge that a combination of the two must result in something quite different from either. A modern critic, Eugene Waith, has analysed the actual process and its effects more minutely and has produced the following list of 'factors responsible for modifying accepted comic and tragic patterns' in the Beaumont and Fletcher plays:

   1. the weakening of the link with actuality to produce a theatrical imitation of life, neither quite familiar nor entirely remote;
   2. the discontinuity of plot which results from sacrificing a single action to a series of situations;
   3. the poses which make many of the protagonists unconvincing or inconsistent.[3]

This is probably a long way from Fletcher's conscious aims, but it seems to be an accurate analysis of what actually happens in the plays, and it certainly helps to explain Fletcher's approach to Chaucer in *The Two Noble Kinsmen*. He was trying to turn *The Knight's Tale* into a tragicomedy like *Philaster*, and he applied the successful method he used on many other stories. It is easier to understand some of the internal inconsistencies of the play when we think of Fletcher's planning 'a series of situations' rather than a single action, and when we realize that he is regularly prepared to sacrifice coherence of character to immediate effect. Philaster himself is not a great deal more consistent or convincing than

---

3. *The Pattern of Tragicomedy in Beaumont and Fletcher* (New Haven, 1952), pp. 135-6.

the Emilia of the combined efforts of Fletcher and Shakespeare, and it would seem, on the evidence of his other plays,
that Fletcher would not have been as worried by the incon-
gruity in the characterization of the play as his critics were to
be later. The discrepancies are the more noticeable because
Shakespeare wrote some of the scenes; otherwise we should
consider them typical examples of Fletcher's narrow-sighted
habit of exploiting the present situation to the full with
almost complete disregard for the rest of the play. Under such
circumstances, it is possible to imagine him writing III. iii
even though he had seen V. i, for example, and to understand
why he adds a passage like the opening section of IV. ii to the
source. Chaucer's poem simply becomes the quarry from
which Fletcher extracts the situations which he proceeds to
elaborate with maximum sensational effect.

   Thus it is not really a valid criticism to say that Fletcher is
using Chaucer inconsistently and without real comprehension, when he is not attempting an interpretation of the poem
but rather adapting its basic story to the successful tragicomic
pattern; he does a similar thing with *The Wife of Bath's Tale*
in *Women Pleased*, as we have already seen. Moreover, his
achievements with *The Knight's Tale* are considerable. The
plot is much more straightforward than those he usually
chooses, and the number of emotional climaxes and theatrical set-pieces is thereby limited. The characters do not rush
quite as quickly from one pose to another as they do in many
of Fletcher's plays, and he sometimes has occasion to exploit
a comparatively simple situation with great effect: III. vi
and IV. ii of *The Two Noble Kinsmen* are equal if not superior
to anything in the Fletcher canon. Philip Edwards has said
that it is Fletcher's art 'not to deal with subtleties of behaviour but to deal subtly with obvious types of behaviour',[4]
and there is ample scope for this talent in the central acts of
the play, where the relationship between the two kinsmen
must be presented in an interesting manner with little help
from the source. One gets the impression that Fletcher knew
what his talents were and how he could best use them on this
story. He cuts out the kind of material which would be in-

4. 'The danger not the death', *Jacobean Theatre*, ed. J. R. Brown and B.
Harris (Stratford-on-Avon Studies 1, London, 1960), pp. 159–77.

congruous with his tragicomic conception and concentrates on the more promising elements. He omits Chaucer's ironic perspective because his kind of tragicomedy requires its pathos to be taken seriously. Altogether he produces a well-constructed fast-moving tragicomedy that might have seemed his best play if the presence of Shakespeare had not set up conflicting aims and standards which act as a constant reminder to readers and audiences that, however excellent Fletcher may be at his own craft, it is one which is bound to seem narrow and limited in comparison.

Shakespeare's romances do *not* 'modify accepted comic and tragic patterns' in the manner of Fletcherian tragicomedy. They can in fact make a more genuine claim to combine the qualities of both. The reason why Fletcher's attempt to do this fails to live up to its pretensions lies, as Cyrus Hoy says, in 'the formal arbitrariness of the definition of tragicomedy'[5] on which it rests. It is not enough, although it is attractively simple, to define 'tragedy' and 'comedy' by whether the principal characters happen to die at the end. Shakespeare does not use discontinuous plots and inconsistent characters, but combines elements from the two genres with a full and, one might say, empirical knowledge of what they really are. Theodore Spencer's distinction between Shakespeare who had 'come out on the other side of experience' and Fletcher who 'never got there' comes to mind: Shakespeare is consistently more serious and seems to go deep while Fletcher plays with surface attitudes and short-term effects.[6]

Shakespeare's seriousness is consistent with that in his other late plays, but in some respects he pushes his themes further in *The Two Noble Kinsmen* and questions some of the values he has hitherto accepted in such a way as to make one feel the play could have been the first of a new set of 'dark comedies' or 'problem plays'. In particular the treatment of love and the attitude towards the gods are worth attention.

Nostalgia for asexual love and a corresponding awareness of the destructive and degrading effects of sexual love and the

---

5. *The Hyacinth Room* (London, 1964), p. 213.

6. T. Spencer, '*The Two Noble Kinsmen*', *Modern Philology*, xxxvi (1939), 255–76.

jealousy which can accompany it are elements in both *Cymbeline* and *The Winter's Tale*, but the latter theme (the negative aspect) is not as strong as in the *Kinsmen* where we see and hear far more of the destructive power of love than its desirability, especially at the end of the play where Shakespeare really seems to harp on what the happy ending has cost. Palamon's prayer to Venus also emphasizes the realistic rather than the romantic side of love which usually dominates in this sort of semi-pastoral tragicomedy. It is again John Danby who, writing of Shakespeare's romances, comments that 'the facts of Mars and Venus cannot be considered in them along with the theories of Diana'.[7] But this is of course exactly what happens in *The Two Noble Kinsmen*, where the dark side of love, its irrational indignity, its cruelty, and above all its cost, are considered alongside the ideals. This naturally makes the play grimmer than the other romances, but in all of them Shakespeare gives his characters a self-awareness that immediately differentiates them from those of Fletcher. Just as Palamon and Emilia are shown to appreciate how dearly they have bought their love, so characters like Leontes and Posthumus are given a serious insight into the significance of their actions. It is this self-knowledge that is one of the more characteristically 'tragic' elements of the Romances and which gives them a level of meaning which is quite alien to the Fletcherian conception of tragicomedy.

Shakespeare makes use of the gods in all his late plays, but again the emphasis is different and somehow darker in *The Two Noble Kinsmen*. The appearance of Diana in *Pericles* is not strictly necessary, and Jupiter's riddle in *Cymbeline* is similarly redundant. We feel that the human beings are quite capable of working things out for themselves. Apollo and his oracle in *The Winter's Tale* again seem more important than they are and it is possible, though an exaggeration, to see all the 'epiphanies' as dramatically impressive methods of externalizing human motives and events. By contrast, the gods in *The Two Noble Kinsmen* are felt to be truly powerful, especially in the prayers in v. i. They are presented as arbitrary and controlling forces, and attempts to rationalize, like

7. Op cit., p. 101.

that of Arcite in I. ii and that of Theseus at the end of the play, seem only to reinforce the impression of human impotence and divine inscrutability. As I have demonstrated above, *The Knight's Tale* contains material both on the darker side of love and on the subservience of individual men to external forces which could have influenced Shakespeare. The characters in his parts of the play, like those of *Troilus and Cressida*, have also an awareness of the power of time, which is again an ingredient of tragedy and a theme inherited by the Renaissance from the Middle Ages.

Thus Fletcher's treatment of the story of Palamon and Arcite owes more to his desire to write a commercial tragicomedy than to any deep interest in the source. This is not surprising, especially if, as seems most likely, the story was not his own choice. In the Shakespearian parts of the play, however, there is considerable evidence for a thoughtful reading of the poem and an attempt to express and elaborate Chaucer's complex attitude and philosophy. Both Chaucer and Shakespeare saw that the story was an absurd one, but they saw that its very absurdity made it serious too. Chaucer, through his device of the narrator, in this case the knight (though it is questionable how far the persona is sustained), uses comic irony to provide a method of distancing and moderating, while Shakespeare's version is more consistently sombre. J. B. Leishman makes an interesting comparison between the two writers in another context when he says that Chaucer never achieved the 'one-sided intensity' of tragedy because he was 'more continuously aware of other kinds of experience which are possible',[8] and hence incapable of taking himself or anyone else seriously for very long or of considering his tragic insights in isolation from the rest of life. He keeps deflating the tragic potential of his material by his comic remarks and ironic perspective, whereas Shakespeare refrains from doing this and the result is profoundly serious.

Philip Edwards says in fact that *The Two Noble Kinsmen* 'gives the most cynical assessment of the progress of life since the writing of *Troilus and Cressida*'[9] and one is lead to

8. *Themes and Variations in Shakespeare's Sonnets* (London, 1961), pp. 142–6.
9. 'On the design of *The Two Noble Kinsmen*', REL, v (1964), 105.

wonder whether the comparison is significant. Undoubtedly Shakespeare saw behind the Chaucerian humour to the dark vision of men blindly pursuing happiness at the instigation of their own lower instincts and the arbitrary and incomprehensible decrees of the indifferent gods. It is not a comforting thought, and it does not fit in with some of the rather sentimental conceptions about Shakespeare's calm and satisfied state of mind at the close of his career. Like *The Tempest*, *The Two Noble Kinsmen* deals with the limitations of some of the qualities affirmed in the other romances, but the scepticism seems greater and is due at least in part to the influence of the source.

6

Conclusions

It cannot be denied that Chaucer was still a major poet for Elizabethan and Jacobean writers and the number of references to his works in the drama proves that their admiration was not mere lip-service to the man best qualified for the position of 'English Homer'. They did read him with pleasure and understanding despite the difficulties set in their way by unfamiliar vocabulary and syntax, badly mangled metres, and misleading apocryphal works. The poems they chose to use most frequently, for example *Troilus and Criseyde*, *The Knight's Tale*, and *The Clerke's Tale*, indicate two important things about their attitude to Chaucer and his works: firstly that they did not think of him primarily as a funny (even bawdy) poet as many people do today but as a serious romantic writer, and secondly, that they did not regard these non-naturalistic medieval romances as impossibly archaic and undramatic.

They used Chaucer's poems in many different ways. Shakespeare is typical of his contemporaries in using Chaucer for a brief reference or quotation, a subsidiary source or a full-scale plot. A single poem can be drawn upon in all these ways; *The Wife of Bath's Tale* for example is an important source for Fletcher's *Women Pleased*, and probably inspired the king's speech on true nobility in *All's Well that Ends Well*, while her *Prologue* lies behind more than one discussion of sovereignty in marriage and a couple of conversations about virginity. Moreover a metaphor from the *Tale* is borrowed to illustrate the pain of exile in *Richard II*. Thus two dramatists demonstrate their appreciation of different aspects of the poem: its romance, its humour, its serious morality, and its occasionally vivid imagery.

The plays based substantially on Chaucer vary widely in

the use they make of him. Sometimes he seems little more than a convenient source for a story, as in both the *Patient Grissil* plays and R. B.'s *Apius and Virginia*. A more thoughtful dramatist like Chapman can extract the romantic comedy (and even some of the dialogue) from *Troilus and Criseyde* while implying a criticism of that poem's claim to be a serious moral tragedy, and Shakespeare is more openly destructive. At the other end of the spectrum we find Beaumont and Fletcher who instead of adding their own interpretation to a plot subtract what is there already and give us a fast-moving but impoverished version. What made all these dramatists (and others whose plays are lost) choose to make use of Chaucer is difficult to decide. Throughout the period he was the only medieval poet to be widely read and thus played an important role in transmitting the narrative materials and styles of an earlier age. His poems are often quite short (for example many of *The Canterbury Tales* and *The Legend of Good Women*) and need little rearrangement to bring out the most effective dramatic points. Above all he was generally available in the four folio editions published between 1532 and 1602—I have suggested above that the 1598 edition in particular encouraged the dramatists to use him.

Shakespeare's use of him remains the most extensive as well as the most interesting.[1] Some of the evidence that has been offered in the past is flimsy, but by now the case that he knew Chaucer very well indeed is a strong one. In a play like *A Midsummer Night's Dream* as many as four Chaucerian works are used in different ways: *The Knight's Tale* for the framing action and parts of the main romantic plot, *The Legend of Good Women* for Pyramus and Thisbe and a brief reference to Dido, *The Merchant's Tale* for the quarrel between Oberon and Titania, and perhaps *The Parlement of Foules* for Theseus's reference to St Valentine's day. Conversely, a single poem by Chaucer, such as *The Knight's Tale* or *The Parlement of Foules* can occur in four or five independent contexts in Shakespeare. His ability to remember passages

1. Both Dekker (if we count the two lost plays) and Fletcher make more use of Chaucer for whole plots, but in both cases it is just plots that are used; they could almost be using summaries of Chaucer rather than the poems themselves.

from Chaucer at unlikely times as well as obvious ones (for example his use of *The Parlement of Foules* in Claudio's speech about the afterworld in *Measure for Measure* as well as in the list of birds in *The Phoenix and the Turtle*) gives us a valuable illustration of one of the ways in which his work is deeper and richer than that of other writers: his powers of association are more complex and daring.

Troilus and Cressida and *The Two Noble Kinsmen* provide further evidence of how well Shakespeare knew Chaucer in the very looseness of his adaptation. He is able to pick out details from several different places in each poem to concentrate an effect in a single scene rather than being obliged to follow his source carefully through from beginning to end. The only other dramatist who displays anything like this familiarity with Chaucer is Chapman who combines two episodes in *Troilus and Criseyde* for a single scene in *Sir Giles Goosecap*. Both Shakespeare's Chaucerian plays differ widely from their originals in tone, though this is more obvious in the case of *Troilus*. By losing the narrator and his ability to modify and distance what he tells, Shakespeare gives us a more consistently dark and uneasy version of each story. *Troilus* without the poet's sympathy and wisdom becomes bitter and sordid, while the omission of an ironic perspective in *The Two Noble Kinsmen* makes the absurdity of its plot more frightening than comic. In the latter case though, one should remember that Shakespeare had exploited the comic potential of *The Knight's Tale* in *A Midsummer Night's Dream*, so the uneasiness is only a part of his reaction and may be due to a reappraisal of his own earlier work as well as to a new interpretation of Chaucer.

In both plays, Shakespeare's use of Chaucer is only one factor in a more complex design. In the case of *Troilus and Cressida* I have argued that the substance and style of Chaucer's poem influenced not just the love-story but the whole play by suggesting many of the thematic links between the two plots which Shakespeare develops. Chaucer's self-consciousness about using a well-known story could also have had a strong effect on Shakespeare's unusual tone and attitude in this play. In *The Two Noble Kinsmen* there is again convincing evidence of the influence of *The Knight's*

Tale on the themes of the play as well as on its plot, though this is sometimes obscured by the presence of Fletcher. A source-study of this play confirms the accepted lines of authorship division and provides some valuable insights into the fundamental differences between Shakespearian romance and Fletcherian tragicomedy. *Romeo and Juliet*, while it is less directly dependant on Chaucer than *Troilus and Cressida* or *The Two Noble Kinsmen*, has many more similarities with *Troilus and Criseyde* than can be attributed to coincidence, and allows us to make some close comparisons between Chaucer and Shakespeare when they are both handling the basic materials of the tragedy of love.

It would be rash to claim that I have found every one of Shakespeare's references to Chaucer, but it is likely that I have (with the aid of many previous writers) assembled a representative selection both of the kind of material and the kind of influence involved. If the methods I have devised for making relative judgements about the validity and significance of different types of parallel are valid they will continue to be applicable as the coral growth of scholarship proceeds. I hope that there will in the future be much more work done on Shakespeare's medieval heritage, a subject too long neglected.[2]

2. After finishing this book I was pleased to discover a new treatment of one aspect of the subject, namely Shakespeare's use of the mystery plays, in Emrys Jones, *The Origins of Shakespeare* (Oxford, 1977).

Appendix

Chronological table of Shakespeare's references to Chaucer

(Dates are taken from J. G. McManaway, 'Recent studies in Shakespeare's chronology', *Shakespeare Survey*, iii (1950), 22–33.)

Date	Shakespeare	Chaucer	Page
1589–91	*1, 2, and 3 Henry VI*		
1592–3	*Richard III*		
1592–3	*Venus and Adonis*		
1593–4	*The Rape of Lucrece*	*The Legend of Good Women*	85–87
1593	*The Comedy of Errors*		
1593–4	*Titus Andronicus*	*The Legend of Good Women*	69, 87
		The Physician's Tale	70–71
		The House of Fame	74
1593–4	*The Taming of the Shrew*	*The Clerk's Tale*	70
		The Wife of Bath's Tale	84
		Troilus and Criseyde	65
1593–4	*The Two Gentlemen of Verona*	*The Knight's Tale*	75
		The Legend of Good Women	69
1594–5	*Love's Labour's Lost*	*The Knight's Tale*	75–76
		The Parlement of Foules	85
		The Book of the Duchess	85
1595–6	*Romeo and Juliet*	*Troilus and Criseyde*	94–110
		The Parlement of Foules	78–79
		The Manciple's Prologue	60
		The Man of Law's Tale	83
		The Squire's Tale	60–61
1595–6	*Richard II*	*The Wife of Bath's Tale*	77
		The Knight's Tale	61
1596	*A Midsummer Night's Dream*	*The Knight's Tale*	88–92
		The Merchant's Tale	92
		The Legend of Good Women	69, 93
		The Parlement of Foules	94
1596	*King John*		
1596–7	*The Merchant of Venice*	*The Legend of Good Women*	66–67
		Troilus and Criseyde	65–66
1597	*1 Henry IV*	*The Nun's Priest's Tale*	73
1598	*2 Henry IV*	*The House of Fame*	74
1598–9	*Much Ado About Nothing*	*Troilus and Criseyde*	64

Date	Shakespeare	Chaucer	Page
1599	Henry V	Troilus and Criseyde	65
1599–1600	Julius Caesar	The Monk's Tale	72–73
1599–1600	As You Like It	The Merchant's Tale	63
		Troilus and Criseyde	65
1595–1600	The Sonnets		
1601	The Phoenix and the Turtle	The Parlement of Foules	85
1599–1602	The Merry Wives of Windsor	Troilus and Criseyde	65
1601–2	Twelfth Night	Troilus and Criseyde	64
		The Parlement of Foules	73–74
1601	Hamlet	The Legend of Good Women	78
1601–2	Troilus and Cressida	Troilus and Criseyde	111–65
		The Parson's Tale	77–78
		The Wife of Bath's Prologue	63
1602–4	All's Well that Ends Well	The Wife of Bath's Prologue and Tale	80–81
		Troilus and Criseyde	65
1604	Measure for Measure	The Parlement of Foules	79–80
1604	Othello		
1605	King Lear	The Monk's Tale	71–72
		Merlin's Prophecy	81–82
1606	Macbeth		
1606–7	Antony and Cleopatra	The Monk's Tale	73
1608	Coriolanus		
1606–8	Timon of Athens		
1608	Pericles	The Man of Law's Tale	83–84
		The Clerk's Tale	83–84
1609–10	Cymbeline		
1610–11	The Winter's Tale	The Clerk's Tale	84
		The Merchant's Tale	62
		The Franklin's Tale	62
		The Nun's Priest's Tale	73
1611–12	The Tempest	The Franklin's Tale	76
1612–13	Henry VIII		
1613	The Two Noble Kinsmen	The Knight's Tale	166–215
		Anelida and Arcite	70

Bibliography

This bibliography contains all works cited in the text and footnotes and is divided into three sections, Texts and editions of medieval and Renaissance writers, Source criticism with specific reference to Chaucer, General criticism and other works cited. Each section is arranged alphabetically by author, with anonymous works in the first section under their titles.

1. Texts and editions of medieval and Renaissance writers

B., R., *Apius and Virginia*, ed. W. W. Greg and R. B. McKerrow for the Malone Society (Oxford, 1911).

BEAUMONT, F., and FLETCHER, J., *The Works of Francis Beaumont and John Fletcher*, ed. A. Glover and A. R. Waller (Cambridge, 1905–12), *Philaster*, ed. A. Gurr for the Revels Series (London, 1969) and 'The Masque of the Inner Temple' in F. T. Bowers (ed.), *The Dramatic Works in the Beaumont and Fletcher Canon*, vol. i (Cambridge, 1966).

BROOKE, A., *The Tragicall Historye of Romeus and Juliet*, ed. G. Bullough in *Narrative and Dramatic Sources of Shakespeare*, vol. i (London, 1964).

C., I., *The Two Merry Milkmaids*, Old English Drama Students Facsimiles (London, 1914).

CAXTON, W., *The Recuyell of the Hystoryes of Troye*, ed. G. Bullough in *Narrative and Dramatic Sources of Shakespeare*, vol. vi (London, 1966).

CHAPMAN, G., *The Tragedies* and *The Comedies*, ed. T. M. Parrot (London, 1910 and 1912).

CHAUCER, G., Sixteenth- and seventeenth-century editions (quotations are always taken from the most recent at the time of the work on which I am claiming an influence) edited by William Thynne (1532), John Stow (1561), Thomas Speght (1598 and 1602). Line numbering from *The Works of Geoffrey Chaucer*, ed. F. N. Robinson (2nd edn, London, 1957).

Common Conditions (anon.), ed. J. S. Farmer, *Five Anonymous Plays* Fourth series, London, 1908).

DAY, J., *The Works of John Day*, ed. A. H. Bullen (London, 1881), revised R. Jeffs (London, 1963).

DEKKER, T., *The Dramatic Works of Thomas Dekker*, ed. F. T. Bowers (Cambridge, 1953–61).

FLETCHER, J. (see Beaumont, F., and Shakespeare, W.)

GOLDING, A., *Shakespeare's Ovid.*, ed. W. H. D. Rouse (London, 1961).

GREENE, R., *The Complete Works of Robert Greene*, ed. A. B. Grossart (London, 1881–6).

HENRYSON, R., *The Testament of Cresseid*, printed in all the early Chaucer editions above. Modern edition by D. Fox (London, 1968).

HENSLOWE, P., *Henslowe's Diary*, ed. R. A. Foakes and R. T. Rickert (Cambridge, 1961).

JAMES I, *Short Treatise on Verse*, ed. G. G. Smith in *Elizabethan Critical Essays*, vol. i (Oxford, 1904).

JONSON, B., *Works*, ed. C. H. Herford and P. and E. Simpson (London, 1925–52). *Complete Masques*, ed. S. Orgel (New Haven and London, 1969). *The Alchemist*, ed. C. M. Hathaway (New York, 1903).

LYDGATE, J., *The Hystorye Sege and Dystruccyon of Troye*, ed. G. Bullough in *Narrative and Dramatic Sources of Shakespeare*, vol. vi (London, 1966). *The Siege of Thebes*, printed in the Chaucer editions of 1561, 1598, and 1602. Modern edition by A. Erdmann for the Early English Text Society (London, 1911).

MARSTON, J., *Plays*, ed. H. H. Wood (Edinburgh, 1934–9).

Parnassus Plays (anon.), ed. J. B. Leishman (London, 1949).

PHILLIP, J., *Patient Grissil*, ed. W. W. Greg and R. B. McKerrow for the Malone Society (Oxford, 1909).

Rare Triumphs of Love and Fortune (anon.), ed. W. W. Greg for the Malone Society (Oxford, 1930).

ROWLEY, W., *All's Lost by Lust*, ed. E. C. Morris (Boston, Mass., and London, 1908).

SHAKESPEARE, W., *The Complete Works*, ed. P. Alexander (London, 1951). Variorum, Arden, New Arden, New Cambridge, New Penguin, and Signet editions as referred to in the text and footnotes. *The Two Noble Kinsmen* (with John Fletcher), ed. G. R. Proudfoot (London and Nebraska, 1970). Earlier editions by H. Littledale (London, 1876, 1885) and W. W. Skeat (Cambridge, 1875).

SIDNEY, P., *An Apologie for Poetrie*, ed. G. G. Smith in *Elizabethan Critical Essays*, vol. i (Oxford, 1904). *Astrophel and Stella*, ed. M. Putzel (New York, 1967).

SPENSER, E. *Poetical Works*, ed. J. C. Smith and E. de Selincourt (Oxford 1912).

WEBSTER, J., *Works*, ed. F. L. Lucas (London, 1927).

2. Source criticism with specific reference to Chaucer

ANDERS, H. R. D., *Shakespeare's Books* (Berlin, 1904).

BALLMANN, O., 'Chaucer's Einfluss auf das Englische Drama in Zeitalter der Königen Elizabeth und der beiden ersten Stuart-Könige', *Anglia*, xxv (1902), 1–85.

BERGERON, D. M., 'The Wife of Bath and Shakespeare's *Taming of the Shrew*', *University Review*, xxxv (1969), 279–86.

BERTRAM, P., *Shakespeare and 'The Two Noble Kinsmen'* (New Brunswick, 1965).

BETHURUM, D., 'Shakespeare's comment on medieval romance in *A Midsummer Night's Dream*', *Modern Language Notes*, lx (1945), 85–94.

BRADBROOK, M. C., 'What Shakespeare did to Chaucer's *Troilus and Criseyde*', *Shakespeare Quarterly*, ix (1958), 311–19.

BUDD, F. E., 'Chaucer, Shakespeare and Harsnett', *Review of English Studies*, xi (1935), 421–69.

BULLOUGH, G., *Narrative and Dramatic Sources of Shakespeare* (London, 1957–75). 'The lost *Troilus and Cressida*', *Essays and Studies*, xvii (1964), 24–40.

CHAMPION, L. S., '*A Midsummer Night's Dream*: the problem of source', *Papers on Language and Literature*, iv (1968), 13–19.

CHUTE, M., 'Chaucer and Shakespeare', *College English*, xii (1950), 15–19.

COGHILL, N., 'Shakespeare's reading in Chaucer', *Elizabethan and Jacobean Studies presented to F. P. Wilson*, ed. H. Davis and H. Gardner (Oxford, 1959).

DENT, R. W., *John Webster's Borrowing* (Berkely, 1960).

FAIRCHILD, A. H. R., '*The Phoenix and the Turtle*', *Englische Studien*, xxxiii (1904), 337–84.

FARMER, R., 'Essay on the learning of Shakespeare', ed. D. Nichol Smith in *Eighteenth Century Essays on Shakespeare* (Oxford, 1903).

FISHER, L. A., 'Shakespeare and the Capitol', *Modern Language Notes*, xxii (1907), 177–82.

FREEMAN, A., '*Richard II*, I. iii. 294–5', *Shakespeare Quarterly*, xiv (1963), 89–90.

HALES, J. W., 'Chaucer and Shakespeare', *Quarterly Review*, cxxxiv (1873), 225–55.

HANKINS, J. E., 'Pains of the afterworld in Milton and Shakespeare', *Publications of the Modern Language Association of America*, lxxi (1956), 482–95.

HENDERSON, W. B. D., 'Shakespeare's *Troilus* and its tradition', *The Parrot Presentation Volume*, ed. H. Craig (Princeton, 1935), pp. 127–56.

HUNTER, J., *New Illustrations of the Life, Studies and Writings of Shakespeare* (London, 1845).

JUSSERAND, J. J., *A Literary History of the English People* (London, 1909).

KIMBROUGH, R., 'The origins of *Troilus and Cressida*', *PMLA*, lxxvii (1962), 194–9. '*Troilus and Cressida*' *and Its Setting* (Oxford, 1964).

KITTREDGE, G. L., 'Notes on Elizabethan plays', *Journal of English and Germanic Philology*, ii (1898), 7–13.

LAWRENCE, W. W., 'The love-story in *Troilus and Cressida*', *Shakespearian Studies*, ed. B. Matthews and A. H. Thorndike (New York, 1916), 187–211.

LEHNERT, M., 'Shakespeare und Chaucer', *Shakespeare Jahrbuch*, ciii (1967), 3–39.

MARKLAND, F., 'The order of *The Knight's Tale* and *The Tempest*', *Research Studies*, xxxiii (Washington, 1965), 1–10.

MAVEETY, S. R., 'Hermione, a dangerous ornament', *Shakespeare Quarterly*, xiv (1963), 485–6.

MAXWELL, J. C., 'Chaucer in the Queen Mab speech', *Notes and Queries*, vii (1960), 16.

MUIR, K., 'Greene and *Troilus and Cressida*', *Notes and Queries*, cc (1955), 141–2. 'Pyramus and Thisbe: A study in Shakespeare's method', *Shakespeare Quarterly*, v (1954), 141–53. *Shakespeare's Sources* (London, 1957).

MUNRO, J. J., *Brooke's 'Romeus and Juliet'* in *The Shakespeare Classics* series (London, 1908).

ORD, H., *Chaucer and the Rival Poet in Shakespeare's Sonnets* (London, 1921).

PEARCE, T. M., 'Another knot, five-finger-tied', *Notes and Queries*, vii (1960), 18–19.

PRESSON, R. K., 'Boethius, King Lear and "Maystresse Philosophie" ', *Journal of English and Germanic Philology*, lxiv (1965), 406–24. 'The Conclusion of *Love's Labour's Lost*', *Notes and Queries*, vii (1960), 17–18. *Shakespeare's 'Troilus and Cressida' and the Legends of Troy* (Wisconsin, 1953). 'The structural use of a traditional theme in *Troilus and Cressida*', *Philological Quarterly*, xxxi (1952), 180–8.

ROLLINS, H. E., 'The Troilus–Cressida story from Chaucer to Shakespeare', *PMLA*, xxxii (1917), 383–429.

ROOT, R. K., 'Shakespeare misreads Chaucer', *Modern Language Notes*, xxxviii (1923), 346–8.

SARRAZIN, G., 'Chaucer und Shakespeare', *Anglia Beiblatt*, vii (1897), 265–9.

SCHANZER, E., '*Antony and Cleopatra* and *The Legend of Good Women*', *Notes and Queries*, vii (1960), 335–6.

SIDGWICK, F., *Sources and Analogues of 'A Midsummer Night's Dream'* (London, 1908).

SMALL, R. A., *The Stage-Quarrel between Ben Jonson and the so-called Poetasters* (Breslau, 1899).

SOELLNER, R., 'Shakespeare and the *Consolatio*', *Notes and Queries*, cic (1954), 108–9.

TATLOCK, J. S. P., 'The Siege of Troy in Shakespeare and Heywood', *PMLA*, xxx (1915), 673–770.

TAYLOR, G. C., 'The medieval element in Shakespeare', *Shakespeare Association Bulletin*, xii (1937), 208–16.

WILSON, F. P., 'Shakespeare's reading', *Shakespeare Survey*, iii (1950), 14–21.

3. General criticism and other works cited

BALDWIN, T. W., *The Literary Genetics of Shakespeare's Poems* (Urbana, Illinois, 1950). *William Shakespeare's Petty School* (Urbana, Illinois, 1943). *William Shakespeare's Small Latine and Lesse Greeke* (Urbana, Illinois, 1944).

BAYLEY, J., 'Shakespeare's only play', *Stratford Papers on Shakespeare*, ed. B. W. Jackson (Toronto, 1963), pp. 58–83.

BOAS, F. S., *An Introduction to Tudor Drama* (Oxford, 1933). *Shakespeare and his Predecessors* (London, 1896).

BRADBROOK, M. C., *Shakespeare and Elizabethan Poetry* (London, 1951).

BROOKE, N., *Shakespeare's Early Tragedies* (London, 1968).

BUSH, D., 'Classical myths in Shakespeare's plays', *Elizabethan and Jacobean Studies Presented to F. P. Wilson*, ed. H. Davis and H. Gardner (Oxford, 1959), pp. 65–85.

CHAMBERS, E. K., *The Elizabethan Stage* (Oxford, 1923).

COGHILL, N., 'The basis of Shakespearean comedy', *Essays and Studies*, iii (1950), 1–28.

DANBY, J., *Poets on Fortune's Hill* (London, 1952).

EDWARDS, P., 'The danger, not the death', *Jacobean Theatre*, ed. J. R. Brown and B. Harris (Stratford-on-Avon Studies 1, London, 1960), pp. 159–77. 'On the design of *The Two Noble Kinsmen*', *A Review of English Literature*, v (1964), 89–105.

ERDMAN, D. V., and FOGEL, E. G., *Evidence for Authorship* (New York, 1966).

FARNHAM, W., 'England's discovery of the Decameron', *PMLA*, xxxix (1924), 123–39. *The Medieval Heritage of Elizabethan Tragedy* (Cambridge, 1936).

HARBAGE, A., *Shakespeare and the Rival Traditions* (New York, 1952).

HAWKINS, H., *Poetic Freedom and Poetic Truth* (Oxford, 1976).

HERMERÉN, G., *Influence in Art and Literature* (Princeton, 1975).

HONIGMANN, E. A. J., *The Stability of Shakespeare's Text* (London, 1965).

HOY, C., *The Hyacinth Room* (London, 1964). 'The shares of Fletcher and his collaborators in the Beaumont and Fletcher Canon, 7', *Studies in Bibliography*, xv (1962), 71–90.

HUNT, M. L., *Thomas Dekker* (Columbia, 1911).

JONES, E., *The Origins of Shakespeare* (Oxford, 1977).

JONES, R. F., *The Triumph of the English Language* (Stanford, 1953).

KERMODE, F., *William Shakespeare: The Final Plays* (London, 1963).

KOTT, J., *Shakespeare Our Contemporary* (London, 1965).

LAWLOR, J., 'Romeo and Juliet', *The Early Shakespeare*, ed. J. R. Brown and B. Harris (Stratford-on-Avon Studies 3, London, 1961), pp. 123–43. *The Tragic Sense in Shakespeare* (London, 1960).

LEECH, C., *The John Fletcher Plays* (London, 1962).

LEISHMAN, J. B., *Themes and Variations in Shakespeare's Sonnets* (London, 1961).

LEVER, J. W., *The Elizabethan Love Sonnet* (London, 1956).

LEWIS, C. S., *The Allegory of Love* (Oxford, 1936).

MACLURE, M., *George Chapman* (Toronto, 1966).

MASON, H. A., *Shakespeare's Tragedies of Love* (London, 1970).

McALINDON, T., 'Language, style and meaning in *Troilus and Cressida*', *PMLA*, lxxxiv (1969), 29–43.

MEADER, J. G., *Courtship in Shakespeare* (New York, 1954).

MISKIMIN, A., *The Renaissance Chaucer* (Yale, 1975).

MUIR, K., *Shakespeare as Collaborator* (London, 1960).

MUSCATINE, C., 'Form, texture and meaning in Chaucer's *Knight's Tale*', *PMLA*, lxv (1950), 911–29.

NELSON, W., 'The teaching of English in Tudor grammar schools', *Studies in Philology*, xlix (1952), pp. 119–45.

PEARSALL, D., *John Lydgate* (London, 1970).

PETTET, E. C., *Shakespeare and the Romance Tradition* (London and New York, 1949).

PROUDFOOT, R., 'Shakespeare and the new dramatists of the King's Men, 1606–13', *Later Shakespeare*, ed. J. R. Brown and B. Harris (Stratford-on-Avon Studies 8, London, 1966), pp. 234–61.

REESE, M. M., *Shakespeare's World and Work* (London, 1953).

SALINGAR, L. *Shakespeare and the Traditions of Comedy* (Cambridge, 1974).

SCHOFIELD, W. H., *Chivalry in English Literature* (Harvard, 1912).

SEVERS, J. B., *The Literary Relationship of Chaucer's 'Clerke's Tale'* (New Haven, 1942).

SIEGEL, P. N., 'Christianity and the religion of love in *Romeo and Juliet*', *Shakespeare Quarterly*, xii (1961), 371–92.

SHAW, G. B., *Shaw on Shakespeare*, ed. E. Wilson (Harmondsworth, 1969).

SMITH, J. O., 'Essence and existence in Shakespeare's *Troilus and Cressida*', *Philological Quarterly*, xlvi (1967), 167–85.

SPALDING, W., *A Letter on Shakespeare's authorship of 'The Two Noble Kinsmen'* (London, 1833).

SPENCER, T., *Shakespeare and the Nature of Man* (New York, 1942). '*The Two Noble Kinsmen*', *Modern Philology*, xxxvi (1939), pp. 255–76.

SPURGEON, C. E., *Five Hundred Years of Chaucer Criticism and Allusion* (Cambridge, 1925).

SWANSTON, H., 'The Baroque element in *Troilus and Cressida*', *Durham University Journal*, xix (1958), 14–23.

THOMPSON, K. F., 'Shakespeare's romantic comedies', *PMLA*, lxvii (1952), 1079–93.

TILLEY, M. P., *A Dictionary of the Proverbs in England in the Sixteenth and Seventeenth Centuries* (Ann Arbor, 1950).

TILLYARD, E. M. W., *Shakespeare's Problem Plays* (London, 1950).

URE, P., *Shakespeare's Problem Plays* (London, 1961).

VYVYAN, J., *Shakespeare and the Rose of Love* (London, 1960).

WAITH, E. M., *The Pattern of Tragicomedy in Beaumont and Fletcher* (New Haven, 1952).

WATSON, C. B., *Shakespeare and the Renaissance Concept of Honor* (Princeton, 1960).

WHITAKER, V. K., *Shakespeare's Use of Learning* (San Marino, 1953).

WHITER, W., *A Specimen of a Commentary on Shakespeare 1794*, ed. A. Over and M. Bell (London, 1967).

WICKHAM G., *Shakespeare's Dramatic Heritage* (1969).

WRIGHT, H. G., *Boccaccio in England* (London, 1957)

Index

Did Shakespeare read Chaucer? This is the first book to address itself specifically to the question of the literary relationship between two of our greatest poets. In the past, some critics have assumed that Shakespeare must have read Chaucer because there was so little other English poetry for him to read, while others have assumed that he could not possibly have done so in view of the remarkable differences between the two poets' versions of the story of *Troilus and Cressida*. In this book, the author makes a careful study of the evidence and establishes beyond doubt that Shakespeare knew Chaucer very well and that there are signs of the earlier poet's influence in almost every play.

Dr Thompson examines in detail the way in which Shakespeare used Chaucer, the plots, situations, themes, and images he borrowed, and the way in which he exploited them by adaptation and combination with other materials. There is a chapter illustrating the ways in which other dramatists of Shakespeare's time drew on Chaucer's work and many other issues are also discussed, such as Chaucer's significant role in the handing down of medieval stories, themes, characters, and concepts, to the writers of the Elizabethan era.